New Cambridge Advanced English

Teacher's Book | Leo Jones

CAMBRIDGE
UNIVERSITY PRESS

PUBLISHED BY THE PRESS SYNDICATE OF THE UNIVERSITY OF CAMBRIDGE
The Pitt Building, Trumpington Street, Cambridge CB2 1RP, United Kingdom

CAMBRIDGE UNIVERSITY PRESS
The Edinburgh Building, Cambridge CB2 2RU, United Kingdom
40 West 20th Street, New York, NY 10011–4211, USA
10 Stamford Road, Oakleigh, Melbourne 3166, Australia

First published 1991
New Edition 1998

Printed in the United Kingdom at the University Press, Cambridge

ISBN 0 521 62941 1 Teacher's Book
ISBN 0 521 62939 X Student's Book
ISBN 0 521 62940 3 Class Cassette Set

Contents

Map of the book   4

Thanks   6

Introduction   7

1 Desert islands   21
A year on a desert island   Joining
sentences – 1   Writing a narrative
The Castaways   Survival
All's well that ends well!

2 Around the world   33
United nations   World Music
The past – 1   Really? That's amazing!
See the world?   Synonyms and
opposites – 1   You can't lose!

3 That's show business!   49
Films, shows and concerts   One of my
favourite films . . .   Adults only
Making an emphasis   Punctuation
Planning ahead . . .   *At* . . . and *by* . . .

4 Enjoy your meal!   60
To whet your appetite . . .   Favourite foods
Appropriate language   Simple + progressive
aspect   Words easily confused
Bring, carry and *take*

5 Travellers or tourists?   70
Travelling abroad   Tourism and tourists
Making notes   A letter of complaint
Travel writers   *High, middle* and *low*

6 It takes all sorts . . .   76
What do they look like?   Politically correct?
Modal verbs   Synonyms and opposites – 2
Personalities

7 Put it in writing   84
Handwriting   A professional writer
Different styles   Long and short sentences
Living with a computer   Formal letters and
personal letters   The differences between
spoken and written English   A tactful letter
In . . . and *out of* . . .

8 Past times   98
The good old days?   The past – 2
Fourteen ninety-nine   Forming adjectives
In other words . . .   *Get*

9 You're as old as you feel   110
The Third Age   Paragraphs   Granny power
Family life   A letter to the editor   Ages

10 Utopia?   118
An ideal home?   The perfect society?
The best of all possible worlds   Articles
Describing a place   Synonyms and
opposites – 3   *Hard, soft, difficult* and *easy*

11 Fame and fortune   129
Role models   Emphasising the right syllable
Charlie Chaplin   Style, tone and content
Sharing opinions   Household names
For and *on*

12 Education and science   142
Science and technology   First day at school
Education systems   The sixth form
Comparing and contrasting   How does it
work?   *Look* and *see*

13 Communication   153
The art of conversation   Joining sentences
– 2   Gestures   You just don't understand!
Advertising   Colours

14 The English-speaking world   161
English in the world   Indirect speech
Spelling and pronunciation 1 – Consonants
I ♥ signs   British and American English
Speaking and *thinking*

15 How strange!   171
Truth or fiction   A good introduction and
conclusion   A sense of humour
Mind control   *Day* and *time*

16 Body and mind   181
How are you?   Prefixes   Spelling
Conditional sentences   Giving advice
First aid   *Hearts, hands, legs* and *feet*

17 Love stories   189
What do you enjoy reading?   Small World
How romantic are you?   First meetings
First paragraphs   Expressing feelings
Four weddings and . . .   Head over heels . . .

18 The natural world   197
Fauna and flora   Compound words
Protecting the environment   The future
and degrees of certainty   Spelling and
pronunciation 2 – Vowels   *Keep, hold,
stand* and *turn*

19 What's in the news?   206
In the headlines   Don't believe everything
you read . . .   Danger – Hippies!   Connecting
words   Crime and punishment   Reports
and opinions   Presenting a radio show
Back, front and *side*

20 The real world . . .   215
Earning a living   A satisfying job
Satisfaction and success   Word order
Great business deals?   Abbreviations and
acronyms   *-ing* and *to* . . .   Applying for
a job   *First, second, third* . . . and *last*

Index   223

Map of the book

	Reading	Interviews	Listening	Word study	Effective writing	Creative writing	Grammar	Speaking & pronunciation	Verbs, idioms & collocations
1 Desert islands	Landings / The Castaways	Pen Hadow, survival expert	A year on a desert island		Joining sentences – 1	Writing a narrative			*All's well that ends well!*
2 Around the world	Japanese beach lovers & Push-button lover		World Music / See the world?	Synonyms & opposites – 1		(Informal letter)	The past – 1	Really? That's amazing!	*You can't lose!*
3 That's show business!	The rage of Rambo	Maev Alexander, actress	One of my favourite films ...	Making an emphasis	Punctuation	Planning ahead ...		Opinions	*At ... & by ...*
4 Enjoy your meal!	Cat canteloupe			Words easily confused		(Instructions + note)	Simple + progressive aspect	Appropriate language	*Bring, carry & take*
5 Travellers or tourists?	Trouble in paradise / Travel writers	Susan Davies, traveller			Making notes	A letter of complaint			*High, middle & low*
6 It takes all sorts ...	Politically correct? / Horoscopes		7 descriptions	Synonyms & opposites – 2		Letter of reference	Modal verbs	Describing people	
7 Put it in writing	Different styles / The unstoppable Albert Sukoff / Spammed & Writing unlimited / The secrets of writing business letters	Isabelle Amyes, writer	Handwriting / The differences between spoken and written English		Different styles / Long & short sentences / Formal & personal letters	A tactful letter			*In ... & out of ...*
8 Past times	The good old days?		Fourteen ninety-nine / In other words ...	Forming adjectives		(Descriptions of 2 historical figures)	The past – 2		*Get*
9 You're as old as you feel	Life begins at 50 / The Greys / Family life	Geoffrey Smerden, U3A organiser	Granny power		Paragraphs	Letter to the editor			*Ages*
10 Utopia?	Island / The best of all possible worlds / Brasilia		An ideal home? / The perfect society	Synonyms & opposites – 3		Letter describing a place	Articles	Describing a place	*Hard, soft, difficult & easy*

	Reading	Interviews	Listening	Word study	Effective writing	Creative writing	Grammar	Speaking & pronunciation	Verbs, idioms & collocations
11 Fame and fortune	Remarkable Charlie Record-breaking lottery winner	Anita Roddick, Body Shop founder	Role models		Style, tone & content	(Letter to a friend) Household names		Emphasising the right syllable Sharing opinions	*For & on*
12 Education and science	The Cat Sat on the test That sixth sense Clock of ages	Wendy Fielder, research scientist	10 clips First day at school How does it work?			(First day at school) (Instructions)	Comparing & contrasting		*Look & see*
13 Communication	Gestures You just don't understand!	Bob Stanners, advertising copywriter	The art of conversation		Joining sentences – 2	Advertising: report			Colours
14 The English-speaking world	English in the world		Indirect speech	British & American English		(Instructions)	Indirect speech	Spelling & pronunciation 1 – Consonants	*Say, speak, call & tell*
15 How strange!	New legends for old Odd, odder, oddest Inhuman nature	Ian Howarth, ex-cult member	A sense of humour		A good introduction & conclusion	(Letter of advice)			*Day & time*
16 Body & mind	Mirror, mirror		5 clips	Prefixes Spelling		First-aid instructions	Conditional sentences	Giving advice	*Hearts, hands, legs & feet*
17 Love stories	Small World In her arms, he melted First paragraphs		First meetings Four weddings		Expressing feelings	(Article about book) Account of a wedding		Storytelling	Head over heels
18 The natural world	Protecting the environment	Cyril Littlewood, environmentalist	10 clips	Compound words		(Report on environment)	The future & degrees of certainty	Spelling & pronunciation 2 – Vowels	*Keep, hold, stand & turn*
19 What's in the news?	Don't believe everything Travelling tribe ...	JoAnne Good, broadcaster	Danger – Hippies!		Connecting words (conjunctions)	Reports & opinions		Crime & punishment	*Back, front & side*
20 The real world . . .	Rosalyn Clark, bus driver Great business deals?		Great business deals?	Abbreviations & acronyms	Word order	(Accounts of day at work) Applying for a job	-ing & to ...	Satisfaction & success: a survey	*First, second, third & last*

I'd like to thank everyone whose hard work, fresh ideas, helpful comments and criticisms have enhanced this book immensely:

The following teachers reported on their experiences of using the first edition:

Dolly Irani in France   Chrysoula Georgouli & Fotini Petrou in Greece   Andrea Marschalek in Hungary   Bernardo Santano Moreno in Spain   Anna Kibort in Poland   Peter Tomkin in the UK

Alison McCabe advised me on the Reading paper of the CAE exam.

The following teachers reported on the new material as it was being written:

Christa Kochuyt Temple in Belgium   Katherine Spence in France   Philip Devlin, Ines Laue & Caroline Mears in Germany   Andrea Marschalek in Hungary   David Massey & Mary Nava in Italy   Karina Schymik & Tadeusez Z. Wolanski in Poland   Teresa Corchado in Spain   Sue Gosling, Nick Kenny, Patricia O'Sullivan, Peter Watkins & Martin Wilson in the UK

Liz Sharman set the ball rolling. Charlotte Adams took over and continued to give her encouragement and support, with help from Niki Browne.

Alison Silver edited the book and guided the project efficiently through to publication. I'm very grateful for her insights and meticulous attention to detail. It was, as ever, a pleasure to work with her.

Hilary Fletcher researched the photographs.

Michelle Uniacke Gibson was responsible for text permission.

Celia Witchard did the illustrations.

Ruth Carim was the proofreader.

Paul Wilson of Sage Associates designed the book with the help of Gecko Limited.

Susie Fairfax organised the Interviews and asked all the right questions.

James Richardson produced the recordings. Andy Taylor was the engineer at Studio AVP.

Sue Gosling wrote the Model versions for the Teacher's Book.

The author and publishers are grateful to The Guardian for permission to reproduce the article on page 141. We have been unable to trace the copyright owner of the image on page 141 and would be grateful for any information to enable us to do so.

From the first edition

First of all, I'd like to say how grateful I am to:

Jeanne McCarten for her inexhaustible patience, support and encouragement throughout my work on this book, Alison Silver for her friendly editorial expertise, Peter Ducker for the design of the book, and Peter Taylor and Studio AVP for producing the recordings.

Thanks very much also to the following teachers who used the pilot edition with their classes and contributed detailed comments on it and who evaluated and reported on subsequent revised units. Without their help, this book could not have been written:

Pat Biagi, Christ Church College ELTU, Canterbury   Jenny Bradshaw   Sylvie Dawid, Beverly Langsch and Monty Sufrin, Migros Club School, Berne   George Drivas, Moraitis School, Athens   Tim Eyres, Godmer House, Oxford   David Gray   Amanda Hammersley, British School of Monza, Italy   Chris Higgins and staff, Teach In Language and Training Workshop, Rome   Tom Hinton   Roger Hunt, International House, Madrid   Ruth Jimack   Christine Margittai   Laura Matthews, Newnham Language Centre, Cambridge   Joy Morris and staff, British Institute, Barcelona   Jill Mountain and staff, British Institute, Rome   Julia Napier   Patricia Pringle, Université II, Lyon   Lesley Porte and Diann Gruber, ESIEE, Paris   Rachelle Porteous, London School of English   Tom Sagar and colleagues, Collège Rousseau, Geneva   Katy Shaw and colleagues, Eurocentre, Lee Green   Elizabeth Sim and staff, Eurocentre, Cambridge   Lynda Taylor   Kit Woods

Finally, thanks to Sue, Zoë and Thomas for everything.

Who is this book for?

New Cambridge Advanced English is for students who have completed an upper-intermediate course and have passed the Cambridge First Certificate in English examination (FCE) – or reached an equivalent level.

Students using this course may be attending classes once or twice a week at a language institute, doing a language course at a university, or attending an intensive EFL course.

They might be preparing for the Cambridge Certificate in Advanced English (CAE) exam. Or they might have no paper qualifications at all in mind and simply want to improve all aspects of their English in order to be able to communicate better in their work, studies or social life. Or the class may consist of both exam candidates and non-exam candidates.

The material in this course is very FLEXIBLE and can be used successfully with all the types of students described above. Throughout the book, there is an emphasis on the acquisition of skills that students will find useful in their everyday lives. *New Cambridge Advanced English* covers all five papers of the CAE exam and many of the task and exercise types reflect the format of the CAE exam, but these tasks and exercises are all relevant and interesting for students who aren't exam candidates. (There are also CAE exam tips in the Teacher's Book for the teacher to announce to exam candidates, but these don't appear in the Student's Book.)

How is it different from the first edition?

New Cambridge Advanced English is significantly different from the first edition. Many of the reading and listening texts, activities and exercises are completely new, but the features that teachers and students have appreciated have been retained. The texts and activities which have been retained from the first edition have been modified so that they work better and are more user-friendly. The new layout and organisation of the pages makes the course easier to use – this helps the students to get the maximum benefit from their work.

CAE exam preparation is more prominent in *New Cambridge Advanced English*, with many exercises that are similar to the CAE exam. All the skills and techniques that exam candidates need to master are covered. But this is by no means a single-minded exam preparation course – it's a course for people who not only want to do well in the CAE exam, but also want to develop their English for use in the real world of work, study and social life. It's equally suitable for students who are not preparing for an exam, and who want to improve their English in the most interesting and motivating ways.

The revisions and changes are based on detailed comments and reports from teachers who had been using the first edition successfully for many years. *New Cambridge Advanced English* is easy for both students and teachers to use and find their way around. The format of each unit provides a more balanced lesson structure and increased flexibility.

New Cambridge Advanced English includes:
- 20 units – odd-numbered units are theme units, even-numbered units are language units
- Four or five double-page spreads in every unit
- Vocabulary development exercises with plenty of opportunities for students to use the new words in discussion tasks and Communication Activities
- Exercises on word study
- Many new and up-to-date reading texts, with pre- and post-reading tasks and discussion questions
- Thorough training in writing skills
- Grammar review with thorough coverage of problem areas
- Many new or revised listening comprehension exercises
- Interviews with experts and people with special knowledge
- Many new or revised speaking exercises and Communication Activities

- Advice, hints and tips on exam techniques in the Teacher's Book, which can be passed on to exam candidates
- Exercises on idioms and collocations, and verbs and idioms

How much time will it take to complete the course?

For students at this level, it's impossible to predict exactly how long each section in a coursebook will take. As a rough guide, the material in the book with its accompanying recordings will provide approximately 80 hours of classroom work, plus further work to be done outside class. Each of the 20 units is likely to take two or three 90-minute sessions, but time can be saved by getting the students to prepare some exercises before the lesson – or by skipping some sections.

If you decide to devote a lot of time to the discussion activities you're likely to need more time. Every class is likely to have its own strengths and weaknesses, which will lead you to spend more or less time on particular sections in a unit. Moreover, some topics may interest your students more than others and consequently there's likely to be more discussion on these than on the ones that are of less interest to them.

The sections in each unit are designed to be used SELECTIVELY. Some sections that deal with aspects of English which your students are already confident in, or which are less relevant for them, may be omitted. You may also like to use supplementary materials and give your students an opportunity to contribute their own input to the course (in the form of discussions about current affairs, texts clipped from magazines or newspapers or student talks, for example).

What are the aims of the course?

The aims of *New Cambridge Advanced English* are:
- To build on the vocabulary that students already know and increase their range of expression
- To improve students' reading skills so that they can read more effectively and appreciate the implications and style of a text
- To improve students' listening skills so that they can understand a wide range of spoken texts and are able to participate actively in discussions and conversations with native and non-native English speakers from all parts of the world
- To improve students' writing skills and encourage them to develop useful practical techniques which will enable them to communicate effectively in writing
- To revise the 'problem areas' of English grammar in a stimulating, helpful and entertaining way
- To improve students' command of spoken English, by providing frequent opportunities for discussion, so that they will be able to participate appropriately and confidently in a wide range of interactions with English speakers
- To increase students' awareness of and sensitivity to degrees of appropriateness in their use of English
- To give students a chance to use their English in class in interesting communicative activities and produce meaningful written work, not just to practise speaking or writing in controlled exercises
- To integrate different language skills in the practice activities, so that each skill is not practised in isolation
- To encourage students to improve their English outside class by reading widely and taking every opportunity to practise their English with native speakers and with each other
- To prepare students for all five papers in the Cambridge CAE exam, if they're taking it

What does the course contain?

There are 20 units in *New Cambridge Advanced English*, each based on a different topic.

The odd-numbered units are 'THEME UNITS', which contain:

- Informative **Reading** texts from a variety of authentic sources, with tasks, exercises and activities to improve students' reading skills. Many of these can be prepared in advance at home. Many of the tasks are similar to the tasks in the CAE Reading paper.
- **Listening** exercises with tasks and activities to help students to improve their listening skills. Many of the tasks are similar to the tasks in the CAE Listening paper.
- **Interviews** with people who have special knowledge of the theme or stories to tell about it
- **Effective writing** exercises to help students to develop useful techniques they can use in their writing – both for exam purposes and for general use
- Realistic **Creative writing** tasks which give students an opportunity to express themselves in writing. Many of the tasks are similar to the tasks in the CAE Writing paper, but are also relevant for students who aren't taking it.

The even-numbered units are 'LANGUAGE UNITS' and they contain:

- Shorter **Reading** texts and/or **Listening** exercises leading to a discussion activity and/or a writing task ($\overline{\Phi}$)
- **Grammar** revision: the 'problem areas' of English grammar are dealt with in a thought-provoking and interesting way
- **Word study** exercises to help students to develop their vocabulary skills
- **Speaking** sections to help students to practise the functional language needed in different real-life situations – and in the CAE Speaking paper

Both the odd- and even-numbered units (i.e. all the units) contain:

- Exercises on the **Vocabulary** connected with the topic of the unit
- Opportunities for **Discussion**
- Work on **Idioms and collocations** or **Verbs and idioms**, including phrasal verbs

There are regular Communication Activities. Individual students are given different information that they have to communicate to each other. These are printed at the end of the Student's Book in random order so that students can't see each other's information. There's a complete list of these on page 16. Not every unit contains a Communication Activity.

The **Teacher's Book** contains:

- Correct or suggested answers to all the exercises in the Student's Book
- Model versions for the Creative writing tasks, which you can photocopy for the students if you wish
- A transcript of all the recordings
- Teaching notes on every section of the Student's Book
- CAE exam advice and tips (for you to pass on to students preparing for the CAE exam)
- Extra activities and exercises for photocopying

READING

New Cambridge Advanced English contains a wide variety of interesting authentic texts taken from newspapers, magazines and from fiction or non-fiction books. These are accompanied by exercises and tasks which will help students to develop their skills in: skimming a text to get the gist, scanning a text to find specific information, note-taking, summarising, coping with unfamiliar vocabulary, distinguishing the main idea from supporting ideas, using the information acquired from a text in a subsequent activity, etc. The passages are all chosen as suitable springboards for discussion, so that the students can react to what they've read and/or talk about their own experiences and opinions.

Before many of the reading comprehension tasks there are pre-reading tasks, preliminary discussion questions or questions about the theme that students may be able to answer from their own previous knowledge. These tasks help students to approach the text with more interest and curiosity than if they merely had to 'Read the text and answer the questions'.

It's essential for students to realise that they don't have to be able to understand every single word in a passage to perform the tasks. They should concentrate on what the writers are trying to say and the information they're communicating. Unfamiliar words in a reading text may be distracting but students should not assume that every single one is important and 'worth learning'. It may be a waste of time looking up every word they don't understand in a reading text.

▼ In some reading exercises the students have to highlight certain words or phrases in a passage. This encourages them to deduce meanings from the context and also to notice how particular words are used.

After the reading comprehension questions there are further discussion questions, to encourage students to use some of the new words they've encountered in the text and share their reactions to its content with each other. In some cases there's a Communication Activity or a writing task arising from the content of the passage.

The first Reading exercise is 1.4 on page 12 of the Student's Book.

LISTENING

The cassettes comprise a variety of recordings: broadcasts, discussions, talks and conversations. These are accompanied by exercises and tasks designed to develop skills in finding the important information in the recording, note-taking, performing another task (in writing or speech) using the information acquired from a text, interpreting a speaker's attitude, etc.

Most of the Listening sections begin with a pre-listening task, preliminary discussion questions, or questions about the topic which students may be able to answer from their own previous knowledge. These tasks help students to approach the recording with more interest than if they merely had to 'Listen to the recording and answer the questions'.

Try to 'set the scene' for students before they hear the recording by explaining where the speakers are and what their relationship is (colleagues, good friends, etc.). Remember that students will be trying to understand disembodied voices coming out of a loudspeaker without the aid of a transcript, and this is much more difficult than being in the same room as a real person who is speaking.

In some of the Listening exercises, students may need help with vocabulary. It's a good idea to read through the transcript in your copy of the Teacher's Book before the lesson, and highlight any vocabulary that you wish to draw your students' attention to.

Most classes will need to hear each recording at least twice to extract all the required information. In some classes, where students are weak at listening, you may need to pause the tape frequently and play certain sections again to help them to understand more easily. However, it's essential for students to realise that they don't have to be able to understand every single word to answer the questions. They should concentrate on what the speakers are trying to say and the information they're communicating, NOT the actual words they're using.

After the listening comprehension task there are often further discussion questions, to encourage students to share their reactions with each other and discuss the implications of what they've heard.

The first Listening exercise is 1.1 C2 on page 9 of the Student's Book.

Interviews

Each theme unit includes an interview with someone who is an expert on an aspect of the topic, or who has some inside knowledge of it. The speakers all speak at their normal speed and make no concessions to foreign learners. The Interviews can be treated in the same way as any other Listening exercise and the same advice given above applies. In the Interviews the questions and tasks focus on HELPING the students to understand the main points that the speakers make – it's the information and ideas they give that are important.

The interviews are:

1.5A   Pen Hadow – an Arctic explorer
3.1 B   Maev Alexander – an actress
5.1 C   Susan Davies – a traveller
7.2   Isabelle Amyes – a television scriptwriter

9.1 D   Geoffrey Smerden – founder of a University of the Third Age
11.6 A   Anita Roddick – founder of The Body Shop
12.1 A   Wendy Fielder – a research scientist
13.5 A   Bob Stanners – an advertising copywriter
15.4   Ian Howarth – founder of the Cult Information Centre
18.3 B   Cyril Littlewood – a conservationist
19.7   JoAnne Good – a radio presenter

VOCABULARY

Each unit includes work on vocabulary, covering some of the vocabulary connected with the topic of the unit. There are various types of vocabulary exercises and activities, including warm-up discussion questions and follow-up activities to encourage the students to use new words they've come across. While doing these activities and exercises, students should be encouraged to ask questions about vocabulary, and to use the relevant vocabulary they already know to discuss the topic.

Some units begin with a vocabulary brainstorming activity, based on a discussion of pictures. Here the students work in pairs or small groups and together build up a list of relevant words and phrases, which they then compare with other students to build up a longer list, learning from each other. As every individual knows or remembers different English words, pooling knowledge is invaluable. The first of these activities is 3.1 A1 on page 24 of the Student's Book.

There are two big problems about introducing new vocabulary:

1   It's difficult to help students to remember vocabulary items – giving them a large amount of controlled oral practice in class is no guarantee that they will remember everything a week later!

2   It takes time for students to develop a sensitivity towards the kinds of contexts and situations in which each vocabulary item can be used: which words are formal or informal, which are used jokingly or seriously, which are used in a derogatory or complimentary sense, etc. Students also need to develop an awareness of the connotations of different vocabulary items, since many broadly synonymous expressions may have quite different connotations.

Unfortunately, there are no quick and easy solutions. What will certainly help is:

● DISCUSSION of the meanings, connotations and usage of vocabulary introduced in class
● Encouraging students to use a DICTIONARY intelligently, particularly studying the examples given after the definitions
● Encouraging students to HIGHLIGHT vocabulary items they don't know and want to remember
● Making sure that students get plenty of EXPERIENCE in reading – not just reading the texts in this book, but popular fiction and journalism
● Systematic use of NOTEBOOKS to store useful new vocabulary items, preferably devoting a separate page to each different topic or category. It's recommended that students should discuss which system of vocabulary storage they consider most effective
● A REALISTIC approach to the problems: it's the students who have to do the remembering – all the teacher can be expected to do is introduce regular revision sessions throughout the course to help them not to forget (these may be described, perhaps disparagingly, as 'vocabulary tests').

The first Vocabulary exercise is 1.4 A2 on page 12 of the Student's Book.

Word study

Each even-numbered unit contains a section on word formation or an aspect of vocabulary building, in addition to the topic-based Vocabulary sections. One of the primary purposes of a course at this level is to encourage students to expand their active vocabulary, which involves them in DECIDING what to learn, according to their own needs and interests. In particular, students who need to concentrate on improving their writing skills will need to increase their range of expression.

The following points are covered in the Word study sections:

2.6   Synonyms and opposites – 1
3.4   Making an emphasis
4.5   Words easily confused
6.4   Synonyms and opposites – 2
8.4   Forming adjectives
10.6   Synonyms and opposites – 3
14.5   British and American English
16.2   Prefixes
16.3   Spelling
18.2   Compound words (nouns and adjectives)
20.6   Abbreviations and acronyms

Verbs and idioms

Almost every unit contains work on idioms and collocations or verbs and idioms.

These sections, which come at the very end of each unit cover phrasal verbs and the collocations in which certain common verbs are used. These can be fitted in when there's a little spare time during the lesson, or set for homework and checked in class later.

These sections deal with the following idioms and phrasal verbs:

1.6   All's well that ends well! – idioms and collocations with *all*
2.7   You can't lose! – verbs and idioms with *lose*
3.7   *At . . .* and *by . . .*
4.6   *Bring, carry* and *take*
5.6   *High, middle* and *low*
7.9   *In . . .* and *out of . . .*
8.6   *Get*
9.6   Ages – idioms and collocations with *age, fresh, new, old* and *young*
10.7   *Hard, soft, difficult* and *easy*
11.7   *For* and *on*
12.7   *Look* and *see*
13.6   Colours – *red, blue, green, black* and *white*
14.6   Speaking and thinking – *say, tell, call, speak, talk* and *think*
15.5   *Day* and *time*
16.7   *Hearts, hands, legs* and *feet*
17.8   Head over heels . . . – *head, brain, mind, face, eye, nose* and *ear*
18.6   *Keep, hold, stand* and *turn*
19.8   *Back, front* and *side*
20.9   *First, second, third . . .* and *last*

GRAMMAR

The Grammar sections in the even-numbered units are designed to revise the main problem areas of English grammar that still cause difficulties for advanced students.

These sections contain a variety of exercises: contrasted sentences where students have to explain the differences in meaning, error-correction exercises where students have to find the 'typical mistakes' and correct them, sentence-completion exercises and other more open-ended tasks. Some of these exercises reflect the task types in the English in Use paper of the CAE exam.

The Grammar sections cover the following areas:

2.3   The past – 1
4.4   Simple + progressive aspect
6.3   Modal verbs
8.2   The past – 2
10.4   Articles
12.5   Comparing and contrasting
14.2   Indirect speech
16.4   Conditional sentences

18.4   The future and degrees of certainty
20.7   *-ing* and *to* . . .

Students should realise that the Grammar sections are intended as REVISION of points that they've covered in previous courses. If they require more detailed rules or guidelines they should refer to a reference grammar book, such as *Basic English Usage* by Michael Swan (OUP). Students should be encouraged to ask questions if they're unsure about any points in the Grammar sections.

WRITING
Effective writing

These sections are designed to develop students' writing skills. Most of the sections include a short writing task of up to 100 words.

The Effective writing sections deal with the following points:

1.2	Joining sentences – 1
3.5	Punctuation
4.2 A	Spelling and punctuation
5.3	Making notes
7.4	Long and short sentences
7.6	Formal letters and personal letters
8.5 C–D	Formal and informal style
9.2	Paragraphs
11.4	Style, tone and content
13.2	Joining sentences – 2
15.2	A good introduction and conclusion
17.6	Expressing feelings
19.4	Connecting words (conjunctions)
20.4	Word order

In an advanced class, each individual student may to a greater or lesser degree be 'good at writing'. It's essential to regard the exercises in *New Cambridge Advanced English* as a starting point. Further remedial work may be necessary for students whose writing skills are particularly weak, or who need to develop specific writing skills (such as essay-writing for academic purposes, or business letters) to a very advanced level. In particular, the feedback you give to students when handing back their written work should take into account each individual student's strengths and weaknesses.

➡ See Correcting written work on page 14.

Creative writing

In most of these sections discussion in class leads up to the actual writing, which would be done at home. At this level it's important for students to feel that they're being given opportunities to communicate and not just being given 'compositions' to write, particularly if their creative writing takes a long time to prepare, write and receive feedback on.

Make sure you allow everyone time to read each other's written work: this is particularly important if creative writing is to be considered as more than 'just a routine exercise'. Any piece of writing should be an attempt to communicate ideas to a reader. If students know that their peers are going to read their work, they're more likely to try to make it interesting, informative and entertaining! If you, their teacher and 'critic', are the only reader, the process of writing is much less motivating.

Students can learn a lot from reading each other's ideas – and from each other's comments on their own work. A piece of written work should be regarded as a piece of communication, not simply an opportunity to spot the grammatical errors that students make.

➡ See Correcting written work on page 14.

The main Writing tasks are in the odd-numbered theme units but there are also Writing tasks in the even-numbered language units, usually connected with a reading passage or listening exercise. If your students are preparing for the CAE exam, most of the Writing tasks should be considered as compulsory – if not, you may prefer to skip some or all of them, depending how relevant each one is to your students' special needs and interests.

Here is a complete list of all the Writing tasks – the main Creative writing sections are in **bold type**:

1.3	**Writing a narrative**
2.5 D	A letter to a friend
3.6	**Planning ahead** . . . and **Writing a review**
4.2 C	Instructions (a recipe) and a note
5.4	**A complaint letter and a note**
6.4 E	A letter of reference
7.8	**A tactful (informal) letter**
8.3 C	Descriptions of the lives and achievements of two historical figures
9.5	**A letter to the editor (of a magazine)**
10.3 C	A description of your own Utopia
10.5 D	A letter describing the attractions of a city
11.5 E	A letter to a friend who has won the lottery
11.6 C	**Descriptions of three household names for a guidebook**
12.2 B	A letter about your first day at a new school or in a new class
12.4 B	A letter to the writer of the article OR an account in the same style as the article
12.6 E	Instructions on how to operate household equipment
13.5 C	**A report on advertisements in a magazine**
14.4 F	Instructions on what to do in case of fire
15.4 C	**A letter giving advice and a note** (based on information in the Interview)
16.5 B	Another letter giving advice
16.6 B	**Instructions for a first-aid manual**
17.5 D	An article describing a favourite book
17.7 C	**An account of a wedding or a family event**
18.3 D	A report on measures to protect the environment
19.6	**Reports and opinions (a report and an opinion column)**
20.1 C	An account of someone's day at work
20.8 B	**A letter applying for a job**

Correcting written work

When marking students' written work it's important to remember how discouraging it is to receive back a paper covered in red marks! The feedback you give to students when handing back their written work should take into account each individual student's strengths and weaknesses – and each student should be praised for making progress during the course.

It's better for students to locate and correct their own mistakes, rather than have corrections written out for them. This is particularly important when you believe that a student has made a careless mistake or a slip of the pen. In many cases, once mistakes are pointed out to students they can often correct them themselves – and they're more likely to remember the point later if they've put some effort into learning it.

A 'marking scheme' like the following is recommended, but whatever scheme you use make sure your students are conversant with the system you're using. The symbols shown here would appear on the side of the page in the margin – so please make sure your students do leave a wide enough margin for your comments!

X = 'Somewhere in this line there's a mistake of some kind that you should find and correct'

XX = 'Somewhere in this line there are two mistakes that you should find and correct'

An incorrect <u>word</u> or <u>phrase underlined</u> = 'This particular word or phrase is not correct and you should correct it'

G = 'Somewhere in this line there's a GRAMMATICAL mistake that you should find and correct'

V = 'Somewhere in this line there's a VOCABULARY mistake that you should find and correct'

Sp = 'Somewhere in this line there's a SPELLING mistake that you should find and correct'

P = 'Somewhere in this line there's a PUNCTUATION mistake that you should find and correct'

WO = 'Some of the words in this sentence are in the WRONG ORDER, please rearrange them'

? = 'I don't quite understand what you mean here'

And remember that all learners need encouragement and praise. So, equally important, use these more positive or encouraging marks liberally:

✓ = 'Good, you've expressed this idea well!' or 'This is an interesting or amusing point'

✓✓ = 'Very good, you've expressed this idea very well!' or 'Very interesting or amusing point!'

If your students are preparing for the CAE exam, you'll need to get a feel for the level of the exam and how marks are awarded. The marking scheme and sample candidates' work can be found in the Teacher's Book for *CAE Practice Tests 3* (or later) and in the CAE Handbook. The latter is obtainable from UCLES, 1 Hills Road, Cambridge CB1 2EU (fax +44 1223 460278), and can be consulted at your local British Council office or resource centre.

SPEAKING
Speaking and Pronunciation

The Speaking sections will help students to develop their sensitivity to degrees of appropriateness and extend their range of expression. (They also practise skills that are relevant for the CAE Speaking paper.)

Although a relatively small number of pages are devoted to Pronunciation, this doesn't imply that phonology is of little importance. Indeed, it requires constant attention, particularly when you're giving students feedback on their performance in spoken activities. At this level, correction is likely to be a more effective method of dealing with phonology than pronunciation exercises. However, bearing in mind the particular pronunciation difficulties of your students, you may wish to devise your own pronunciation drills or use supplementary materials which focus on their particular problems.

The Speaking and Pronunciation sections deal with the following areas:

2.4 Really? That's amazing! (expressing reactions)
4.3 Appropriate language (formal and informal styles)
6.1 What do they look like? (describing people)
11.2 Emphasising the right syllable
11.5 Sharing opinions
14.3 Spelling and pronunciation 1 – Consonants
16.5 Giving advice
17.4 First meetings
18.5 Spelling and pronunciation 2 – Vowels
19.5 Crime and punishment (discussion in the style of the CAE Speaking paper)
20.3 Satisfaction and success (conducting a survey)

But speaking and discussion are encouraged on pretty well every page in *New Cambridge Advanced English*! For example, most of the grammar exercises can be done in pairs and discussed as if they're problem-solving tasks.

Discussion opportunities

Every unit contains a variety of questions for students to consider and then discuss in small groups. These should be regarded as 'discussion opportunities', and if your students have little to say about some of these questions, they may be omitted. Conversely, if they have a lot to say, these discussions may go on for quite a long time. In other words, the amount of time that should be devoted to these is unpredictable. The discussion questions may be dealt with in any order, not necessarily starting with the first.

The first sets of discussion questions are in 1.1 A (a warm-up, scene-setting discussion) and 1.1 D (a follow-up discussion).

Communication Activities

All these Communication Activities involve an information gap, where each participant is given different information which has to be shared with a partner. Each part is printed on a different page to make it more difficult for students to see each other's information – they have to find it out from each other by telling each other and asking questions.

Here's a complete list of the Communication Activities at the end of the Student's Book:

Section	Description	Communication Activities
1.1 E	Desert island stories	1 + 19 + 35
2.5 B	Continuations of newspaper articles	2 + 20
6.1 E	Describing people in photos	3 + 22
6.2 A	Continuation of newspaper article	12 + 32
7.1 B	Information about graphology	4 + 23
7.7 B	Conversational and written styles	10 + 29
11.4 B	Marilyn Monroe and James Dean	14 + 37
12.6 D	Movie projector and movie soundtrack	6 + 25
14.2 B	Indirect speech exercise	7 + 26
15.1 E	Urban legends	8 + 27
15.2 D	Describing paintings	18 + 34
16.5 A	Giving advice	11 + 15 + 28
16.6 A	First aid	9 + 16 + 31
17.5 B	Synopses of books	13 + 21
18.1 C	*Woof!* and *The Transformation*	5 + 24
19.1 D	Newspaper stories	17 + 30 + 36

Working in pairs or groups

Many of the exercises in *New Cambridge Advanced English* are designed to be done by students working together in pairs, or in small groups of three or four. They are NOT designed to be quickly done 'round the class' with each student answering one question in turn.

There are several advantages to this approach:

● Students get an opportunity to communicate their ideas to each other while they're discussing each exercise

● Students are more likely to remember answers they've discovered or worked out by themselves than answers other students give – or answers the teacher announces to the class

● Students working in groups are more active than if they're working as a class: they talk more and do more thinking too. If a class of, say 20, were doing a 10-question exercise 'round the class', half of them wouldn't answer a single question.

● If an exercise is done 'round the class', the less confident or more sleepy students can simply answer 'I don't know' when their turn comes and go back to sleep the rest of the time. Moreover, weaker students can be lulled into a false sense of security by writing down all the correct answers and kidding themselves that they've 'done' the exercise. The exercises and activities in *New Cambridge Advanced English* are designed to help students to LEARN, not to test their knowledge or catch them out, and the idea is NOT for students to say to themselves 'Another 44 pages/exercises to go and then we've finished'!

One drawback of doing exercises in pairs or groups is that it does take time. However, as many of the exercises can be done as homework, time can be saved by setting some exercises to be done at home. Then, back in class next time, students can begin the session by comparing their answers in pairs or groups, and discussing as a class any problems they encountered.

Another possible problem is that errors may go uncorrected and that students might even learn 'bad habits' from each other. This can be dealt with by vigilant monitoring of students as they're working together and encouraging students to correct each other's mistakes – which they should be able to do quite efficiently at this level. This is covered in more detail in the section that follows.

However, the main problem is that, unobserved, the students may decide not to speak English but their mother tongue, especially if they're particularly interested in a topic and want to have their say in a discussion.

There is only one solution to this: insist that ENGLISH is the ONLY language that may be spoken in your classroom. The students have the rest of the week to speak their own language and your lesson is their main (perhaps their only) opportunity to talk English. You'll need to make this ground rule clear at the beginning of the course – and make sure from Day One that everyone in the class sees the wisdom behind the rule and agrees to cooperate. Even so, they may need reminding of the 'rule' at regular intervals during the course.

Mistakes and correction

Although work on improving students' accuracy is an essential aspect of a language course, particularly at an advanced level, it's far more important for learners to be able to communicate effectively. It's very difficult to develop confidence if one is afraid of making mistakes, and if students are corrected too frequently they may become 'mistake-conscious'. In real life, after all, people have to communicate with each other IN SPITE OF the mistakes they may be making and their less-than-complete command of English.

Students should certainly be corrected when they make serious errors, but it's usually best to point out any mistakes that were made after the groups have completed an activity, rather than interrupting during the activity. While students are working together in pairs or groups, and you're going from group to group listening in, you may be able to make the occasional discreet correction without interrupting the flow of the discussion, but normally it's better to make a note of some of the errors you overhear and point them out later.

You may hear your students making mistakes in pronunciation, grammar or style, but rather than mentioning every mistake you notice, it's more helpful to be selective and to draw attention to specific points that you think your students should concentrate on improving. It may be less confusing to focus on just one type of error at a time by, for example, drawing attention to pronunciation errors after one activity and then to vocabulary errors after another. Accuracy is something that takes a long time to develop and it can't be achieved overnight!

If they're working in pairs or groups, interrupting them to point out their mistakes may be counter-productive: it may break the flow of the conversation, discourage them from speaking English together or inhibit their attempts at communication. It's better in this case to 'store up' your comments on their mistakes (by making notes as you patrol the class) and then point out the anonymous students' mistakes you've overheard at the end of the pair- or group-work activity.

OTHER MATERIAL

Students at this level have specific needs and interests that a general coursebook can only partly cater for. You may need to find supplementary materials (particularly topical reading or listening texts) from other sources. Video recordings of BBC news programmes are particularly useful, especially the short reports and interviews they contain.

Students should also possess an up-to-date English to English dictionary:

the *Cambridge International Dictionary of English* (CIDE), the *Longman Dictionary of Contemporary English* (LDOCE), the *Oxford Advanced Learner's Dictionary* (OALD) and the *Collins COBUILD Essential English Dictionary* are all comprehensive and relatively portable.

A bilingual pocket dictionary may be useful while travelling, but isn't adequate for students studying at this level.

Although *New Cambridge Advanced English* revises the main problem areas of English grammar, students should also have access to a comprehensive grammar reference book. *Practical English Usage* by Michael Swan (Oxford University Press) is easy to use and highly recommended. Or, if your students' grammar is weak, you may prefer them to do extra grammar practice using *English Grammar in Use* by Raymond Murphy (Cambridge University Press).

CAE examination preparation

New Cambridge Advanced English is a complete CAE exam preparation course, covering the skills and techniques that candidates need to do well in all five papers of the exam. But the underlying philosophy of the book is that the exam is a stepping stone, not the students' final goal. Of course, everyone wants to do well in the exam, and their career may depend on a good result, but they also want to improve their English so that they can use it afterwards in real life – in their work, studies and social life.

Candidates who are taking the CAE exam need to be familiar with what to expect in each paper. Pages 19 and 20 may be photocopied for them as a handout.

For full details of how the exam works and four sample papers, please consult the Student's Book and the Teacher's Book of *CAE Practice Tests 3* (or later) published by Cambridge University Press. It's also worth consulting the latest edition of the CAE Handbook: this is obtainable from UCLES, 1 Hills Road, Cambridge CB1 2EU (fax +44 1223 460278), and can be consulted at your local British Council office or resource centre.

With any exam there are some special techniques that have to be mastered, which may not be required in real life situations. If your students have taken FCE since 1996 they'll already be familiar with most of the types of exercises and tasks that are required in CAE. The main difference is that the CAE versions are harder! But if they haven't taken FCE there are some tasks which may require extra work – a case in point is the 'gapped text' in the Reading paper, which demands a technique that even native speakers find tricky, and which is unlikely to be needed in real-life reading tasks. For more information on this, see page 139 in the Teacher's Book.

Students taking the CAE exam should devote more time to the **Creative writing** sections than students who have no exam in mind. They should also do most of the extra **Writing tasks** in the even-numbered units, which non-exam students can skip.

Many of the exercises and tasks in *New Cambridge Advanced English* reflect the format of the CAE exam. This is pointed out throughout the Teacher's Book whenever relevant in a note like this:

CAE exam	In the Teacher's Book, whenever an exercise reflects the format of part of the CAE exam this is noted in a box like this.

Because *New Cambridge Advanced English* is also designed for students who aren't taking the CAE exam, exam advice and tips are given in the Teacher's Book, not the Student's Book:

CAE exam	Exam hints and tips are given in the Teacher's Book, not the Student's Book, because they are only relevant for exam candidates. Pass these tips on to your students.

Exam candidates should also spend extra time using *CAE Practice Tests 3* (or later), which are actual past papers from previous CAE examinations. This is particularly important during the weeks before the exam takes place when candidates need to do some exam papers under exam conditions (without dictionaries and observing the specified time limits).

CERTIFICATE IN ADVANCED ENGLISH

The CAE examination consists of five papers, each of which has equal weighting of 20% of the total marks. The format of the exam is fairly similar to the First Certificate exam, which some students may already be familiar with.

In December 1999 the numbering (but not the content) of some papers in the exam will change: the pre-December 1999 names are given *in italics* below. However, a new word-formation task will be introduced as Part 4 of the English in Use paper at that time, replacing the note expansion task (*Question 6*).

Paper 1   Reading (1 hour 15 minutes)

This paper consists of four parts, each containing one or more texts. The texts are taken from newspapers, magazines, non-literary books, leaflets, brochures, etc. The tasks test a wide range of reading skills and strategies. There are between 40 and 50 multiple-matching, gapped text and multiple-choice questions altogether.

Paper 2   Writing (2 hours)

This paper consists of two parts, each with a writing task of approximately 250 words. Tasks include writing a newspaper or magazine article, a leaflet or brochure, a formal or informal letter, a report, a review, a competition or guidebook entry, a character reference, an information sheet or a memo. Question 5 is oriented towards work.

Part 1   consists of a compulsory task based on a substantial
(*Section A*)   reading input.
Part 2   consists of one task selected from a choice of four.
(*Section B*)

Assessment is based on content, organisation and cohesion, accuracy and range of language, register and effect on target reader.

Paper 3   English in Use (1 hour 30 minutes)

This paper consists of six tasks which test the ability to apply knowledge of the language system, including grammar, vocabulary, register, cohesion, spelling and punctuation.

(*Until December 1999 the paper is divided into three sections: A, B and C. After December 1999 the paper will be divided into six parts (Part 1 – Part 6). These comprise multiple-choice cloze, open cloze, error correction, word formation, register transfer and gapped text tasks. Until December 1999 Question 6 is a note expansion task.*)

Paper 4   Listening (about 45 minutes)

This paper contains four recordings which test a wide range of listening skills by means of matching, sentence completion, note-taking and multiple-choice questions. There are between 30 and 40 questions altogether and each piece is heard twice, except in Part 2.

(*Until December 1999 the paper is divided into four sections: A–D. After December 1999 these will be renamed Part 1 – Part 4.*)

Paper 5   Speaking (about 15 minutes per pair of candidates)

The CAE Speaking paper is conducted by two examiners (an interlocutor and an assessor), with pairs of candidates. The four parts of this paper are based on visual stimuli and verbal prompts and are designed to elicit a wide range of speaking skills and strategies from both candidates. Each part of this paper lasts 3–4 minutes.

Grammar and vocabulary, discourse management, pronunciation, interactive communication and global achievement are assessed.

This is the first 'Theme unit'. In common with the rest of the odd-numbered units, there is a special emphasis on reading and listening skills and on writing skills.

(1.1) A year on a desert island   Listening and Speaking

➡ In this section students have to speak, read and listen – they'll also participate in a Communication Activity. See page 10 of the Introduction for more information on the Listening activities, and pages 15 to 16 for more about Speaking and Communication Activities.

Ⓐ This brief discussion is a warm-up before the students read the short text in B and then do the listening exercise in C. Allow a little time for feedback from the pairs or groups: ask each pair or group to 'report back' on what they decided the answers to the questions were. Correct any misunderstandings but don't take too long.

➡ Whenever the symbol 👥 (Work in pairs) or 👥👥 (Work in groups) is used in the Student's Book instructions, please feel free to overrule this from time to time if you prefer to do the activity as a class, particularly if you have a small class. Also, many of the exercises which *don't* have a 👥 symbol can be done in pairs, if you prefer.

➡ If you have an odd number of students in the class, one 'pair' can consist of three students – this applies to all subsequent 👥 exercises too.

Ⓑ Keep the same pairs for this. As these are questions for discussion, some of the answers are a matter of opinion. The suggested answers below are for the benefit of students who are all at sea and can't find an answer – they shouldn't be considered as 'correct answers'.

SUGGESTED ANSWERS

- By boat (in a small aluminium dinghy)
- There were many small islands, all looking alike
- Three
- blue . . . white . . . blue . . . bottle green . . . white . . . blue – dazzlingly bright sunshine, heat, clean sea
- . . . small hills … muffled in dense dark green [vegetation]. Huge boulders . . . a wide open bay . . . a long straight beach with light coloured sand . . . palm trees – a perfect tropical, unspoilt island

> After *Castaway* (1983) Lucy Irvine wrote about her earlier life in *Runaway* (1986). She has also written a novel, *One is One* (1989).
>
> After *The Islander* (1984) Gerald Kingsland wrote about his further travels in *The Voyager* (1987).

▼ Ⓒ Before playing the recording, read through the transcript and highlight any vocabulary items that you'd like to draw your students' attention to later.

The recording is in THREE PARTS, separated by a short pause and indicated by ★★★ in the Transcript below. The first part is about the couple's preparations, the second part about their life alone together, and the third about other visitors to the island and the end of their stay on the island.

As it's a spontaneous conversation, the speakers hesitate a lot, repeat themselves frequently, and often interrupt each other.

1 Allow everyone time to read through the questions before playing the recording to them. Answer any questions about vocabulary that are raised. Encourage them to 'guess' some of the answers, basing their guesses on their ASSUMPTIONS about what is likely to have happened in the story. Then, when they listen to the recording, this can confirm or contradict the answers they anticipated and make the task of listening more realistic. This may help to simulate the real-life situation, where a listener often approaches a text with some previous knowledge of the subject matter.

2 Arrange the class into pairs so that they can quickly compare their answers later. Make it clear to everyone that the task isn't intended to catch them out but to help them to listen out for the main points that are made.

Set the counter on your cassette player to zero. Then, to give everyone a chance to get used to the voices before they have to concentrate on answering the questions, play the first 20 seconds of the first part of the recording through first, then rewind the tape back to the beginning (zero). Then play the whole of the first part.

Get everyone to compare their answers in pairs before going through the correct answers. If there is much disagreement about any of these, play the relevant sections of the recording again. If everyone thinks they have every answer right this won't be necessary. If everyone is unsure about some answers (and if there's time) the whole of the first part should be played through again.

3 After resetting the counter to zero, play the second part of the conversation and afterwards ask everyone to compare their answers. If necessary, play the second part again.

Again, reset the counter to zero and now play the third part of the conversation.

ANSWERS (L = Lucy, G = Gerald, L + G = both of them)

wrote *Castaway*	L	wrote *The Islander*	G
was 24 years old	L	was 51 years old	G
had lived on another island	G	had worked in a tax office	L
caught fish	L + G	tried to grow vegetables	G
did the cooking	L	was going to write a novel	G
was bad-tempered	G	went off for long walks alone	L
fell in love with the island	L	wrote a diary	L
was badly bitten by insects	G	could hardly walk	G
lost a lot of weight	L + G	had an irritating voice	L
lost touch with reality	L + G	drank salty water	L + G
did repairs for local islanders	G	went to another island for Christmas	L + G
wanted to stay longer	G	wrote a best-selling book	L

Transcript 9 minutes 40 seconds

HELEN: . . . Oh, you know what, I wanted to record that film *Castaway* on TV last night.

TIM AND JANE: Oh!

HELEN: I forgot to set the video. Did you guys see it?

TIM: No, no but I've...I've read the book written by Gerald Kingsland. I mean the...he was the man on the island.

JANE: And I've read...I've read the other one by Lucy Irvine. Um...she was the woman, you know.

HELEN: Oh, right. So you can both tell me the story . . .

TIM: Mm, OK.

JANE: Yeah. OK, well, there was this...there was this woman, Lucy Irvine, um... and she had a really boring job...er... working in an income tax office. And she was looking for an escape and she saw this...um...this ad in *Time Out*, you know, one of those...um...you know, looking for adventure type ads . . .

TIM: Yeah, but . . .

JANE: . . . a...and it said – no, hang on – it said...er...the ad said something like: 'Writer wants "wife" for year on...on... on desert island'...um...er...you know, so . . .

TIM: Yeah, but...but...but i...i...it started a long time before that . . .

JANE: Well, no, yeah, yeah, yeah, no, no, then...then she responded . . .

TIM: No, no. Yeah, I know, but Gerald Kingsland's dream was...was to experience life on a desert island and...er...way before that, he tried to find a suitable island: first the...the Cocos Island off the coast of Costa Rica. He spent some months there with his sons and a…a female companion, they all lived together for a whole summer, it…and it was very beautiful. But, it…it was, I mean, it was an inhabited island, not a deserted island. Um…he wanted to go, where he wanted to go was…um…Robinson Crusoe's original island, but his companion fell ill before they could get there. So, that's when he went back to London and he advertised in *Time Out*, and he interviewed dozens of applicants and chose Lucy Irvine. He was 51, and she was 24!

JANE: Yeah, that's right. And um…and they actually…they got permission to…um…er…to…to stay on the island for a year, and it was…it was an island called Tuin Island and…um…I think it's in the Torres Strait, which…um…that's between sort of North Australia and Papua New Guinea. Um…but they could only stay on the condition that…er…that they got married . . .

TIM: Married, yeah.

JANE: So…so they…they got married in Australia, and that was just…just before they went…just before they went off to the island, er . . . But, this is the big thing, you see, Lucy told Gerald that…um…she…she wouldn't sleep with him . . .

★★★

TIM: The island itself wasn't very big and it just had…um…er…just one small spring of fresh water. Er…plenty of fish of course, being an island. Um…er…there were coconuts and some fruit. I mean, i…it was very dry, there wasn't much rain. Um…their survival rations were what: just a few kilos of rice and a bit of cooking oil, some tea? So they, I mean, they'd have to depend on the island's resources for food. So, I mean, when . . .

JANE: Yeah, and then they…they had a very clear…er…sort of definition between what they…each of them would do. So…um…he…he was in charge of…um…growing things: he planted…he planted seeds and vegetables. And…um…and…he…he got all the firewood. And…um…and then also of course he was writing this book…he was writing this novel. And…um…and she did all the cooking, and…er…she…she…she collected fruit and stuff like that. And…um…and…they…but they both went fishing, er…and that was their only…that was the only protein that they managed to . . .

TIM: Yeah, but, while…um…while Gerald was trying to write and…er…trying

to…trying hard to make a sort of garden grow, Lucy went off by herself all day, sort of wandering around the island and swimming. He…he disliked the island because it was…um, well, he thought it was very flat and not as beautiful as…um…other tropical islands he'd visited. So, I mean, there was the . . .

JANE: But, you know, while…while he was…while he was…um…staying in the camp, I think Lucy just felt that she had to…had to get away from him. You know, she…because they just weren't getting on. And so she'd go off on these long walks just to get away from him and his…because he was a really bad-tempered guy. And she kept a diary, and…um…and she absolutely loved the island, she thought it was beautiful and mysterious. And…um…and so she just…she just couldn't understand what…why he couldn't appreciate the place. You know, he thought…he thought it was boring, she thought it was beautiful. And…and the other thing was: the real bone of contention was that he…um…he wouldn't build a…a permanent shelter to…er…you know, in place of their tent.

TIM: Yeah, but…but…because Gerald didn't want to rush into anything. They'd got a whole year ahead of them, there was… there was no point in building a permanent shelter sort of straight away.

JANE: Yeah, OK. Yeah, but I mean, this was a big…this was a big issue between them. You know, he…he wouldn't build a…a shelter, and he said that it wasn't…that it wasn't a priority, it wasn't important.

TIM: A…and meanwhile, they both had to spend the night in one small tent. And Gerald was bitten by sandflies and the bites turned into…er…tropical ulcers. They were so painful he could hardly walk and the sea water just made them worse, so that was just awful.

JANE: Yeah, and they just got…they just got…they lost more and more weight. Um…got…they got really weak because they just weren't – you know, OK, they were eating fish – but they weren't getting enough carbohydrates, you know . . .

TIM: Potatoes . . .

JANE: No, that's right, there was no…no bread, no potatoes. And they j… and they weren't getting their vitamins either. And…and…and then on top of that it also…it just didn't rain at all, so the vegetables didn't grow. And…and there was just this huge tension growing between them.

TIM: Yeah, well, because, according to Gerald, Lucy just talked too much – she did! And she always seemed to be telling him what to do all the time.

JANE: Yeah, yeah, but…but according to Lucy, Gerald just didn't do anything. You know, he just…he just didn't seem to appreciate that they had to survive and um…and also he just didn't…he just didn't appreciate the beauty of the island.

TIM: Mm, yeah, and the other…b…the spring, which was, you know, the water supply was drying up, so there wasn't any water. And they…they both seemed to be losing touch with reality, they were sort of walking around in a dream just, you know, losing it really.

★★★

JANE: Yeah, and then…um…I think sort of around that time there were these er…these…two…two men turned up on the island, um…they were…um . . .

TIM: Yachtsmen.

JANE: Yeah, that's right. What were they called?

TIM: Peter and…er . . .

JANE: Derek.

TIM: Peter and Derek, yeah.

JANE: And…um…they were…er…they were sailing to Singapore …in a catamaran. And they had some…and they had some antibiotics which they gave to them and that…I think that helped with his ulcers, didn't it?

TIM: Yeah, one…one of the men asked Gerald how he could stand Lucy's bossy tone of voice and the…the constant talking!

JANE: Yeah, and…er…and they both…they both had a word with Lucy and tried to persuade her to…to…that she should leave him…um…because they said that he was, you know, bad-tempered and…and hopeless and weak, and…um…and old. And…um…but…but she…she wouldn't go, er…she was absolutely determined to…to stay there for the year.

TIM: And then…and then some weeks after that, there was a fisherman from a…from a nearby island, Ronald Lui. Er…he came to the island and he noticed their…that their…um…fresh water was salty – they hadn't noticed it because it had been happening gradually, you see, with the spring drying up. Well, you eventually go mad if you…if you drink salt water. So…er…he gave them all the water that he'd got with them, and…er…then he sailed back to his island to…to bring

more water over. So, you know, he was…saviour . . .

JANE: And then, finally, Gerald…G…Gerald went ahead and built them a proper house. And…um…and then Ronald, the…the fisherman, he…he brought them…er…an old sewing machine . . .

TIM: Sewing machine, yeah.

JANE: Yeah, and…er…Gerald repaired it. And… er…he was…he was…he was really good, you know, that was one thing he was good at, he was…he was a good repairer . . .

TIM: That's it, he used to fix it.

JANE: And…um…so…er…they brought him lots of . . . You know, he became sort of like the handyman and lots of more things were brought for him to repair, like…er…there was outboard motors and generators . . .

TIM: Generators.

JANE: . . . and things like that, yeah. And… um…he…and he set up this sort of barter system, so he…he fixed their things and they gave him rice and flour and stuff like that. And…um…and slowly he started to get better and he sort of…he regained his self-respect as well.

TIM: Yeah, and then…um…at the end of the year they left the island to visit Ronald's island for Christmas. And then the rainy season came straight after it, I mean, huge storms and very very rough seas. So they…they couldn't get back to their island because the sea was too rough. Um…and then when it calmed down, then they returned to the island and they spent the last months of their time quite happily really, didn't they?

JANE: Yeah. And I think when…er…when they actually decided, when, you know, when…when the year was up…um… Gerald really wanted Lucy to…er…to…to stay with him and live on…er…on Ronald's island, but…er…she . . . No way!

TIM: She wasn't…she was having none of it!

JANE: Well, I think she thought she was too young for him, you know, rightly so. And she wasn't in love with him, so they…they parted. And…um…and then she went home and wrote…er…*Castaway*, and it was a huge success, it was a best-seller.

TIM: Yeah, and…but Gerald Kingsland never did finish his novel, but he did write his story in a book called *The Islander*, which is what I've read. So…and…and he didn't go home, he just…he just kept on travelling, you know, and he's still travelling now . . .

D This group discussion gives everyone a chance to air their views. Ask each group to report back on their discussion at the end. The amount of time you allow for this will depend on how much time you have available – and how interested or involved everyone gets in their discussion.

E1 In this Communication Activity each student has different information which must be shared with a partner and there is an 'information gap' to bridge.

Draw everyone's attention to the instructions in the Student's Book: this is NOT a reading aloud exercise but a chance to share information with each other.

Student A looks at **Activity 1** on page 180, which tells the story of *The Blue Lagoon*.
Student B looks at **Activity 19** on page 186, which tells the story of *The Swiss Family Robinson*.
Student C looks at **Activity 35** on page 191, which tells the story of *Robinson Crusoe*.

➡ If your class numbers aren't divisible by three, and it's necessary to form a group of four, two students could 'share' the Blue Lagoon story in Activity 1.

At the end of the activity, when each group member has told his or her story, ask for feedback from the class:

● Do they have any questions?
● What did they find easy/difficult about the activity?
● If they could do it again, what would they do differently?

2 If most or all of your students are taking the CAE exam (or a similar exam with a substantial written emphasis) this writing task should be set as homework.

However, if your students' main priority isn't improving their writing skills – and if they don't have time to do more than one writing task in one unit – it could be skipped. There's a 250-word writing task in 1.3 which should not be skipped, and a 100-word task at the end of 1.4.

CAE exam   1.1 **E2** is similar to Question 6 in the English in Use paper, which requires candidates to expand notes into full sentences. In the exam they have to write separate sentences, rather than a single complete paragraph as here. This task type will be replaced in the exam with a 15-item word formation task after June 1999.

These exam notes are a recurring feature of the Teacher's Book. If some or all of your students are taking the CAE exam, you should convey the information and advice in the exam notes to your class. If none of them are taking the exam, these notes can be disregarded.

(1.2) Joining sentences – 1   Effective writing

➡ See page 13 of the Introduction for more information about the Effective writing sections.

The exercises in this section are intended as revision of work your students are likely to have done in previous courses. They will also help you to diagnose what kind of mistakes your students make in their writing.

A Ask the class to comment on the styles used in the six examples. The connecting words are simply words used to connect two or more ideas in the same sentence – they include conjunctions, adverbs and prepositions.

SUGGESTED ANSWERS

Connecting words used:
As because because by the time while followed by after
During and then, after

As our train was late … and *During our lunch …* are perhaps the preferable versions because they're easier to understand, but this may be a matter of opinion.

B1 This exercise, together with B2, helps to raise the students' awareness of how in speech we tend to narrate events in chronological order, using simpler shorter sentences than in writing. This should be done in pairs but if it is more convenient to set this as homework, make sure pairs of students have a chance to compare their ideas together in class at some stage.

SUGGESTED ANSWERS (Many variations possible – the connecting words are in *bold italics*.)

2 It was a cold, damp morning, *and* I couldn't get my car to start, *so* I knew that I would have to push it down the hill. The car gathered speed *and then* I jumped in *and* managed to start the engine, *but* I still arrived late for work.

3 Her interest in politics made her decide to stand for parliament *and* she won the by-election with a large majority, *but* she lost at the next general election and *so/then* she gave up politics for good.

4 They went dancing together *and then* they went to a café. They spent a long time drinking coffee and talking, *so* they got home very late.

5 The airport was closed because of fog, *so* many flights were delayed *and* this caused inconvenience to hundreds of passengers. Our plane didn't take off *and* we had to spend the night in the departure lounge.

6 The ransom money was paid *and then* the hostages were released. The kidnappers were trying to get out of the country, *but* all the ports and airports were being watched *so* they were caught by the police.

2 It might be a good idea to discuss with the class how the endings could change. There are many different ways each story could turn out differently – just one is given in each suggested answer below.

SUGGESTED ANSWERS (The connecting words are in *bold italics*.)

2 I arrived on time for work *even though* I hadn't at first been able to get the car to start one cold, damp morning. I decided to push the car down the hill *and* managed to start the engine *after* jumping in as it gathered speed.

3 Her interest in politics made her decide to stand for parliament *and* she won the by-election with a large majority. *After* keeping her seat at the next general election, she remained in politics.

4 They got home quite early *because* they hadn't spent a long time drinking coffee and talking in a café *after* they had been dancing together.

5 Our plane took off on time *because* the airport reopened *as soon as* the fog cleared. Otherwise many flights would have been delayed, *which* might have caused inconvenience to hundreds of passengers, *and* we might have had to spend the night in the departure lounge.

6 The kidnappers escaped from the police *even though* all the ports and airports were being watched *while* they were trying to get out of the country. They had *eventually* released the hostages *when* the ransom money had been paid.

CAE exam In the Writing paper candidates are rewarded for writing more complex sentences (as in **B2**) rather than using an over-simple style as in **B1**.

C This can be done in pairs in class or set for homework. Any of the conjunctions listed in B2 in the Student's Book can be used.

SUGGESTED ANSWERS

2 Once they had found some driftwood and built a bonfire on the beach, they caught some fish and grilled them over the fire.

3 After they had gathered palm leaves, they built themselves a rough shelter.

4 After suffering a sleepless night because of all the insects, they began to lose heart.

5 They made mosquito nets because they wanted to protect themselves the following night.

6 They were very glad when they found wild bananas growing on a hillside and, after eating them, they started to look for a supply of drinking water.

7 As they were unable to find any fresh water, they were afraid they would not be able to survive on the island.

8 Although they hoped to collect some rainwater to drink, there was so little rain that they were in despair.

9 After they had built a raft from the remaining driftwood, they set sail across the ocean.

10 In the end, as the raft started to sink, man-eating sharks began to circle ominously round them.

CAE exam   **1.2 C** is similar to Question 6 in the English in Use paper, which requires candidates to expand notes into full sentences. This task type will be replaced in the exam with a 15-item word formation task after June 1999.

Finally, ask the class what they found most difficult in this section and, if necessary, do some remedial work.

➡ There's more practice on using past tenses in 2.3. Joining sentences – 2 is 13.2.

(1.3) Writing a narrative   Creative writing

➡ See pages 13–15 of the Introduction for more information about the Creative writing sections and Correcting written work.

A Encourage everyone to make notes before they start writing. This can be done by students working together in pairs or groups.

B1 Make sure everyone follows the instructions, so that the activity in B2 is set up suitably.

2 After the group work, collect everyone's work and mark it. Treat this exercise as a way of diagnosing your students' writing skills. Try to make comments on each person's work and help them to be aware of their strengths and weaknesses in writing.

➡ If possible, photocopy your students' work and store the copies safely. Later in the course you can show them this work – and help them to realise that they've made a lot of progress.

The model answer on the next page can be photocopied, if you wish, as a model for your students to see. It conforms to the requirements of the CAE exam and would get an impression mark in 'Band 5' (the highest grade), to which your students may aspire.

See pages 18–19 in the Introduction for more information about the CAE exam and how it's marked.

Before the next lesson

If possible, get everyone to prepare the text on pages 12–13 as homework and highlight the unfamiliar words (step C1). Reassure everyone that, although the text is a poem, it is written in a fairly conversational style. Indeed, take away the line breaks and it reads quite like a short story.

(1.3) MODEL VERSION

I found myself lying on a sandy, palm-fringed beach. As I opened my eyes the palm fronds waved above me fragmenting the deep blue sky. How had I got here? I had absolutely no recollection of airport terminals, suitcases, disembarking from a cruise ship, hotels, companions. I was wearing jeans and a T-shirt and no shoes, water lapping my feet in a relentless fashion. What was going on?

I got up unsteadily, a dull ache at the base of my skull causing me to move my head carefully as I scanned the surroundings. Nothing in sight but white sand, sun glinting on milky blue water and palm trees and other vegetation along the shore, their denseness forming a formidable barrier to easy exploration of the interior. On the horizon sky met sea with no hope-bearing vessels to break the monotony.

In my dark clothes the heat was intolerable. I threw off jeans and T-shirt and decided I had to find out more about this place. Where was I? Was this an island or the coastline of some large country? I had to find a hill or some high point to get an idea of what kind of place I was in. I didn't dare risk the lush vegetation inland – what poisonous or aggressive creatures might be lurking there? Or even, terrible thought, what warlike tribe of cannibals?

"Get a grip!" I told myself and set off along the fine sand towards what I thought must be the east.

+ on a fresh page . . .

After walking for several hours with a searing thirst developing and the dull ache in my skull splitting my head in two, I met a man.

"Welcome to Club St Lucia," he said.

© **Cambridge University Press, 1998**

(1.4) *The Castaways*   Reading

➡ See page 9 of the Introduction for a description of the Reading sections in the book. In common with most 'Reading' sections in the book, students are also expected to speak and write during this section – however, the main emphasis is on reading and the reading passage is central to the section.

A 1 This is a warm-up discussion, encouraging everyone to revise some of the vocabulary they encountered in 1.1 and preparing them for the theme of the poem.

2 This vocabulary exercise can be done in pairs or alone – paragraphs 2 and 4 explain some of the references in the poem which might otherwise fox some students.

ANSWERS

1 surviving   circumstances   tension   nerves   **2** shipwrecked   remote
3 isolation   companion   servant   **4** rescued   lonely   pirates

> **CAE exam** **1.4 A2** resembles Part 1 in the English in Use paper, where candidates have to choose a suitable word to fill each gap in a text from a choice of four. In the exam there are only four words to choose from for each gap, and the words all have similar meanings, so more careful analysis of meaning is necessary.

The poet Adrian Mitchell was born in 1932. His poems are simple and topical, and easily accessible. He is committed to poetry as performance and much of his work contains social comment. His collected verse is published in *For Beauty Douglas: Collected Poems 1953–1979* and *Blue Coffee: Poems 1985–1996*. There's also a paperback collection: *Adrian Mitchell's Greatest Hits*.

B The poem is recorded – play the tape as the class follow the text in their books. Reassure everyone that, although the text is a poem, it is written in a fairly conversational style. (3 minutes 40 seconds)

C1 Ask everyone to highlight any unfamiliar words in the poem using a fluorescent highlighter. This symbol is used throughout the book whenever this has to be done.

➡ Point out to everyone that useful vocabulary is also to be found in other places in the Student's Book – for example, in the instructions and within the exercises. Looking back at 1.4 section A2, for example, students might have highlighted *magician* and *creatures* in paragraph 2.

2 There are no 'correct answers' here: even what is 'useful' or 'pointless' may be a matter of opinion.

3 This discussion will encourage students to think about the implications of the poem. Make sure there is time for feedback afterwards and make it clear that there are no 'right answers' when it comes to interpreting a poem.

4 This writing task is probably best set as homework. However, if your students don't have enough time to do it (and especially if they aren't going to take the CAE exam) it could be skipped or covered as a further discussion topic.

Leo Jones *New Cambridge Advanced English*

(1.4) MODEL VERSION

I like the poem because it's entertaining and packed full of ideas. You'd expect a tale of air crash survivors to be tragic and depressing but there's no pessimism and no account of any difficulties. The survivors have no problem coping with their new life (apart from Mary, the widow). They organise life according to their tastes and talents and rapidly convert the desert island into a modern state, with public and commercial institutions. Mary seems to be the only one to worry about how they've changed the unspoilt beauty of the place. It's a poem that tells a good story.

1.5 Survival

➡ This is the first of 11 interviews with experts or people who give a different point of view about the topic of the unit. The next one is an interview with an actress in Unit 3.

A Although the theme of survival relates to previous sections in this unit, the speaker talks about survival in the Arctic, not on a desert island.

Play the first 30 seconds or so of the recording for everyone to get used to the speaker's voice. Then rewind to the beginning and play it right through, possibly pausing it from time to time for everyone to have a breather and write down their answers. They'll probably need to hear it twice to get them all.

Afterwards ask the class for their reactions to what they've heard. What kind of person do they think Pen Hadow is and what was their impression of him?

SUGGESTED ANSWERS

1 rediscover/reinvent **2** the cold **3** solo attempts **4** calmly confident **5** lose your cool/panic/get depressed **6** engines **7** pack/drifting/floating ice **8** rougher **9** they would be ashamed/humiliated (as professional explorers they'd lose credibility) **10** strapped themselves to the deck **11** hypothermia **12** 50 hours **13** a few miles **14** the Arctic **15** a couple of years

> **CAE exam** **1.5 A** is similar to one of the tasks in the Listening paper where candidates have to complete sentences with a word or short phrase. Other tasks in the exam require candidates to fill gaps in a chart or table, or fill the gaps in notes with a word or phrase (note-taking), multiple-choice questions, or a multiple-matching task.

B There's quite a lot to discuss among these questions, so try to leave plenty of time. Point out to everyone that they can discuss the questions in any order, not necessarily starting with the first.

Transcript 6 minutes

PEN: I'm Pen Hadow and…er…my profession is a polar guide and I run a small specialist guide service called the Polar Travel Company. I'm also a polar explorer.

INTERVIEWER: What do you really enjoy about going to the Arctic?

PEN: It's so different, it offers so many…er…ways of broadly getting back to the basics of oneself and then to some extent rediscovering oneself, reinventing oneself even. I think people find it hugely invigorating and enervating and refreshing, all those things. Quite apart from the obvious things of the wildlife and the landscapes and, and so on, you know, and the sense of achievement in what they've been doing.

INTERVIEWER: And what do you not enjoy so much?

PEN: The cold. I do not enjoy the cold any more than anybody else. But I'm used to it, I know how bad it can be, I know that if it's bad that it could get a great deal worse. I've made two solo attempts on the north geographic pole – a more God-forsaken,

isolated…er…pressured scenario is hard to imagine. Um…but again I would say that I don't enjoy the cold but at least I know when my toes go numb, my fingers go numb I know that that doesn't necessarily mean I've got frostbite so I understand what's going on and understanding is…is a, you know, is a long way to being confident and once you're confident that's a long way to not making mistakes…er…if one's sort of calmly confident. Um…hypothermia is one of the bigger problems and one of…one of the things that triggers that is getting into a state about things, um…losing your cool and then getting in a flap and then getting depressed about the situation and it's a very difficult slide to get out of, um…especially if you're on your own. So…um…I think just through experience I've learnt a lot and therefore feel a lot more comfortable about being cold.

INTERVIEWER: What's the most dangerous situation you've been in, or one of them?

PEN: Um…I was once on…I was on this rubber boat…um… adrift in the Denmark Straits, which . . . we'd read the Admiralty sort of…er…report if you like o…on conditions to be expected in the Denmark Strait, which is the strait that separates western Iceland from eastern Greenland. And it said: 'This is the…one of the most dangerous stretches of water in the world. Seas can be expected to be mountainous on several occasions, you know, during …during the autumn, um…30 metres or more, which is sort of 90- to 100-foot waves. And…um…we were late in the season for various reasons we couldn't avoid, um…and we were given a clear weather window of about two days, maybe three days, and it was going to take us two days to make the crossing. And…er… essentially, both our engines…um…seized, so we were adrift in pack ice…in drifting ice that comes…drifts out of the Arctic Ocean down the east coast of Greenland in the East Greenland Current. And…er… then the wind started to get up and we were in this rubber boat in amongst all these big plates of ice and…um…the seas got bigger and bigger and I just thought, 'Well, this is it. This isn't…this is going to be a serious challenge a…and ultimately it's not a challenge that may…it may go beyond a challenge.' You just get wiped out, there's nothing you can do. Um…and we were both very anxious not to use the search and rescue sort of system that we always have as a backup because of the shame and the humiliation really of having to use it, um…as professional explorers. And…um…so we sat it out. And in fact what happened was that we drifted deeper and deeper into this pack ice as the swell got bigger and bigger. We started off in relatively open seas, um…and there were…there were waves raking the boat and we were strapped, there was no protection, no cockpit, anything like that, it was an open deck. And we…er…used ratchet straps, we strapped ourselves to the deck and these waves were just raking the boat and stripping off…stripping gear out of the boat. And…er…my colleague had…um…quite serious hypothermia at the time and…er…in fact we got into the same…um…er…bivouac bag, trying to keep each other warm. And…er…we drifted deeper and deeper into the… into the floating pack and…er…it acts like oil on troubled waters. In fact it was much better to be in there…um…than it was to be out in the…in the more open sea. And…er…in…in the morning it was flat calm. So we were out for fifty…we were adrift for fifty hours and…um…we actually drifted to within a few miles of our dest…final destination, which we could see across the…across the open water. That's about as bad as it's got!

INTERVIEWER: Yes! That sounds pretty bad I think.

PEN: Yes.

INTERVIEWER: How do you think you'd survive if you were on a desert island?

PEN: Love it! Nothing I'd like more – send me there now!

INTERVIEWER: Where would you find one in . . .?

PEN: Ooh, the Arctic.

INTERVIEWER: In the Arctic, yes.

PEN: Yes, I would like plenty of ammunition…um…and a few basic provisions and I'd…and I'd…and I'd look forward to surviving a couple of years on my own, before my rescuers found me. I'm beginning to think that I was destined for a desert island, so if you'd like to send me there I'd be very happy.

All's well that ends well!   **Idioms and collocations**

➡ See page 12 of the Introduction for more information about the Idioms and collocations / Verbs and idioms sections.

Although the Idioms and collocations / Verbs and idioms sections come at the end of each unit, they can all be done at ANY stage, depending on the time available. They can, for example, fill a convenient 10–15 minutes at the end of a lesson and be completed as homework.

➡ Point out to everyone that just doing these exercises is not going to 'teach' them the expressions. The exercises revise expressions they may already know and introduce new ones – learning the idioms they consider to be useful is up to them and it will take time for such idioms to be incorporated into their active vocabulary.

Ⓐ **SUGGESTED ANSWERS**

2 all over   **3** it's all the same   By all means   **4** all in   **5** all in
6 All at once   all but   **7** All being well   **8** all right   **9** all right   **10** all the same
11 all told / in all   all at once   **12** First of all   above all

Ⓑ **SUGGESTED ANSWERS**

1 First of all   **2** all being well   **3** all the same   **4** All the same   **5** all over
6 all the same   **7** By all means   **8** Above all

➡ As pointed out in the note in the Student's Book, students should make their own decisions about what vocabulary is useful for them to learn. Highlighting will help to draw attention to vocabulary when they are reviewing a unit.

FINALLY . . .

Recommend to everyone that they should spend half an hour reading through the whole of this unit at home before going on to the next one. In this way, new vocabulary is more likely to 'sink in' and be remembered permanently.

This is the first of the 'Language units': in common with the rest of the even-numbered units, there is a special emphasis on grammar revision, word study and speaking skills. But there is also some listening and/or reading in these units too.

(2.1) United nations   Vocabulary

➡ If possible, take a large map of the world, a globe or perhaps an atlas into class for this section.

A1 This exercise contains a number of tricky nationality words, even for students whose geographical knowledge is good. Some of the countries are included because they will be referred to later in this unit.

Note that we are concerned with nationality words, not the word for a native or resident of the cities (e.g. *Muscovite, Viennese, Cairene*, etc.) in this exercise.

ANSWERS
Bombay – an Indian   Bratislava – a Slovakian   Bucharest – a Romanian
Budapest – a Hungarian   Cairo – an Egyptian   Havana – a Cuban
Jakarta – an Indonesian   Johannesburg – a South African   Karachi – a Pakistani
Kiev – a Ukrainian   Kuala Lumpur – a Malaysian   Lagos – a Nigerian
Lima – a Peruvian   Ljubljana – a Slovenian   Manila – a Filipino/Filipina
Moscow – a Russian   Oslo – a Norwegian   Prague – a Czech   Riyadh – a Saudi Arabian
São Paulo – a Brazilian   Seoul – a (South) Korean   Sofia – a Bulgarian
Sydney – an Australian   Toronto – a Canadian   Vienna – an Austrian

2 It might be intriguing or amusing to start off with some vehicle nationality plates from the countries already mentioned in A1. Write them on the board and see if anyone can guess where they come from:

(SLO)	(RO)	(BG)	(CDN)	(DZ)	(A)	(TR)	(ZA)
Slovenia	Romania	Bulgaria	Canada	Algeria	Austria	Turkey	South Africa

For non-European students, many of the nationality plates may be enigmatic! Encourage everyone to guess the ones they don't know because in doing so they'll be coming up with the names of other countries. (The answers in brackets show what a person would be called, though this isn't what the exercise asks for.)

ANSWERS   (country · nationality adjective (a person))
CH = Switzerland · Swiss (a Swiss)   D = Germany · German (a German)
DK = Denmark · Danish (a Dane)   E = Spain · Spanish (a Spaniard)
GR = Greece · Greek (a Greek)   I = Italy · Italian (an Italian)
NL = Holland/the Netherlands   P = Portugal · Portuguese (a Portuguese)
       Dutch (a Dutchman/woman)   S = Sweden · Swedish (a Swede)
PL = Poland · Polish (a Pole)   CD = diplomatic corps · foreign (a diplomat)
SF = Finland · Finnish (a Finn)

3 SUGGESTED ANSWERS
Europe: Albania, Andorra, Belgium, Belorussia, Croatia, Cyprus, Estonia, France,
           FYRM (Former Yugoslav Republic of Macedonia), Georgia, Great Britain,
           Iceland, Ireland, Latvia, Lithuania, Malta, Moldavia (Moldova), Monaco,
           Yugoslavia (Serbia & Montenegro), etc.
Africa: Angola, Cameroon, Ethiopia, Ghana, Ivory Coast, Kenya, Morocco,
           Mozambique, Senegal, Sudan, Tanzania, Tunisia, Zaïre, Zambia,
           Zimbabwe, etc.

Asia: (West) Afghanistan, Armenia, Azerbaijan, Iran, Iraq, Israel, Kyrgyzstan, Syria, Tajikistan, Turkmenistan, United Arab Emirates, Uzbekistan, etc.

(North) China, Japan, Kazakhstan, Mongolia, North Korea, Taiwan, etc.

(South) Brunei, Burma (Myanmar), Cambodia, Nepal, Singapore, Sri Lanka, Vietnam, etc.

Latin America: Argentina, Bolivia, Chile, Colombia, Costa Rica, Ecuador, Mexico, Nicaragua, Panama, Paraguay, Uruguay, Venezuela, etc.

This could be started on the board and then completed for homework. The list can include countries mentioned in A1 and A2, as well as new ones from A3 – but only ones they know the whereabouts of (so probably not Kyrgyzstan). However, make sure they don't include *too* many nationalities that are already well-known to them (e.g. China, Japan, USA, etc.).

B SUGGESTED ANSWERS (To show what the students might come up with.)

Country	nationality	a person	the people	language(s)
Argentina	Argentinian	an Argentine/ Argentinian	the Argentines/ Argentinians	Spanish
Belgium	Belgian	a Belgian	the Belgians	French and Flemish (Dutch)
Canada	Canadian	a Canadian	the Canadians	English and French
Croatia	Croatian	a Croatian	the Croatians	Croatian
Estonia	Estonian	an Estonian	the Estonians	Estonian
Iceland	Icelandic	an Icelander	the Icelanders	Icelandic
Kenya	Kenyan	a Kenyan	the Kenyans	Swahili and English
Mexico	Mexican	a Mexican	the Mexicans	Spanish
Nepal	Nepalese	a Nepalese	the Nepalese	Nepali
New Zealand	New Zealand	a New Zealander	the New Zealanders	English and Maori
Scotland	Scottish	a Scot	the Scots	English and Gaelic
Wales	Welsh	a Welshman/ woman	the Welsh	English and Welsh
etc.				

➡ Before they begin C, your students may need reminding of some useful expressions they can use in discussions and when giving reasons. The following page may be photocopied, or you may prefer to write selected expressions on the board so that the students can note them down.

C This group discussion will encourage everyone to daydream about world travel. Reasons are important. Start the ball rolling by explaining why YOU would love to visit a couple of countries one day:

I'd love to go to Thailand because . . .
Somewhere else I'd really like to visit is Nepal, because . . .

➡ There's further discussion on nationalities in 2.5 C.

CAE exam	In the Speaking paper of the exam candidates are involved in a discussion. Explaining and giving reasons are important aspects of this, as well as asking each other to justify their opinions.

Leo Jones *New Cambridge Advanced English*

SHARING OPINIONS   UNIT 2

Asking for someone's opinion:

> What do you think about . . .?   What are your views on . . .?
> What are your feelings about . . .?   What do you feel about . . . ?

Giving your own opinion: ### Asking someone else if they agree:

> I'd say that . . .   > . . . What do you think?
> I can't help thinking that . . .   > . . . Do you see what I mean?
> It seems to me that . . .   > . . . Do you agree?
> In my view . . .   > . . . Do you go along with that?
> The way I see it . . .
> If you ask me . . .
> Would you agree that . . .?

Saying whether you agree: ### Saying you don't agree:

> That's just what I think.   > I don't really agree.
> I couldn't agree more.   > I don't entirely agree.
> That's true.   > I think I see what you mean, but . . .
> I absolutely agree.   > That's true in a way, I suppose, but . . .
> That's just what I think.   > That's one way of looking at it. On the other hand . . .

Asking someone to give their reasons or explain what they mean:

> I don't quite follow. Do you mean . . .?   I'm not quite with you. Are you saying . . .
> I'm sorry, could you explain why?   I'm sorry, what do you mean exactly?
> Why do you think that . . .?   Can you explain why you think that . . .?

Giving reasons and justifying opinions:

> The reason why I think . . . is because . . .   The reason for that is . . .
> That's because . . .   I think it's because . . .
> Well, you see, . . .   The main/basic reason is . . .
> If I could just explain: . . .

THIS DOCUMENT MAY BE PHOTOCOPIED.   © Cambridge University Press, 1998

A1 Ask everyone to read the paragraph about Oumou Sangaré. Ask them whether her music would appeal to them – and why or why not.

Play the 30-second clip from Oumou Sangaré's album *Worotan* (World Circuit Records, 1996). Ask everyone to give their reactions to what they hear.

2 Before playing the recording for the first time, find out if anyone has heard of any of the artists mentioned. (If the whole recording seems too long to play in one go, there are two possible places where you could pause the recording marked with ★★★ in the Transcript – if you do this, the students could compare their answers thus far before you play the next part.)

ANSWERS

Ali Farka Touré	Mali
Elio Revé	Cuba
Fong Naam	Thailand
Gilberto Gil	Brazil
Inti Illimani	Chile
Joe Arroyo	Colombia
Juan Luis Guerra	Dominican Republic
Khaled	Algeria
Ladysmith Black Mambazo	South Africa
Márta Sebestyén	Hungary
Nikos Ksidakis	Greece
Nusrat Fateh Ali Khan	Pakistan
Oumou Sangaré	Mali
Papa Wemba	Congo (Zaïre)
Paul Simon	USA
Ruben Blades	Panama (now USA)
Youssou N'Dour	Senegal

3 Before playing the recording again, allow everyone time to read through the sentences – can they already guess some of the missing words? If so, they could pencil them in.

ANSWERS

1 popular cultures **2** living played revived **3** West Africa **4** unimaginative fresh **5** families generations **6** dance **7** haunting **8** instruments **9** invented producers **10** hand-made

B This follow-up discussion gives students a chance to find out about each other's tastes in music – 'foreign countries' include the USA and the UK in this case. If you have different nationalities in your class, encourage them to find out about each other's popular music.

Transcript   8 minutes

[Music: clip from *Worotan* by Oumou Sangaré]

PRESENTER: That lovely song was sung by a woman from Mali called **Oumou Sangaré**. She's one of the biggest stars of what's come to be known as World Music. But what is World Music? The music critic Tony Brown and the performer Judy Harvey are here with me in the studio. Tony, what is World Music?

TONY: Well, it's popular music that comes from cultures other than Western Europe and the USA. It includes popular music from all over the world, that is rooted in other cultures, as well as classical music and folk music from other cultures. However this all depends where you are: for us in Europe *samba* is World Music, but for people in Brazil it's their own popular music with its own big stars, such as **Gilberto Gil**.

JUDY: It's been referred to as *living* traditional music, which means that it's real and it's still being played and enjoyed – it's not being r...revived or...or rediscovered.

PRESENTER: So I suppose we're talking about all kinds of music that are neither Western classical music, nor Anglo-American popular music?

JUDY: Nor jazz, that's right.

PRESENTER: So is this a recent trend: Western people discovering music from other cultures?

TONY: No, not at all. Since the nineteenth century many of the popular Western dance crazes, like the polka, the waltz, the tango, samba, have originated in folk music from other countries. The dances and their rhythms were taken by middle-class people wanting to be shocked by sexy new rhythms. The ideas were imported from other countries or from their own under-classes: for example, the blues came from the poor black people of North America. Most of what we consider to be purely American popular music, rock 'n' roll, jazz, is all rooted in West Africa. The slaves took their traditional music and rhythms with them to America.

PRESENTER: Mm, there was an upsurge of interest in South African music after the famous American singer **Paul Simon** released his *Graceland* album in 1987, wasn't there?

JUDY: Mm, it…it's true that Paul Simon did increase public awareness of South African music: bands and groups from the townships like Soweto. **Ladysmith Black Mambazo**, for example, are an extraordinary group of singers who sing unaccompanied, using their voices as instruments. But Paul Simon didn't start the whole thing. Actually, there had been a growing interest dating from the mid-eighties among enthusiasts and musicians who were, well, a lot of them were finding Anglo-American popular music increasingly unimaginative and…and commercial.

PRESENTER: Where is this more imaginative music coming from?

TONY: Well, from all over the world: anywhere people are still creating music and improvising, where the music is still alive and fresh and not organised and managed by big business interests and marketing. If we just look at West Africa, where music-making is still very much alive, there are all sorts of different traditional styles and unusual instruments: er…different kinds of percussion instruments and string instruments too, like the *kora* – that's a…a wonderful 21-stringed West African harp-lute. It has quite a magical sound.

JUDY: As Tony said earlier, many of the people who are becoming well-known in the West are already superstars in their own countries – their music's based on local traditions dating back hundreds and hundreds of years where particular families have carried on the tradition of music-making for, well, for generation after generation. Er…two of the biggest names are **Youssou N'Dour** from Senegal and **Ali Farka Touré** from Mali. Both of them belong to families of musicians and have been performing since they were very young children, just like Oumou Sangaré herself. Often they've combined their traditional instruments from Africa with Western instruments, like…er…electric guitars, i…in strikingly unique, original ways. And this kind of crossover between Western rock music and World Music is very popular.

★★★

PRESENTER: And where else in Africa does this World Music come from?

TONY: Well, all over. For example, the *soukous* music of the Congo is…is very special: **Papa Wemba** is very well-known, fantastic dance music.

JUDY: And the music of North Africa is becoming much better known. Er… Algeria has its own special popular music called *rai*: and…er…**Khaled** is one of its most famous stars.

TONY: There's a wide range of Latin American music too. For example, Cuba is the home of *salsa* and *son-changüi*: **Elio Revé** and his Orquesta Revé – it's really marvellous music, it really makes you want to dance. *Salsa* was exported to the USA via Puerto Rico. One of the most famous *salsa* stars is er…er…**Ruben Blades** from Panama, but now based in the USA. *Salsa* is amazingly popular throughout the whole of Latin America: **Joe Arroyo** in Colombia is a big star who blends *salsa* with *cumbia*. And…er…there's *merengue* music from the Dominican Republic and the big star there is **Juan Luis Guerra**. This is all wonderful happy music.

JUDY: Mm, the music of the Andes is wonderful too in a totally different way. The musicians use pan-pipes and flutes and harps, it's beautifully haunting music, it often sounds very sad. A well-known band there are **Inti Illimani** from Chile.

★★★

PRESENTER: What about the rest of the world?

JUDY: Oh, traditional folk music is still kept alive in many parts of Europe. Er…for example the music of Hungary, which uses instruments and sounds and voices with some wonderfully haunting songs: **Márta Sebestyén**'s songs from Hungary and Transylvania are haunting. And

Greece has a very strong tradition of its own music, known as *rembétika*: **Nikos Ksidakis** is one of its most famous musicians.

TONY: Asian music is not so well-known in the West but that's changing. Indian classical music has influenced rock music since the Beatles discovered the *sitar*. Er…more recently, the melodies and rhythms of **Nusrat Fateh Ali Khan** from Pakistan: these are devotional Muslim songs, they… they're fascinating. But there are so many different cultures in Asia. For example, the classical Thai music of **Fong Naam**, who are…are brilliant. Oh, and the wonderful gamelan music of Indonesia too. The marvellous thing about music from Asia i…is the wide range of instruments that are used that…that sound so different from Western musical instruments.

JUDY: Mm, and the term 'World Music' was actually invented by a group of record producers in 1987, so that record shops would have a convenient special section where customers could find this kind of music. Record buyers didn't even know where to find it in the few shops that did

stock it! And this kind of music tended to be only available as imports and was hard to come by anyway.

PRESENTER: Where is World Music recorded?

TONY: W…the recordings are made all over the world, some on location, some in studios. Many of the big stars record in Western studios, particularly in Paris, or in…er…Peter Gabriel's Real World Studio down in a little village in Wiltshire.

JUDY: Peter Gabriel invested £5 million in a studio in the heart of the English countryside – er…his motto is 'high-tech and hand-made' – where musicians from all over the world can make music and record it using the latest recording techniques.

TONY: You can find all kinds of World Music on labels like RealWorld, and also on EarthWorks, Hannibal Records, Stern's Africa, World Circuit, GlobeStyle – there are lots of them. You just have to browse around in your local record shop to see the range that's available – it's filed under World Music.

JUDY: Yes, all you have to do is discover it for yourself!

PRESENTER: Thank you both.

(2.3) The past – 1   Grammar

➡ See page 12 of the Introduction for more information about the Grammar revision sections in this book.

This section revises the basic uses of the simple past, present perfect and past perfect. There is more work on tenses in 4.4 and 8.2.

A This type of exercise occurs in most Grammar sections – the idea is not only to make students aware of shades of meaning expressed through grammatical structures but also to give them a chance to discover what they already know, what they're unsure of, and what they don't know.

The suggested answers below can be amplified by referring to a grammar reference book, such as *Practical English Usage* by Michael Swan (OUP) or *English Grammar in Use* by Raymond Murphy (CUP).

SUGGESTED ANSWERS

1 *When we heard the song we started singing.*
   = the song hadn't finished, we heard the beginning and then joined in with the rest of it
   When we had heard the song we started singing.
   = we listened to the whole of the song and then began to sing (maybe a different song)

2 *Did you enjoy your holiday?*
   = your holiday is probably over now and you're back at work/home now
   Have you enjoyed your holiday?
   = you are still technically on holiday but it's nearly over

3 *I never enjoyed travelling alone.*
   = this was the situation at the time in the past I'm talking about
   I had never enjoyed travelling alone.
   = this was the situation before an event that happened in the past which perhaps changed my mind

I've never enjoyed travelling alone.
= this is true now and it always has been (but I'm thinking about the past)
I never enjoy travelling alone.
= this is true now (but I'm not thinking about the past)

4 *She lived abroad for two years.*
= in the past but now she's probably living in this country
She had lived abroad for two years.
= this was the situation before another event occurred
She has lived abroad for two years.
= she's living abroad now after two years there
She still lives abroad after two years.
= she's still living abroad now (but I'm emphasising that she is *still* there)

B The whole of this part can be done in pairs or small groups – or alone. The purpose of this exercise is to help everyone to identify the different meanings (**a** to **f**) of the various past forms used in the examples and to make sure they can use similar forms accurately. It's not particularly challenging because, even at this level, students may need reassuring of the basic uses of past tenses. However, dreaming up examples might take some time and is best done in pairs or groups.

Discuss any problems before starting C1.

SUGGESTED ANSWERS   (+ another example for each meaning)

1 was
Did   see/watch
+ I *went* to Spain last summer and I *had* a wonderful time there.

2 a
Did   take
+ I'm spending the night with my friend tonight because I *missed* the last train home.

3 d
Have   been
Have   read
+ I*'ve* visited three countries in Europe but I *haven't been* to Asia.

4 c
has been   have been
+ She's over the moon because she*'s* / she *has passed* her driving test.

5 b
couldn't / wasn't allowed to   had forgotten / hadn't got / didn't have
+ I didn't get cold because I *had packed* my warmest clothes.

6 f
hadn't been invited / hadn't gone / hadn't come
+ She told me that she *hadn't* ever *been* to Nepal, but she *had been* to India in 1997.

C1 Discuss any questions arising from the examples here before starting C2.

2 This exercise can be done by students in pairs, or to save time, set as homework and discussed in class later.

SUGGESTED ANSWERS   (Some of these are debatable.)

already	2 4	a little while earlier	4	a long time ago	1
a moment ago	1	all my life	2	always	3 4
at midnight	1 4	by midnight	4	by now	2
by the end of the year	1 4	for two months	3 4	in the morning	1 4
in 1997	1 4	just now	1	last year	1
never	1 3 4	not long ago	1	not long before that	4
recently	3	so far	2	still	2
this afternoon	2	this week	2	this year	2
till now	2	till midnight	1 4	until today	2
when I was younger	1	yesterday	1 4	yet	2

3 Demonstrate what everyone has to do by writing two more examples on the board, one a beginning and one an end:

> *Recently I . . .*
>
> . . . *yet.*

Ask the class to suggest various ways in which the first might continue, and the second might start:

Recently I . . . went to visit my uncle / received a card from my friend / had a Chinese meal. No one has asked me a difficult question / made any mistakes / had lunch   . . . yet.

D Point out that errors like the ones in this exercise may well be the kinds of mistakes that members of the class make in their own writing.

SUGGESTED ANSWERS

2 It's six years since their eldest son *was* born.

3 What a delicious Indian meal that was – *did you cook* it yourself?

4 Where *did you get* that marvellous Persian rug?

5 I couldn't look up the word because I *had lost* my dictionary.

6 That is the funniest story I *have* ever heard.

7 It *has been* a long time since I wrote to my friends in Mexico.

8 I *haven't finished* yet, can I have a few more minutes, please?

9 By 1965 most African countries *had* become independent from colonial rule.

10 He *had had* three cups of tea by the time I arrived.

CAE exam | 2.3 **D** is similar to the 'proofreading' task in the English in Use paper, where candidates have to read each line of a text and decide if there is a mistake in it. In the exam this is a continuous text with only one word wrong in each line (or no words wrong), not several words as here. The mistakes in the exam may be spelling or punctuation mistakes, extraneous words, or incorrect vocabulary or grammar.

This type of exercise also gets students into the habit of proofreading their own written work to spot careless mistakes before handing it in – also very important in the exam.

E This is an 'activation' exercise to give you and your students a chance to see how well they can use the structures they've been studying. Go round the class listening to each group and correcting any relevant errors, i.e. mistakes in using past tenses.

(2.4) Really? That's amazing!   Speaking

 See page 15 for more information about the Speaking sections in this book.

 A Although this is a 'Speaking section', there are two Listening exercises which help the students to get to grips with different tones of voice used to express feeling.

 Play the tape, perhaps pausing momentarily after each clip for students to think for a moment before they note down each answer.

ANSWERS

surprised:	8	12	not surprised:	9		
interested:	7	13	uninterested:	(1)	14	
disappointed:	11		relieved:	6		
annoyed:	4		excited:	(2)	10	
pleased:	5		sympathetic:	3	15	

> **CAE exam**   **2.4 A** is similar to the kind of task that candidates will encounter in Part 4 of the Listening paper, where the questions test understanding of the speaker's identity, opinion, topic – or language function, as here.

Transcript   1 minute 40 seconds

1
MAN: There's a party on Saturday night!
WOMAN: Oh, wonderful.   *(lack of interest)*

2
MAN: There's a party on Saturday night!
OTHER MAN: Oh, wonderful!   *(excited)*

3
MAN: I think I've lost the front door key.
WOMAN: Oh.   *(sympathetic)*

4
MAN: I think I've lost the front door key.
OTHER MAN: Oh.   *(annoyed)*

5
MAN: It's all right, I've found the key in my bag.
WOMAN: Oh good.   *(pleased)*

6
MAN: It's all right, I've found the key in my bag.
OTHER MAN: Thank goodness.   *(relieved)*

7
WOMAN: Did you know that Great Britain is the world's eighth largest island?
MAN: Really?   *(interested)*

8
WOMAN: Did you know that Great Britain is the world's eighth largest island?
OTHER WOMAN: Really?   *(surprised)*

9
WOMAN: Did you know that Great Britain is the world's eighth largest island?
MAN: Really?   *(not surprised)*

10
MAN: The show is on tomorrow.
WOMAN: Really?!   *(excited)*

11
MAN: The show is on tomorrow.
OTHER MAN: Ohh!   *(disappointed)*

12
WOMAN: It's his forty-second birthday tomorrow.
MAN: Fancy that!   *(surprised)*

13
MAN: That film I wanted to see was on TV last Saturday.
WOMAN: I see.   *(interested)*

14
MAN: That film I wanted to see was on TV last Saturday.
WOMAN: I see.   *(not interested)*

15
MAN: That film I wanted to see was on TV last Saturday.
WOMAN: How annoying!   *(sympathetic)*

B1 Point out that some of these expressions are used to express different reactions – and with an appropriate tone of voice an expression like 'Good heavens!' could be used to express practically all the reactions listed.

SUGGESTED ANSWERS

ANNOYANCE	How annoying! How infuriating! What a nuisance!
DISAPPOINTMENT	What a nuisance! What a pity! Oh dear! What a shame!
EXCITEMENT	Fantastic!! How exciting! That's wonderful!
INTEREST	How interesting! Really!
PLEASURE	I *am* pleased! Fantastic!! That's wonderful!
RELIEF	Phew! That *is* good news! Thank heavens! Thank goodness!
SURPRISE	That's amazing! Good lord! Fancy that! Really!
SYMPATHY	What a pity! Oh dear! What a shame!

2 SUGGESTED ANSWERS

ANNOYANCE	That's typical!
DISAPPOINTMENT	I'd been looking forward to …
EXCITEMENT	Great! How thrilling!
INTEREST	That's interesting!
PLEASURE	Oh, good!
RELIEF	Thank goodness for that!
SURPRISE	Good heavens!
SYMPATHY	I'm sorry to hear that.

C Play the second part of the recording and PAUSE the tape after each remark (shown with a ★ in the Transcript). Ask members of the class to suggest various ways in which they might react to what they've heard, using the expressions they've studied in B.

Transcript   1 minute 30 seconds

NARRATOR: Imagine that the people you're talking to are friends of yours and reply to them appropriately.

MAN: Did you know that there's an underwater mountain in the Pacific Ocean that's the same height as Mount Everest?

★

WOMAN: You know that job I applied for teaching in China? Well, I've been accepted and I start in September!

★

MAN: I've got to babysit tonight, so I'm afraid we won't be able to go out together.

★

MAN: You know those notes you lent me? Well, I'm afraid I've lost them. You'll have to write them out again.

★

WOMAN: I've got us all tickets for that show – you know, the one we thought was sold out.

★

MAN: I've already made arrangements for that evening, so I won't be able to come with you to the show.

★

MAN: You know Bill and Maria? Well, I've just found out that they're getting married in April!

★

WOMAN: Did you know that the book *Robinson Crusoe* is based on a true story?

★

MAN: As it's your birthday next week, we've all decided to take you out for a meal. Our treat!

★

MAN: Remember I told you I'd lost your notes? Well, I've just remembered where I put them – they're in my briefcase.

★

D1 And finally a chance for everyone to practise using the expressions. Make sure the class is divided into pairs of pairs, so that they can combine into groups of four later. If necessary, some 'pairs' can be groups of three to start with.

2 Combine the pairs into groups for them to react to each other.

➡ We return to the theme of reacting to events in 2.6 Synonyms and opposites – 1.

2.5 **See the world?**   **Listening and Reading**

 Before playing the recording, give everyone time to look at the task and try to anticipate what the attractions might be.

 You'll probably need to play the recording more than once. During the second listening the students should check their answers so far and fill in the gaps that are still open.

> **CAE exam** In the Listening paper, a recording like this is heard twice with a pause before the second playing. Reading the questions before you hear it makes it easier. The task in **2.5 A** is similar to an exam task.

SUGGESTED ANSWERS (Several main attractions are mentioned for some places – the students are only required to note down one for each place.)

Theme park	Main attraction
Tokyo Disneyland	Main Street USA World Bazaar
Huis Ten Bosch, Nagasaki	devastating Dutch flood
Sea Hawk Resort & Hotel, Fukuoka	hotel in the shape of an ocean liner
Garasunosato, Hiroshima	Venetian canals gondola rides
Russian Village, Niigata	Russian buildings Russian food Russian Orthodox cathedral
Shingo-mura, Aomori Prefecture	'Jesus Christ's Tomb'
German Happiness Kingdom, Hokkaido	medieval buildings German food and drink
Canadian World, Hokkaido	Anne of Green Gables' farm
Shakespeare Country, Marayuma	Shakespeare's Village Shakespeare's Birthplace
Tobu World	replica of the Eiffel Tower/Parthenon/ St Basil's Cathedral/Statue of Liberty
Epcot World Showcase, Florida, USA	O Canada movie etc.

Transcript   5 minutes 30 seconds

PRESENTER: …tourists go to Japan to experience Japanese life, and Japanese tourists travel the world to experience life in other countries. But if you live in Japan you can travel the world without ever leaving home. There are theme parks which show you the highlights of different countries around the world. The reason why these 'little countries' are so popular is that everyone welcomes strangers and everyone speaks Japanese. Here's Tony Peterson.

REPORTER: The first theme park and the most famous is **Tokyo Disneyland**, which was opened in 1983. You can see an idealised America and experience the American way of life in 'Westernland' and in 'Adventureland' – including a

'Main Street USA', which has stores and places to eat American food, just like in the other Disneylands. There's also a 'World Bazaar' where you can experience other countries' food as well and buy their products.

Nagasaki has an amazing theme park called **Huis Ten Bosch**, which is a miniature Holland – 152 hectares of windmills, tulips and old-looking brick houses, together with a palace, a castle, ships and museums. One of its attractions is a devastating Dutch flood featuring thunder, lightning and 600 tons of very real, very wet water – it's very popular. Really enthusiastic and rich tourists can buy the ultimate souvenir:

a real Dutch-style house built right in the theme park, where they can actually live.

Nearby in the city of Fukuoka you can stay at the **Sea Hawk Resort and Hotel** – a huge hotel in the shape of an ocean liner ready to set sail for the five continents of the world. The rooms are all decorated in the style of different continents and your journey around the world starts the moment you step on board. Different restaurants serve food from all five different continents too!

Garasunosato near Hiroshima is known as the 'Venice of Japan'. You can go on gondola rides, and you can wander beside the canals and eat typical Italian food.

Niigata is the closest place to Russia on the north coast of Honshu, due north of Tokyo. It has its own **Russian Village** where you can see Russian houses and taste Russian food and drink vodka – and you can actually worship in a Russian Orthodox cathedral.

Or if you go to Aomori Prefecture further north still, you can visit 'Jesus Christ's Tomb' at **Shingo-mura**. Some Japanese believe that it was Jesus's brother who was crucified, not Jesus himself. Jesus escaped, came to Japan, married a Japanese woman and had three daughters. So you can go on a pilgrimage to visit his tomb.

From Aomori, you can cross the sea to the island of Hokkaido. There you can visit **German Happiness Kingdom**– you can see replica medieval buildings and experience German food and drink and see people dressed in traditional costumes.

Also on Hokkaido is **Canadian World** which offers 'the sense of romance, exoticism and nostalgia implicit in 19th-century Canada'. One of the most popular books in Japan is *Anne of Green Gables* – here you can see Anne's farm and buy Anne of Green Gables cakes, home-made jam and other souvenirs.

Now, a favourite destination in England for Japanese tourists is Stratford-upon-Avon – but now they can take just an 80-kilometre train ride to Marayuma and visit the **Shakespeare Country** theme park. There they can visit Shakespeare's Village, go inside a replica of Shakespeare's Birthplace and Mary Arden's House, as well as experiencing what life was like in Elizabethan England.

But, if you really want to save time, go to **Tobu World** where you can see scale models of more than a hundred famous buildings from around the word: the Eiffel Tower in Paris, the Parthenon in Athens, St Basil's Cathedral in Moscow, the Statue of Liberty in New York, and so on.

But this kind of thing isn't limited to Japan. If you're in Florida you can go to Disney's **Epcot World Showcase**, where you can walk from country to country or take a ferry across the lake. Each country has a treasure (a building typical of the country), musical entertainments, places to eat and shops to buy souvenirs. Some have a ride. In Norway you can experience a storm at sea. In Mexico you can sail through the 'River of Time' and experience the history of Mexico. In Canada, you can see a 360-degree CircleVision movie called *O Canada*. You can even visit the United States (sponsored by American Express and Coca Cola) where you can see 'an amazing and moving summary of America's struggles and triumphs' performed by animatronic figures representing famous people from American history. You can go to an English pub or have afternoon tea in the United Kingdom, drink in a German beer garden, sit at a French sidewalk café, eat in Alfredo's Restaurant in Italy – and you can visit Japan, where apart from eating at Japanese restaurants you can see a five-storey pagoda. It's not the whole world, though, because only eleven countries are represented there.

PRESENTER: Oh dear, it sounds absolutely dreadful!

REPORTER: It really is.

B Both the news reports are about Japan, and neither of them presents a negative image of Japan. Most Japanese students welcome the chance to read about their own country and see themselves as others see them. However, some Japanese students in a multinational class might possibly feel that they are being made fun of – if you think this would happen, this Communication Activity could be skipped.

In this Communication Activity student A looks at **Activity 2** and student B at **Activity 20**. The two students read a different article before rejoining the group. The idea is to exchange information and not to read the texts aloud word-for-word. Make sure, therefore, that everyone has enough time to study their text before they start sharing its contents.

C The discussion on 'national stereotypes' may be done as a class, rather than in groups, if time is short. This kind of discussion may need to be handled carefully if your students are particularly prejudiced against certain nationalities. Some more questions if they aren't:

- How would you describe 'a typical American', 'a typical Japanese', 'a typical German' or 'a typical English person'? Have you ever met any of them?

D This writing task is most appropriate for students who are preparing for the CAE exam. In a non-exam class this might perhaps be skipped.

The extra information on the next page can be photocopied for the students if they need more advice on writing personal/informal letters.

CAE exam	In the Writing paper candidates will have to write at least one letter – this might be an informal letter as in **2.5 D**, or a formal one.

Leo Jones *New Cambridge Advanced English*

(2.5) MODEL VERSION

Dear Philippa,

I'm writing to tell you something about the beautiful island of St Lucia in the hope that you'll consider joining me in visiting it next summer.

It is one of the Windward group and lies towards the lower half of the chain of Caribbean islands which runs southwards from Cuba in the north to Tobago in the south. The climate is comfortable, about 28–30 degrees Celsius most of the year, rather humid and with frequent but short-lived rain.

It's quite small, less than 40 km long by 15 km wide. It is a very green island and it isn't very densely populated. The interior is mostly mountainous (with a tame volcano bubbling away) and covered in tropical forest. The east Atlantic coast is rather wild but the west side has beautiful sandy beaches and clear blue seas, great for snorkelling or scuba diving. There's a wealth of wildlife in the sea and on land and if you are lucky you might see the St Lucian Parrot, the island's national emblem.

It's got a very interesting history too, having been fought over for about 250 years by the Dutch, French and English, which means there's a fantastic mixture of culture and language. For someone like you the St Lucian patois is really fascinating, it's a blend of French, some African grammar with a bit of Spanish as well!

The people are great – laid-back, friendly and full of fun. You'd love the music too, steel bands everywhere and "jump-ups" (street parties) in the villages on a Friday night.

I do hope you'll consider coming with me.

© Cambridge University Press, 1998

A PERSONAL LETTER   UNIT 2

An informal letter or fax to a friend or acquaintance is different from a business letter, or a letter to a person you haven't met. For a start, you probably share experiences in common and, depending how well you know each other and how recently you've been in touch, some information can be omitted if you both already know it. Informal letters are often chatty and reflect some features of conversation.

Contractions are used a lot in informal letters:

there's   he's   I'd have / I'd've   we've   haven't   needn't

If something is obvious or irrelevant it can be left unsaid by using phrases like these:

As you know   . . . and so on.   etc.   Well, I don't think I need to say any more!
You can guess how I felt!

To make an informal letter sound friendly and spontaneous, some features of spoken English can be used:

Well, ..., you see, . . .   – believe it or not!   I must say that . . .
Mind you, . . .   Did you hear that . . .?   Oh, I forgot to mention that . . .

Different punctuation is used:

– dashes are used a lot
For emphasis, words are <u>underlined</u> or may be written in CAPITALS
More exclamation marks and question marks are used than in a business letter
As already mentioned, things can be left unsaid . . .

Little drawings or diagrams can be added:

This is how to get to my house:

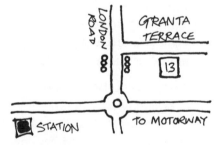

Informal language is used:

lots of   loads of   ever so many   awfully   terribly   frightfully   dreadfully

. . . and take a look at 7.6 on page 63 in the Student's Book for more on formal and personal letters.

. . . and look at 4.3 on page 34 for more on using appropriate language.

© Cambridge University Press, 1998

(2.6) Synonyms and opposites – 1 **Word study**

➡ See page 11 of the Introduction for more information about the Word study sections in this book.

Ⓐ1 Make sure everyone understands the way the chart works before beginning A2. Deal with any questions that arise. Write the four headings on the board to show everyone what they'll have to do in A2.

2 Encourage everyone to choose which three groups of words to work on – with any luck different pairs will choose different ones and be able to look at other pairs' charts with more interest. As SURPRISED is the shortest, it's likely that almost everyone will have that in common.

The purpose of this exercise is to increase students' awareness and sensitivity – there are no fixed rules about the meanings of words like these and there's no such thing as an exact synonym in many cases.

SUGGESTED ANSWERS (Many of these are open to discussion or argument – a couple of extras are given in the appropriate column in *bold italics*.)

slightly	'normal'	very	extremely
dissatisfied	ANNOYED	indignant	furious
irritated	cross	*angry*	livid
resentful	discontented		*wild*
	grumpy		*mad*
	upset		
	put out		
taken aback	SURPRISED	amazed	astonished
dismayed		shocked	horrified
		startled	stunned
			thunderstruck
unworried	CALM	impassive	serene
	composed	indifferent	
	detached	unemotional	
	relaxed	unmoved	
	nonchalant	unruffled	
		self-controlled	
glad	HAPPY	delighted	overjoyed
satisfied	cheerful	exhilarated	thrilled
pleased	light-hearted	on top of the world	
amused		pleased as Punch	
		jubilant	
disappointed	UNHAPPY	dejected	desperate
dissatisfied	discontented	miserable	heartbroken
fed up	down in the dumps	wretched	inconsolable
sorry	feeling down	*gloomy*	*depressed*
disgruntled	feeling low		
glum	upset		

Ⓑ1 Perhaps give everyone a little help with this by brainstorming some ideas as a class before they continue in pairs. There needs to be an even number of pairs, so that they can combine into groups of four (or five).

2 Combine the pairs into groups.

This section can be done at any stage, not necessarily at the very end of the unit. The exercises can be done in pairs in class, or as homework.

A ANSWERS

2 lost my head   was at a loss

3 losing myself in   have lost interest

4 were lost without

5 lost face   lose any sleep over

6 lose my balance

7 lost their lives

8 lose weight   lose heart

9 lost my nerve

10 have lost touch (with each other)

11 lost patience   lost my temper with

12 is (such) a bad loser   have lost count of

B ANSWERS

1 lost interest

2 lost touch (with each other)

3 lose heart

4 losing face

5 lose your head

6 lost my way

7 lose patience with them

8 lost his nerve / his balance

FINALLY . . .

Draw everyone's attention to the note on page 23: encourage them to highlight the most useful new expressions (or other vocabulary) in this section – and in the whole unit.

Recommend to everyone that they should spend half an hour reading through the whole of this unit at home before going on to the next one. In this way, new vocabulary is more likely to 'sink in' and be remembered permanently.

3.1 Films, shows and concerts — Vocabulary and Listening

A 1 Looking at the photos and brainstorming vocabulary enables the students to pool ideas, reminding them of words they already know and encouraging them to think of ideas they can't express in English. Their questions arising from this activity will help them to widen their vocabulary.

There's no way of predicting what your students will remember or want to know, but here are some words that might come up:

CINEMA: director, star, Western, comedy, thriller, sequel, extra, bit part, cameo appearance, Oscar

TV: sitcom, talk show / chat show, series, serial, entertainer, presenter, host, quiz show

STAGE: stage, actor, lighting, curtain, performance, play, tragedy, classical, ballet, opera, box office, auditorium, stalls, circle, balcony

MUSIC: symphony, concerto, recording, chamber music, orchestra, conductor, soloist, piano (see A4 for instruments)

2 The discussion prepares students for the exercise in B and leads them gently into the theme of the unit. If preferred, this can be done with the whole class, rather than in groups.

3 This exercise can be done in pairs, or solo.

When they've filled all the gaps, ask everyone to look again at the words that don't fit anywhere:

action   award   cartoon   cast   flashback   plot   scene   sequel   set

What do they mean and when would they be used?

ANSWERS

In a movie, the names of the stars, the producer, the person who wrote the *screenplay* and the *director* are given in the opening *credits*, but you have to wait till the end to see the complete *list* of characters and the actors who *played* them – and the name of every individual member of the film *crew*. Some films are shot in a *studio*, others are filmed on *location*. Foreign-language films can be shown with *subtitles* or they may be *dubbed*.

A really exciting movie depends on good photography, good *editing* (the way the film is cut with perfect timing so that each *shot* surprises you), exciting *stunts* (car chases, fights and falls), *special effects* (visual techniques which make the fantasy seem like reality), and the *soundtrack* (music and sound effects).

4 SUGGESTED ANSWERS

POP OR ROCK BAND: drums, electric guitar, bass guitar, keyboard, synthesiser, saxophone, etc.

SYMPHONY ORCHESTRA:

STRINGS: violin, viola, cello, double bass

WOODWIND: clarinet, flute, oboe, French horn, cor anglais, bassoon

BRASS: trumpet, trombone, tuba

PERCUSSION: timpani, cymbals, bass drum, xylophone, glockenspiel, triangle, etc.

B Allow everyone time to look through the questions before they hear the interview. Can they guess any of the answers? If they can, they could pencil them in now.

Play the recording. It may help to pause it a couple of times during the interview to give everyone a chance to catch their breath.

ANSWERS

1 44 **2** 1,000   staying fresh and spontaneous **3** voice   movements   confidence **4** 21 **5** become herself again **6** chatting to the audience **7** live theatre **8** talent   voice   memory **9** push   gypsy   mixers **10** a drug/an addiction

CAE exam	In Part 3 of the Listening paper there's often a task which requires candidates to focus both on opinions and on stated information, as here in **3.1 B**.

Transcript   6 minutes

INTERVIEWER: . . . St Martin's Theatre in the Number one dressing room where *The Mousetrap* is playing and I'm sitting here talking to Maev Alexander who plays Molly, the leading lady. Maev, how long has this play been running?

MAEV: 44 years, it's just about coming up to its 45th, which is astonishing.

INTERVIEWER: And you've just celebrated, how many performances?

MAEV: One...I've just done over a thousand, now, which is...I can't quite believe. And that's...I can't quite believe from the point of view of: 'Am I still keeping it as fresh as it was when I'd done the first week?' And that's the...that's the challenge for me of doing it again and again and again and again, is keeping the spontaneity going.

INTERVIEWER: And you've...you've enjoyed it all the way through?

MAEV: Yes, it's a...it's...Molly is a wonderful part to play. She's got a very good story to tell. I get to do a little bit...a nice bit of light comedy at the beginning, I get to scream, I get to cry, I get to have a fight with my husband. It's very cathartic.

INTERVIEWER: It doesn't affect your home life?

MAEV: My husband says that I'm always very nice when I'm playing Molly because she's a nice lady.

INTERVIEWER: So what are the skills that you think are essential for an actor?

MAEV: Obviously to have a good strong voice that can project to the back of a big theatre, um...but is also flexible enough to be soft in a television studio or in...in a film set. I also think it's important that you know how to move differently for different parts. That may sometimes be a question of the period it's set in, and people move in different ways in different styles of costume. It may be to do with your age, it may be to do with your station in life. Um...I think it's very important that you adapt your movement to the person you're playing. You need a pretty extraordinary temperament, I think. Er...one that will give you the confidence to stand up on a stage in front of lots and lots of people and pretend to be somebody else. Um...but also preserve the kind of vulnerability that's needed to be sympathetic.

INTERVIEWER: When was your first big break?

MAEV: I'd been out of college for a year and I'd done two seasons in repertory theatre and I was spotted by the Royal Shakespeare Company and asked to join them. At the age of 21 it was a dream come true! It was something I'd . . . I love playing Shakespeare, er...it's not an easy thing to play and not everyone is successful at it. I love the poetry and I think, relative to a l...to a lot of people, I'm good at Shakespeare. And to be a member of the Royal Shakespeare Company at the age of 21 was just heaven on three legs!

INTERVIEWER: Do you find it difficult...um... switching back into reality when the curtain comes down?

MAEV: Not at all, er...a play is a journey that lasts for the length of the play and when the curtain comes down and the audience has done their bit in applauding and...and we have bowed and said thank you to them for that, that's the end of that whole. And I'm then 'me'. I don't think I've ever found a part where I've really carried it home. Um...what I have done recently that was difficult was: we had a failure of the lighting box during a performance of *The Mousetrap*. All the lights went out and there was nothing for it but for me to stop and explain to the audience that there had been a technical failure. And I chatted to them till they got the lights back on, and I then had to switch back in to the play from having chatted to the audience and I found that enormously difficult to do in the middle of a play.

INTERVIEWER: But the audience must have loved you for that.

MAEV: Well, the audience...audiences...if you share it with them, if you let them know what's going on, they love a mistake and they…as long as it's handled well and I don't know what I said to them, I was so nervous, but I do remember at one point saying, 'Well, you've got to remember: this is live theatre!' and got a round of applause. But again so many people see television, see movies. Um…fewer people see live theatre and to be reminded that this is happening here and now was probably quite thrilling.

INTERVIEWER: And finally, what would you…um…say to a young person who announced that they wanted to be an actor?

MAEV: I th…I wouldn't recommend it, I really wouldn't. It is a hard life, it's got huge job insecurity. I have no more…I have no more job security now than I had when I was 17, which is horrifying, and I'm now 48 and in any other profession I'd have gone up the hierarchy. But that doesn't happen, there's no pecking order in theatre. I would ask a young person who was thinking of being an actor to consider very seriously the fact that it's not just a matter of having the talent to pretend to be other people, to convince people that you are someone else. It's not just a matter of having a good voice. It's not just a matter of having the kind of memory that can remember lines. It's a question of having the kind of personality that will continue to push to get work, a personality that can sell itself. And be able to live literally the life of a gypsy. You never know where you're going to be next, you could be working at the other end of the country. The kind of person that doesn't mind making a home wherever they're dumped. You've got to get on with people, you've got to be a good mixer. Er…there are so many difficulties that don't happen to people who are in regular jobs.

INTERVIEWER: But despite the difficulties, what are the things that keep you wanting to be an actor even when the chips are down?

MAEV: It's extraordinary. It's like a drug, it's like an addiction, I can't…I can't not, I can't give it up.

C Encourage further questions on vocabulary during the follow-up discussion. Remind everyone that WHY is an important and useful question. It encourages the other person to say more – and gives you a little more time to think while he or she is speaking.

(3.2) One of my favourite films ...   Listening and Speaking

A1 The four movies are all from the same idiosyncratic writing/directing team: the Coen Brothers. Each was written by Joel and Ethan, produced by Ethan and directed by Joel. It doesn't matter if your students haven't heard of them, they aren't mainstream film-makers but they are extraordinary. Their other films include: *Raising Arizona*, *Blood Simple* and *The Big Lebowski*.

Play the recording, perhaps pausing between each speaker.

ANSWERS

Miller's Crossing	Gabriel Byrne	Tom Reagan
	Albert Finney	Leo, a gangster
	John Turturro	Bernie Birnbaum, a bookie
Barton Fink	John Goodman	Charlie Meadows
	John Turturro	a playwright/scriptwriter
The Hudsucker Proxy	Charles Durning	Waring Hudsucker
	Jennifer Jason Leigh	a journalist
	Paul Newman	Sydney J. Mussberger
	Tim Robbins	Norville Barnes
Fargo	Steve Buscemi	a bad guy/thug
	William H. Macey	Jerry Lundegaard
	Frances McDormond	the police chief

2 Play the recording again. This time everyone makes notes.

SUGGESTED ANSWERS   (Several scenes and features are mentioned here, but the students are only expected to have one.)

Miller's Crossing	– when Bernie Birnbaum is about to be shot, and pleads for his life, saying: 'Look into your heart!'
	– when the hat rolls away from the camera through the woods
	– that you never really know if it's real
Barton Fink	– when the hotel goes up in flames (and you realise Charlie Meadows is the Devil)
	– that it's funny, black, clever and haunting
The Hudsucker Proxy	– when Waring Hudsucker leaps from the top floor of the Hudsucker Building
	– when Norville Barnes invents the hula hoop
	– when Jennifer Jason Leigh's character falls for Norville
	– the sets, particularly the huge clock
Fargo	– that the police chief is a pregnant woman
	– that it avoided the usual Hollywood clichés
	– that it's very very funny

3 Allow time for everyone to compare their reactions – films like the ones described aren't everybody's cup of tea.

B The discussion widens to cover films that your students have seen. It may help to jog everyone's memories if you make a list of some well-known films on the board, taking suggestions from the class for each of the seven categories. (There isn't a category for violent films, because that's what 3.3 is about.)

Transcript   7 minutes

NICK: One of my favourite films is *Miller's Crossing*, which I think was made in about 1990. It's a sort of gangster film set in the thirties or forties and it's set in a town that you never really find the name of – it could be Chicago, it could be New York. It's all that sort of 'film noir'…er… style. It's basically about…um…the boss of the mob, who's a character called Leo played by Albert Finney and he's got a deputy…er…played by Gabriel Byrne, who's called Tom Reagan. And basically… um…these two characters are after the same woman, and I think the main part of the plot is…is the fact that they're in competition for…for…um…for one woman. Er…there's also another character called Bernie Birnbaum played by John Turturro…who…John Turturro, who's a sort of two-timing bookie, and there's an amazing scene where he's about to be shot and he pleads for his life. And there's a scene where he's down on his knees and he just keeps saying, 'Look into your heart. Look into your heart. Can you do this thing?' and it's a very striking scene. There's lots of fantastic images like… um…the famous one of a hat, some…I think somebody's just been shot in the woods or something, and this hat…er…blows and rolls and rolls and rolls away from the camera, er…it's a

wonderful image, sort of rolling with the leaves. And…um…it's just…it's full of great images and a very strange feel to it, you never really know if…if it's real.

JULIET: My favourite film is *Barton Fink*, which came out in 1992, and…um…stars John Turturro as the eponymous hero. Um…he's a writer who has had a great success with a…a play, he's actually a playwright. Um…and…er…and he's summoned to Hollywood to…er…to write a…a movie about a…a wrestler. Um…and…i…i…it's a…it's a very…it's a strange, slightly surreal piece, um…it's set in the…set in the sort of 1930s, 1940s, not…not…not entirely…um…the…clear which. And it…it's both a film about the…the…the sort of corruption of… of…er…of money and of…and of Hollywood and how Hollywood attempts to corrupt people with good intentions and who have…er… you know, who are well-meaning. Um…er…but it's also got this…this…er…this…this strange character played by John Goodman. Er…he plays…er…Charlie Meadows, who occupies a room in the hotel where John Turturro is…er…is…is…is staying. And…um…and he's this peculiar sort of man, he's both the 'Common Man', the ordinary sort of the ordinary man, but he's also got slightly sort of Satanic… er…um…overtones to him. And…um… and the film…the…the film has this sort of apocalyptic ending when the hotel goes…goes up in flames and suddenly you realise that John Goodman, who you'd thought was sort of like the good guy next door turns out in fact to be the Devil. Um…it's a…it's a…it's both funny but also very very black, um…and it's…it's remarkable to look at and it's just a very clever haunting film.

SHARON: My favourite film is *The Hudsucker Proxy* and it came out in 1994. And…um…it's sort of set in a…in a magical kind of 1959 New York City and it starts out with…er…Tim Robbins, who's playing… er…Norville Barnes, the sort of innocent. Um…and he's…he arrives at this…er… industries called the Hudsucker Pr…er… Hudsucker Industries, um…and he…he starts in the…in the mail room, um…and just as he sort of starts his job…er…the firm's founder, who's played by Charles Durning, um…Waring Hudsucker, actually takes a…a suicide leap from the top floor. And…um…Paul Newman who's the executive…um…of Hudsucker Industries, um…Sydney J. Mussberger, he wants the board to take control of the company but he realises that the only way for this to happen is if they make the stock plummet until they can afford to buy it themselves. And so what he does is he actually gets Norville Barnes, Tim Robbins, er…to become President of the company. Um…and a lady journalist… er…played by one of my favourite actresses, Jennifer Jason Leigh, exposes… er…Norville as…as this president that's been put in place by…er…Paul Newman and…er…then she feels guilty about doing this and…and she actually falls for…um…Norville. And what actually… what happens is that Norville comes up with this idea…um…which actually ends up making the…er…the company an enormous amount of money. And the…

the idea that he actually comes up with is the hula hoop, which was…um…a rage in the fifties. And…and it…um…causes all the stock to rise, and um…then forces Paul Newman to have to actually become even…even more sleazy and…and tricky. Um…and I guess I like it because it…it's…um…the sets are quite extraordinary…um…and there's this huge clock that sort of…um…is the…is the centre of the set piece of the…of the Hudsucker Building. And…um…and… er…it's…er…it's…unfortunately it was one of the Coens'…er…least successful films, but for me I…I think it's my favourite and…and sort of…and…um… and one that really deserves more…er… more attention than it…than it got.

ADAM: One of my favourite films is *Fargo*, er…which was made just in 1996, and in fact I believe they won a…an Academy Award for its…er…its female lead, um… played by…er…Frances McDormond, um…who's actually the wife of the director of the movie, which probably helped her get the role, but nonethess she was very good. Um…it was extraordinary to have a police chief played by a pregnant woman for a change, which just cut across all of the…all of the usual things we see in…in police dramas. And now this is one of the things that was so good about the movie is that it steered away from all of the clichés we're used to seeing in Hollywood movies. There were some very good…er…performances in it – apart from the lead, um…there was also an actor called William H. Macey as Jerry Lundegaard, um…I think we'll see a lot more of him. And another actor who played the bad guy, Steve Buscemi, who was one of the most neurotic thugs you'll ever see – er…we've also seen him in *Reservoir Dogs* and a variety of other films, usually playing more or less the same character. Um…it was a really very very funny movie.

(3.3) **Adults only**   **Reading**

To save time in class, perhaps get everyone to read the article at home before the lesson. Though by now a very old film, Rambo is a character who has become a byword for violence, as witnessed by this entry from the *Cambridge International Dictionary of English*:

Ram•bo /£ ˈræm-bəʊ, $-boʊ/ *n* [C] *pl* **Rambos** someone who uses, or threatens to use, strong and violent methods against their enemies • *The Americans responded, Rambo-***style***/Rambo-***like***, by threatening to attack immediately if their conditions were not met.* • Rambo was originally a film character known for his violence, who was played by Sylvester Stallone in several films.

A 1 First, a chance for everyone to air their views on violence and, possibly, Sylvester 'Sly' Stallone. How has his image changed since making the *Rambo* and *Rocky* films?

2 This is not an easy passage, so we begin with a straightforward gist reading task. The gender of the writer is a matter of opinion, on the evidence of the passage – but if you look at page 58 in the Student's Book you'll see another article by the same writer. S/he is not a fan, that is clear from the tone of the text.

B Remind everyone that highlighting words in this way will help them to remember them.

ANSWERS

¶1 articulated = expressed

¶2 articulate = speaking clearly   oafish = idiotic   garrulous = very talkative
preposterous = ridiculous-looking

¶3 perpetrated = committed

¶4 inexhaustible = never-ending

¶8 brief = instructions   gleefully = joyfully

C The questions can be answered in writing, or discussed in pairs. (They aren't CAE exam-style questions.)

SUGGESTED ANSWERS

1 Everything: the lack of dialogue, the female assistant not being played by an Oriental, the violence, the way the audience's worst instincts are played upon, etc.

2 Nothing

3 His body and his preoccupation with exposing it, his voice

4 Difficult: this is a matter of opinion. Probably the arrow shot through a guard's head impaling him to a tree (ugh!)

5 They enjoyed the film and cheered and howled their approval

6 According to the writer, Americans who dislike foreigners and have strong patriotic/nationalistic feelings about the nation's defeat in Vietnam

7 It boosts the American self-image

8 The deliberate mistakes make the concept of 'Rambo' the all-powerful warrior seem more ridiculous

D 1 Play the recording as the students do the matching task. You may have to play it a couple of times.

ANSWERS   (The names have been rearranged to match the opinions.)

Ishia	Everyone knows that violence on TV isn't real.
Tim	Family members no longer communicate with each other.
Karen	People become envious of the lifestyle shown on TV.
Kate	People copy crimes shown or described on TV.
Melinda	Violence on TV is bad for children.
Andrew	We don't know what effect violence on TV may have on children.

2 The groups react to what they've heard and continue their discussion about violence on screen. (In a class of mature students you might consider expanding the discussion to cover sex and violence. Should viewers be protected from explicit sex on TV?)

CAE exam	In Part 4 of the Listening paper candidates will have to do a matching task, as here in **3.3 D**.

Transcript   2 minutes

NARRATOR: First we hear from Andrew.

ANDREW: W...I think all the killing and...and the violence you get o...on television now a...and in films, not only in the...in the drama but in...on the news bulletins as well could have a very devastating effect on...on children who see it. We've no idea how it affects them or...or how they might be upset by it or even if it may affect their behaviour.

NARRATOR: Kate

KATE: I was...er...watching the Geraldo Rivera Show...um...and...and I just turned it on...he was doing this show about massacres in schoolyards...gave me chills and...and I...b . . . – I'm from Stockton, California, that's my hometown – I left and a week later over the news I heard that a guy had taken a rifle and shot five Vietnamese children dead in a schoolyard about ten blocks from my dad's house and I'm sure he was watching that...the same show. I'm sure that's what put it in his head.

NARRATOR: Karen

KAREN: Well, I don't think it's surprising that there's so much crime because I mean just look at all these ads and all the television programmes they promote such a lifestyle that everybody envies it and just wants to copy it.

NARRATOR: Melinda

MELINDA: Well, I don't let my children watch television. Um...you know, you can't even watch the news without seeing terrible scenes of violence and I just don't think it's very good for them.

NARRATOR: Tim

TIM: Well, the basic problem about...er... television in general is that...er...it destroys family life, there's no conversation, nobody ever talks to each other, nobody communicates, all they do is sit and vegetate.

NARRATOR: Ishia

ISHIA: Well, I mean, I think the thing is that...that people are really too...too sensible to be taken in by everything that they see on the television – I mean, they know it's only...the violence is only pretend, anyway.

3.4 Making an emphasis   Word study

A This exercise shows the effect of using emphasising adverbs and adjectives.

SUGGESTED ANSWERS

Our class picnic *very* nearly turned out to be a *big* disappointment because of the *heavy* rain and the *large* number of people who dropped out at the *very* last minute, but to everyone's *total* amazement it was a *great* success and we all had an *extremely* enjoyable time. Every *single* one of the people who stayed at home must have felt *really* fed up when we told them about it later.

Omitting all the intensifiers makes the account rather limp:

Our class picnic nearly turned out to be a disappointment because of the rain and the number of people who dropped out at the last minute, but to everyone's amazement it was a success and we all had an enjoyable time. Every one of the people who stayed at home must have felt fed up when we told them about it later.

B1 Sort out any questions before starting B2. Explain that the purpose of the exercises on this page is to enrich the students' active vocabulary – and to consider the collocational restrictions on the use of intensifying adverbs and adjectives. It's very hard to formulate rules about these restrictions and it may be best to rely on a feeling for what sounds right.

It may help to know that *awful* and *superb* are 'absolute' adjectives (there aren't degrees of awfulness or superbness), so they aren't usually quantified with words like *very* or *fairly*. *Not* + adjective can't be intensified – though we could perhaps say *really not bad*.

2 After everyone has finished, ask the class how the adjectives in the 'very' group are different from the ones in the 'absolutely' group. Can they think of some more words to add to each group (e.g. very good, very interesting, very difficult – absolutely impossible, absolutely incredible, absolutely sensational)?

SUGGESTED ANSWERS

very or **extremely**	clever cross different disappointing enjoyable happy helpful impressive moving powerful proud sleepy surprised
absolutely	amazed amazing brilliant catastrophic disastrous fantastic idiotic marvellous perfect remarkable superb wonderful

C Again, we're looking at which words collocate with others. The answers below include alternatives, but the students are only required to choose one collocation – the one that feels most comfortable. It is possible to imagine situations where practically any combinations can be used. For example, if we call someone a great smoker or a great drinker it suggests we might admire them for the amount they smoke or drink.

SUGGESTED ANSWERS

deep	love pride sigh snow trouble understanding
big	difference improvement success surprise
large	amount number proportion quantity
heavy	drinker pressure sigh smoker snow traffic
high	power pressure price proportion quality speed strength
strong	opinion sense of humour smell
absolute/complete/total	catastrophe failure fool idiot nonsense power success
great	amount anger catastrophe difference excitement friend fun happiness improvement love number pressure proportion quantity sense of humour show skill speed strength success surprise trouble wealth

D1 Divide the class into an even number of pairs, so that pairs of pairs can be formed later. Some 'pairs' can be groups of three. Maybe write another example on the board if the students need more inspiration:

She was ...... disappointed to discover that he was such a ...... drinker.

2 Each pair passes their 'exercise' to another pair. Allow time for them to see each other's work afterwards.

EXTRA ACTIVITY

1 *Work in pairs*   Make a list of some films, actors, books, songs, musicians and food that you really like AND some that you really dislike.

2 *Join another pair*   Ask for their reactions to the items on your list.

(3.5) Punctuation   Effective writing

A It's sharp eyes as well as sharp wits that are required for this exercise and its punctuation!

SUGGESTED ANSWERS

1 *. . . his sister's friends and colleagues*
= the friends and colleagues of his (one) sister
. . . his sisters' friends and colleagues
= the friends and colleagues of his (several) sisters
. . . his sisters, friends and colleagues
= his (several) sisters and his own friends and colleagues

2 *Her brother, who works . . .*
= she has only one brother
Her brother who works . . .
= she has more than one brother and only the one who works in America is a film extra

3 *Rambo . . .*
= the character was dreadful
'Rambo' . . .
= the film was dreadful

4 *I don't watch television – much!*
= probably ironic or self-mocking, the speaker probably watches more than he or she should
I don't watch television much.
= straightforward statement

5 *They said it was marvellous.*
= straightforward statement
They said it was marvellous!!
= I think that's amazing
They said, "It was marvellous."
= those were the exact words they used
They said it was marvellous?
= I find that hard to believe
They <u>said</u> it was marvellous . . .
= but they probably had some reservations
<u>They</u> said it was marvellous . . .
= but someone else said the opposite

B This can be done in pairs or possibly set for homework.

SUGGESTED ANSWERS

1 mother's sister   father's sister/uncle's wife

2 '97   (at the age of 18)

3 it's   its

4 Don't   they're

5 Winona Ryder   Michelle Pfeiffer   Meg Ryan   (or whoever, with Capital Letters)

6 When commas are used, it makes a long sentence easier to read, doesn't it?

7 When the film was over, we stayed in our seats, watching the final credits. / When the film was over, we stayed in our seats watching the final credits. / When the film was over we stayed in our seats, watching the final credits.

8 There are four members of my family: my mother and father, my sister and me.

9 "Well, that's all, thank you very much, ladies and gentlemen," the lecturer said at the end of the lecture. "Does anyone have any questions?"

10 'Barton Fink' was a wonderful film; the director was Joel Coen.

11 'Fargo' was a great film – we all enjoyed it.

C 1 This can be done in pairs. All the necessary full stops are already there. Note that there are two hyphens missing as well as other punctuation.

2 This can be done by students working alone before they join a partner to compare paragraph breaks. (There's more on the use of paragraphs in 9.2.)

SUGGESTED ANSWERS (This is the original article – a few more commas are possible, and different paragraph breaks may also be possible.)

> *A Nightmare on Elm Street* made one experienced journalist scream with terror at the preview screening I went to. The noise frightened me more than the film itself, written and directed by Wes Craven, an ex-professor of humanities.
>
> "It's all very spooky but not at all bloody," says Wes of this teen-orientated horror film, which has a ghostly and ghastly murderer attacking the children of Elm Street not in their waking hours but in their dreams.
>
> John Saxon and Ronee Blakley don't believe all this, and he, a policeman, goes looking for a real madman. But we know better, and so does Heather Langenkamp as their daughter. Langenkamp, apparently known in America as the world's most promising Scream Queen, screams louder than the journalist. I just cringed.
>
> I think Craven has done better, though one has to admit that it's a good idea followed through with efficiency and state of the art special effects. Perhaps my trouble was that I wanted the Evil One to win. I can't stand those awful kids.

> **CAE exam** In the 'proofreading' task in the English in Use paper (Part 3), candidates have to read each line of a text and decide if there is a mistake in it. This question may require them to spot misspelt words or punctuation mistakes, as here in **3.5 C1**. In the exam there would be one mistake or no mistakes in each line, not several as here.

(3.6) Planning ahead . . .   Creative writing

The activities in this section give students a chance to exchange views on the need for planning and methods of planning. Encourage students to decide which of the guidelines they should follow, rather than telling them what to do.

> **CAE exam** In the Writing paper the examiners are looking for well-planned compositions which have clearly taken into account the target reader and the relevance of the ideas and information to the task. An unplanned, irrelevant piece of writing, even if it is written in accurate English, does not get good marks.

Ⓐ It's up to students to accept or reject these guidelines. But, of course, they may want to ask your advice. This is just ONE possible way of rearranging the steps, others are equally valid:

1 Write down your AIM: what is the main purpose of this piece of writing?

2 Think of your target reader: what does he or she want to find out from you?

3 Make notes of all the points you might want to make.

4 Decide which points are irrelevant and should be left out.

5 Decide which points are relevant and should be included.

6 Rearrange the ideas in the order you want to make them in your writing.

7 Decide which points each paragraph will contain.

8 Write an outline in note form.

9 Decide on your style and layout.

10 Choose a title or heading, if necessary.

11 Check the facts and figures: can you spell all the names correctly?

12 Write a first draft and check it through carefully, correcting any mistakes you notice.

> **CAE exam** In an exam your first draft *is* your final draft – so it must be checked carefully.

B The 'review' of *Independence Day* wasn't planned – the ideas were just written down as they occurred to the writer. This would only be acceptable in an informal letter to a close friend who knows how your mind works.

Reassemble the class and ask them to suggest how it could be improved.

C Doing this together encourages students to make notes, rather than just think about it.

D1 Students can choose to write a favourable review or a harsh one – or a balanced one.

2 Remind everyone that the purpose of showing each other their work is to get a reaction to the content of their review – is it interesting, readable, understandable, etc.? When you mark their work you'll also be taking account of these aspects, but you'll probably be focusing more on how the language can be improved – grammar, spelling, vocabulary, punctuation, etc.

CAE exam	The writing task in **3.6 D** is similar to the kind of tasks that candidates may have to choose from in Part 2 of the Writing paper.

Leo Jones *New Cambridge Advanced English*

(3.6) MODEL VERSION

When people visit big cities they usually plan to 'take in a show'. There are several on offer at the moment here. Andrew Lloyd Webber's "Starlight Express" has been running for at least 10 years so is one of those on the tourist trail. It has one major feature to recommend it, which is that the action all takes place on roller skates, and to accommodate this a special roller-skating track has been constructed that goes all around the audience. The stage is peculiarly tilted to allow the skaters to perform acrobatics. There is an extension of the stage which projects forwards into the front stalls, so that those with seats next to the extension have the skaters thundering past them from time to time. So there is certainly novelty value.

What about the story and the music? Well, if I explained the story I don't think it would sound credible. Suffice to say, all the characters are trains who/which fall in love with or hate each other! There are jealousies and fights and love scenes and I must admit, though I hate to, a very exciting race between the main rivals, showing off the power of their engines (skates). Forget the music and the lyrics. I think even Sir Andrew would admit that this was not his finest musical hour.

The skating, acrobatics and costumes are excellent. There is not much call for acting but it's an unusual and interesting theatrical experience.

(3.7) *At . . . and by . . .*   Idioms

ANSWERS

1 at the last moment	8 at least / at any rate	14 By all means
2 at a loss	9 at a loss	15 By the way
3 at cross purposes	10 at any moment / at any rate / at least	16 by any chance
4 at short notice at least		17 by sight by name
5 at the expense of	11 at our expense	18 by myself
6 at all times	12 at a glance	
7 at random	13 at long last	

(4.1) To whet your appetite . . . Vocabulary

A 1 This is a warm-up discussion – and a chance for students to recall useful vocabulary and find out what they still need to learn to discuss this topic. Reassemble the class for questions on vocabulary.

2 There's no predicting what the students will note down, but here are some words that might come up:

delicious tasty mouth-watering refreshing appetising
mixer wooden spoon food processor chopping board bowl wok saucepan
grater oven/stove hob
fizzy still mineral water spirits soft drink red, white, rosé draught beer
freshly-squeezed

B When everyone has finished filling the gaps, ask them to look at the words they didn't use:

loaf sandwich slice wholemeal

When would they be used?

ANSWERS

1 sell-by date last/keep additives protein/carbohydrate carbohydrate/protein vitamins

2 recipe dish ingredients vegetarians main course/starter/appetiser snack

3 set meal menu dessert bill/check tip/service charge water rumble

C Encourage questions on vocabulary during this discussion.

Leo Jones *New Cambridge Advanced English*

EXTRA ACTIVITY Unit 4

Preparing food Vocabulary

Match the foods in the first column with the ways of preparing in the second and cooking in the third column. Then write six sentences like this:

. . . are/is usually . . . and then . . .
Onions are usually peeled, chopped or sliced and then fried.

FOOD	PREPARATION	COOKING
onions	beat	bake
pancake batter	chop	boil
bread dough	grate	eat raw
carrots	grind	fry
cheese	knead	grill/broil
cream	mix	roast
dough	peel	serve
a lemon	stir	steam
a lettuce	slice	stew
potatoes	squeeze	
rice	toss	
walnuts	whip	

THIS DOCUMENT MAY BE PHOTOCOPIED. © Cambridge University Press, 1998

4.2 **Favourite foods**   **Spelling and Punctuation**

 A This text is written in American English, but shouldn't cause any difficulties. As the illustration shows, a *cantaloupe* is a melon. A *gopher* (line 16) is a small squirrel that lives in holes in the ground (and also the person in an office who is sent to fetch things *or* do small jobs).

ANSWERS

4	vaguely	**13**	✓
5	coffee	**14**	imagine
6	borrowed	**15**	cantaloupe.
7	neighbours'	**16**	✓
8	✓	**17**	chicken, milk
9	✓	**18**	cat?
10	carefully	**19**	idea (*there could be commas before* nor *and before* but)
11	cat, who	**20**	✓
12	its		

> **CAE exam**   Part 3 in the English in Use paper is similar to **4.2 A**.

B Allow plenty of time for this and encourage everyone to explain their reasons, not just to make lists.

C This is the only writing task in this unit. You may prefer your students to do it later on.

They may need some guidelines on writing recipes to help them to get started:

Recipes usually list the ingredients separately, and each step of the procedure is numbered and imperatives are used to give the instructions (see model version below).

The accompanying 'note to Tim' is really just a very short informal letter (see the extra information on personal letters in Unit 2 on page 46 and the model version below).

> **CAE exam**   Question 1 (Part 1) in the Writing paper often requires candidates to write a longer and a shorter piece. The shorter one may be a note, as here in **4.2 C**. However the task in Part 1 would include an input text and more information, so the format of **4.2 C** is more like one of the questions in Part 2.

(4.2) MODEL VERSION

Dear Tim,

I know you liked Rösti when you had it with us and also at the local restaurant. It's a dish that doesn't require unusual or exotic ingredients so you should be able to find everything you need in your local supermarket. It's also something of a national dish! Here's my recipe – it's different from the traditional version because I use a microwave to make sure the potatoes are properly cooked.

I hope you enjoy it!

RÖSTI

Ingredients

1 kg waxy potatoes
1 large sweet onion
200 g bacon
oil
pepper

Method

1 Peel the potatoes, then grate them and put them in a covered dish in the microwave for 10 to 15 minutes (on high) until they are nearly cooked.
2 Chop the onion and bacon and fry them gently in a non-stick pan.
3 Mix the potatoes with the bacon and onion. Add some ground black pepper.
4 Fry the mixture for about 5 minutes in a large non-stick frying pan until the underside is a golden brown. To turn the mixture, put a large plate over the upper side, quickly turn the pan upside down so that the mixture falls onto it. Then slide the mixture carefully back into the pan to brown the uncooked side. This will take about another 5 minutes.
5 Serve the Rösti with fried eggs or sausage and a green salad.

(4.3) Appropriate language   Speaking

This section revises some aspects of English usage that are probably fairly well-known to your students. As pointed out in the Student's Book, deciding whether a particular remark is appropriate or inappropriate depends on the WHOLE situation and, indeed, there are degrees of appropriateness. Encourage everyone to discuss what 'feels' appropriate. It's naive to expect there to be easily-learnt 'rules' about this in English – or in any language, for that matter.

1 In 1, 3, 4, 6, 7 and 10 the replies are inappropriate, in 2 and 5 it's not the replies but the opening remarks that aren't appropriate. In 8 and 9 both remarks are inappropriate. There are lots of better replies and opening remarks that your students may come up with.

2 Play the recording, which gives just ONE better version, and not necessarily the best. Pause the recording after each one and discuss the alternatives that everyone suggests. Ask everyone to pay attention to the tone of voice used, as well as the words the people say.

Transcript and Suggested answers 1 minute 30 seconds

NARRATOR: These are improved versions of the conversations. Notice the tone of voice used, as well as the words the people say.
8-YEAR-OLD: Hello.
ADULT: Hello. Is your mummy at home?
NARRATOR: Or . . .
ADULT: Can I speak to your mummy?

1
SHOP ASSISTANT: Can I help you?
CUSTOMER: No, it's all right thanks, I'm just looking.

2
GUEST: The meal was absolutely delicious.
HOSTESS: Oh, good. I'm so glad you enjoyed it.

3
YOUR BOSS: Yes, come in.
YOU: Is it all right if I come in half an hour late tomorrow?

4
BOSS: Do you see what I mean?
NEW EMPLOYEE: Yes, but I'm not sure I quite agree.

5
FRIEND: Sorry, I must just make a phone call.
YOU: Fine.

6
STUDENT: Have you had time to mark my composition?
TEACHER: Yes, it was quite good and I've…er… underlined the mistakes you've made.

7
WAITER: Are you ready to order now?
CUSTOMER: Not quite, we'd just like a little longer to study the menu.

8
WIFE: Oh, can you give me a hand with the washing-up, please?
HUSBAND: Sure, just a minute.

9
WAITER: Did you enjoy your meal?
CUSTOMER: Yes, thanks, it was very good.

10
PATIENT: Good morning, doctor.
DOCTOR: Hello, what seems to be the trouble?

B1 Ask the class to suggest some other remarks that would fit in each category. For example:

VERY FORMAL	I would like to say what a pleasure it is to make your acquaintance. It was most kind of you.
FORMAL	I am very pleased to have met you. Thank you so much.
NEUTRAL	Good night. Thanks very much.
INFORMAL	Cheerio. Thanks a lot.
FAMILIAR	Bye now. Lovely!

2 Doing this activity will help to sensitise students to different registers. Ask them to say which remarks are more likely to be used in conversation rather than writing (2 to 5).

SUGGESTED ANSWERS (Some of these are debatable.)

1 *A lot of people like fish and chips.* — NEUTRAL
Lots of people like curry. — INFORMAL
A significant number of people prefer sandwiches. — VERY FORMAL
Loads of people like fried chicken. — FAMILIAR
Many people enjoy hot dogs. — FORMAL

2 *Good to see you.* — FORMAL/NEUTRAL
It's a pleasure to make your acquaintance. — VERY FORMAL
Hi there. — FAMILIAR
Pleased to meet you. — FORMAL

3 *I'd like to introduce myself. My name's . . .* — FORMAL/NEUTRAL
May I introduce myself, I'm . . . — NEUTRAL
I'm . . . – what's your name? — INFORMAL/FAMILIAR
My name's . . . – who are you? — INFORMAL/FAMILIAR

4 *Do you feel like a drink?* — NEUTRAL
May I offer you a drink? — FORMAL
Like a drink? — INFORMAL
Would you like me to get you a drink? — FORMAL

5 *Can I have tea, please?*	NEUTRAL
I'd like a cup of tea, please.	NEUTRAL
Tea, please.	FAMILIAR
Would it be possible for me to have some tea?	VERY FORMAL
6 *One should always try to be polite.*	FORMAL
You should always try to be polite.	NEUTRAL
7 *Give my best wishes to your parents.*	FORMAL
Oh, love to Jim, by the way.	FAMILIAR
Please give my best regards to your wife.	FORMAL
Give my love to Mary, won't you?	INFORMAL
Remember me to your husband.	FORMAL
Say hello to Sally from me.	FAMILIAR

C1 Answer any questions arising before starting C2.

2 Encourage everyone to come up with examples of actual situations they might really find themselves in.

To give a complete list of all the possible situations in which each term might be used would take up a lot of space and be pretty boring to read! So, trust your own feelings here. To save time, pick out the more 'extreme' item in each list and give an example of when you might use it – or explain why you would never use it.

In the suggested answers below the expressions have ONLY been rearranged very roughly according to their formality – for more information consult *CIDE, LDOCE, OALD* or *COBUILD*.

SUGGESTED ANSWERS

1 youngsters   boys and girls   children   kids

2 human beings   population   citizens   persons   people   ladies and gentlemen
   men and women   everyone

3 male   person   gentleman   man   chap   fellow   guy   boy   bloke

4 female   person   lady   woman   girl

5 nutrition   cuisine   cooking   banquet   feast   food   meal   something to eat

6 appetising   delicious   wonderful   superb   tasty   nice   quite nice   yummy

D Arrange the class into groups of four or five. If possible, try to arrange the groups so that students who don't usually work together are together. This activity gives everyone a chance to try out some of the formal language they've encountered in previous sections – and to see how they manage with small talk.

1 The issue of what topics are suitable when talking to strangers is quite complex, and rather personal. Clearly there are no hard-and-fast rules about this, but probably politics and religion are no-go areas, and your own family might be too personal a topic to talk about at the start of a first encounter.

If your students ask you for advice, tell them which of the topics *you* would feel comfortable talking about. The purpose of a social conversation with a new person is to discover what you do have in common, so that you can exchange experiences.

If the other person is older or senior to you, you might be more deferential and ask her or him exploratory questions to try and discover what you have in common, or at best what you both feel comfortable talking about together.

2 Split each group into pairs (or a pair and a group of three). Allow everyone enough time to talk for a few minutes. Signal the end by announcing: 'Oh, the train's moving again now!'

3 Rearrange the original groups so that the 'strangers' change places. Now the former stranger plays the part of the younger person and vice versa. Again allow enough time for everyone to talk for a few minutes. Signal the end by announcing: 'Oh, here comes the waitress!'

➡ Students should be aware of the need for appropriateness in their conversation and writing. Look out for inappropriate language in their next piece of written work and draw their attention to it. This point is taken up again in 7.6.

EXTRA ACTIVITY

This might be a suitable time for a role-play 'cocktail party' to practise using appropriate small talk. The instructions which follow are addressed to students and may be photocopied if wished.

To add realism and help the activity go well perhaps play a tape of soft music during the 'party'.

Leo Jones *New Cambridge Advanced English*

EXTRA ACTIVITY	**Unit 4**

Socialising
Speaking

Imagine that you and the other members of the class have been invited to a formal buffet dinner – but that you DON'T know each other. You should spend a few moments talking to each of the other 'guests' and then move on and talk to another person, as shown below. First look at the useful gambits you can use.

Imagine that you are wearing your best suit or your best dress.

1 Greet each other, comment on the party and introduce yourselves:

Hello, are you enjoying yourself?

It's a great/lovely/nice party, isn't it?

These ...... are really delicious, aren't they?

This really is a lovely/nice/magnificent house/flat/room, isn't it?

Haven't we met before somewhere?

May I introduce myself, I'm . . .

I don't think we've been introduced. My name's . . .

Hi/Hello, I'm . . .

How nice to meet you.

Pleased to meet you.

2 Talk for a few moments:

How well do you know our hostess/host?

Do you know that lady/man/girl/fellow over there?

What do you do (for a living)?

Do you come from this part of the country?

3 Make an excuse, take your leave and find another guest to talk to:

Well, it's been very nice/enjoyable/interesting talking to you.

Well, I suppose I'd better circulate.

I've just seen someone I haven't talked to for ages, will you excuse me?

Excuse me, I must just go and have a word with our host/hostess.

I think I'll just go and get another drink/some more to eat – can I get you something?

Well, see you later, I hope.

© Cambridge University Press, 1998

(4.4) Simple + progressive aspect

The work in this section is intended as revision. Refer to *Practical English Usage* or *English Grammar in Use* for more information on the simple and progressive aspect.

A **SUGGESTED ANSWERS**

1 *. . . the train had just left.*
= we were too late: the train had departed a short time before we got to the station
. . . the train was just leaving.
= we were late: the train was departing so we had to jump on at the last minute (or we missed it)

2 *He stood up when . . .*
= she came in and then he stood up
He was standing up when . . .
= he stood up, she came in and he continued standing

3 *He usually prepares . . .*
= he waits till she returns and then starts cooking
He is usually preparing . . .
= he starts cooking before she returns and when she comes in he hasn't finished
He has usually prepared . . .
= he starts cooking before she returns and is no longer cooking when she comes in

4 *I've been reading . . .*
= reading only some of it, probably not all
I've read . . .
= all the book and now I have finished

5 *I'm not having dinner . . .*
= I don't intend/plan to have dinner till 8 o'clock this evening
I don't have dinner . . .
= I never have dinner till then, as a general rule

6 *They always ask . . .*
= straightforward statement
They're always asking . . .
= and I feel amused/surprised/annoyed by their asking

7 *We'll be having . . .*
= this is our plan OR we'll be in the middle of breakfast at that time
We'll have . . .
= we'll start breakfast at that time

8 *Will you join us . . .*
= I'm inviting you
Will you be joining us . . .
= I'm asking about your plans/intentions

9 *I think you're being silly.*
= what you are doing now is not sensible
I think you're silly.
= nothing you do is sensible: you are a silly person

B Make it clear that this exercise consists of three stages:

1 developing a feeling for what is correct

2 filling the gaps and

3 writing examples

There's no need to 'explain the rules' for each example, as long as everyone agrees that a different form is either wrong or has a different meaning.

SUGGESTED ANSWERS   (+ an example for each)

2 have/eat/serve   I'm having/eating/serving
He usually has lunch with his friends, but today he's eating alone.

3 eats   explodes/becomes ill/is sick
Rambo shoots his crossbow and kills the guard.

4 are   arriving/coming
Are you staying at home tonight or are you coming out with us?

5 was eating/drinking   choked
He sang to himself while he was driving to help himself to stay awake.

6 wasn't expecting
Last night we were discussing where to go this summer for our holidays.

7 didn't hear/find out/receive
I didn't want to go out until the TV programme was over.

8 was being   was/remained
His car was being repaired so he had to take the bus.

9 arrived/came/rang the doorbell   was   having/taking
He nearly fell asleep while he was driving, which could have been fatal.

10 been learning/studying   learnt/learned/read/spoken
She's been driving for ten years and during that time she's probably driven 10,000 km.

11 has lived/has been living
I've been doing most of the cooking ever since we got married.

12 they been
Have those letters been posted yet?

13 will/'ll be having dinner   will/'ll go out for a walk
I'll be working hard while you're enjoying yourselves.

14 will/'ll be arriving
When do you think you'll be ready to leave?

15 Will
Will you read this through and tell me what you think, please?

C **SUGGESTED ANSWERS**

1 We usually *have* lunch out on Sundays.
2 We can take a picnic but what will we *do* if it starts to rain?
3 She stayed at home because she *had* a cold.
4 While I *was driving* along I suddenly remembered that I had left the freezer door open.
5 ✓ *no errors*
6 Breakfast is normally *served* in the dining room but today it *is being served* in the coffee shop.
7 Who *does* this recipe book that's lying on the table *belong* to?
8 She *disliked* vegetarian food at first but now she *enjoys* it whenever she *has* it.

D This discussion will help students to use the forms more freely. Listen in to each group and correct or make notes of any relevant errors you overhear.

Preparation

It will save a great deal of time if some of this section can be prepared as homework. Ask students to check the meanings of any unfamiliar words in A and B in a dictionary beforehand.

A Make sure everyone understands what to do. If possible, take a few English-English dictionaries into class for this activity, then students can refer to them instead of relying too much on you.

There are no suggested answers here – use a dictionary to check any you're unsure of!

B Perhaps change the pairs around so that everyone has a different person to talk to. This activity takes quite a long time.

Tell everyone that if some differences are 'obvious' and not in the least confusing for them, they should skip those words and move on to the next group of words.

There are no suggested answers here – use a dictionary to check any you're unsure of!

> **CAE exam**   Part 1 in the English in Use paper often includes four alternative words to choose between that are easily confused, like the ones in **4.5 B**. These may be words that look similar to each other but have different meanings, or uses. Candidates should beware of words that are 'false friends' in their language when doing this task.

C 1 If possible, prepare for this by making a list of 'false friends' that confuse your students, depending on their mother tongue(s). If nobody can think of any now, postpone this until the next lesson and ask them to note some down for homework.

2 Presumably the group who thought of the words already know the differences!

4.6 *Bring, carry and take*   **Verbs and idioms**

A ANSWERS

2 them round

3 it down

4 them back

5 it up

6 them away

7 it apart

8 them out

9 it off/away/out

B ANSWERS

2 brought up

3 brought out

4 brought her round to

5 bring the matter up

6 brought on/about

7 bring our dinner forward

8 carry on with

9 got carried away

10 carrying on with

11 carried out

12 take (it all) in

13 takes up

14 take it on

15 took him on

16 took it for granted   take part

17 take-off   taken in   take a day off

18 take her for granted

19 take to

20 take back

Draw everyone's attention to the two notes on page 39.

Five | Travellers or tourists?

(5.1) Travelling abroad   Vocabulary and Listening

A1 When the pairs have noted down their words combine them into groups for them to compare notes. Some words that might come up:

hotel   package tour   excursion   seaside   sun, sea and sand   activity holidays
charter flight   scheduled flight   coach   cruise liner   jumbo jet   duty free   suitcase
luggage carousel   receptionist   sea view   balcony   half board   bed and breakfast
accommodation   camping   caravan   youth hostel

2 Besides finding out 'which' and 'what', encourage everyone to explain 'why'!

B1 This can be done in pairs or alone.

2 The words that don't fit anywhere are *controlling*, *travel*, *view* and *visa*.

Some other words that might fit are given *in italics* in the suggested answers.

SUGGESTED ANSWERS

1 journey/trip/*travels*   port/*harbour*   crossing   sightseeing/*seeing the sights*   resort/*town*
vacation/*holiday*

2 isolated/remote   shy/reserved/*unfriendly*   hospitable/*friendly*   costumes
customs/traditions   unspoilt/*peaceful*   commercialised/*touristy*   hikers/*walkers*
scenery/*views*

3 frontier/border   customs   declare   guilty   immigration   checking (NOT controlling)
passport   smuggler/terrorist

 C Before playing the recording allow everyone time to read through the questions and try to anticipate what some of the answers might be.

SUGGESTED ANSWERS

1 adventure   **2** exactly   **3** chatting   **4** wrong   **5** nightmare   **6** cattle   **7** coffee
8 dropped   **9** nowhere   **10** desperate   **11** yard   **12** snakes   **13** bedding   **14** hut   **15** fox
16 frog   **17** shower   **18** comfy   **19** stream   **20** rock

CAE exam	In the exam it won't be so easy to predict the answers in a listening exercise. However, by looking at the context it's often possible to predict the *kind* of word that's missing: adjective, noun, adverb, number, name, etc. Being able to predict the content in this way facilitates the listening task.

Transcript   6 minutes 30 seconds

SUSAN: My name's Susan Davies, and I'm a researcher and travel writer.

INTERVIEWER: Susan, tell me…um…first of all when did you start travelling?

SUSAN: I think the first proper journey I went…er…was when I was 30, I was quite old. I went to Australia, spent a year there and on the way back I went to Thailand and travelled all round there, up into the north, down to the south, in Bangkok.

INTERVIEWER: What is it that you enjoy most about travelling?

SUSAN: I think it's the sense in adven…of adventure. Most of the travelling I've done, I've done on my own, not particularly out of choice or because I'm so ghastly I can't get people to travel with me but just because I like…I like the adventure, I like the feeling of…um…being able to do exactly what I want. And also I think as a writer you…I've met many more people travelling alone. I think…um…one person on their own is much more accessible than two or three. People don't come up and talk so much if you're a mem…member of a couple or a group. Whereas as one person you get chatting to people in shops, or at…in 'bars, or at…er…just travelling…just…er…on coaches, buses, trains. So it's much more interesting.

INTERVIEWER: There must be something that you don't enjoy quite so much.

SUSAN: I…yes, I think…um…travelling alone has its advantages, it also has its disadvantages in that when something goes wrong, if I'm with someone it can be quite a laugh and quite jolly. But when it goes wrong and I'm on my own it is actually a…a nightmare because it's much more difficult to be brave.

In Australia I spent some time working on a cattle station because I wanted the 'full Australian experience' and through someone I'd met at a coffee bar in Sydney I'd got the address of this place way up in the centre of Queensland… er…near Emerald. And I rang and said, 'Oh, I'm going to be…you know… passing through Queensland next week, can I come and work for you?' 'Oh yes,' they said, 'Er…get the Greyhound and ask them to drop you off at Willows Creek.' And I thought, 'Ooh, well yes OK.' So I did this and travelled overnight through Queensland and I said to the driver, 'I need to be dropped off at Willows Creek.' Not expecting him to take me literally. He pulled in, in the middle of what seemed like a dirt track and said, 'This is Willows Creek.' And there was no one, you know, a long straight road, no one coming left, no one coming right. So I got out and I stood there and…um…the ow…the wife of the owner of the farm did eventually arrive but I was there for what felt like an hour and a half, in fact it was probably only five minutes. Now, if someone had been with me we'd have laughed and it wouldn't have felt quite so desperate. But I can remember thinking then, 'What on earth am I doing? I'm in the middle of literally nowhere and I don't know the people that are meant to be coming, and there's no one coming along this road and I think I might have blown it.'

And…um…the first night I was there I had…um…a meal with the family in the homestead, as it was called, and then… um…they gave me a kerosene lamp and said…um…basically waved me goodnight and said, 'Do mind when you're walking across the yard for the snakes.' And I laughed and she looked at me and she said, 'Oh no, this is the time of year, you know, they like lying in the yard because…er…it's warmer.' And she said, 'And for goodness sake shake your

bedding out because they do get cold and…er…sometimes they do slide in because it's very warm.' And I did at that stage think, 'I am out of my depth. This is not what I came to Australia for. And also I hate snakes, what on earth am I doing here?' And as I walked across… um…sort of making sure my feet made a huge sound so that the vibrations would presumably wake up these lazy old snakes that were lying asleep in the middle of the dark yard, my lamp did catch one of them slithering away. And I screamed and of course no one came because they didn't hear. And anyway I got into the hut as it was, absolutely pitch black, um…shook my bedding, got into bed, you know …thinking all the time that I was just going to be pounced on by loads of cold snakes. And then I heard the sound of wings and the wings went 'Prrrr' and then 'Bang'. I thought, 'What on earth is that?' And then 'Prrrr-bang'. And I just thought, 'This is a nightmare. I am actually in the middle of some terrible Dracula film, something terrible is happening.' And I…I burrowed down even further and in fact eventually fell asleep and the next day I went in to have breakfast and I said…um, 'Oh, I think there might have been a bird in the room last night and I thought what sort of bird would that be?' And they laughed and said, 'Oh no, that's not a bird, that's a flying fox,' which is a type of…um…bat, er…because they…er… said, 'Oh yes, they live in there.' And I thought, 'Gosh here I am, I'm sharing the hut with snakes, flying foxes,' and they…um…told me that there was a frog that lived in the loo. And after that I thought, 'No, I really don't want to use the loo if there's a frog living in there. I'd rather…actually rather go outside,' which is what I did even though there might be snakes.

INTERVIEWER: Do you ever foresee a time when you would be tired of travelling?

SUSAN: I hope not, I hope I don't ever find that. But I suppose having done certain things, I know what I like and I know what I don't like and I don't feel I have to do things just to…that are character-forming. And also I quite like a hot shower and a comfy bed. But that's not to say I couldn't…um…I couldn't manage washing in a stream and sleeping on a rock, I know I could, but…er…whether I could in another 40 years, I don't know.

D Some more questions you might like the class to discuss:
- If you could live in a different country, which would you choose?
- If you could choose a different nationality to adopt, which would it be? Why?
- If you could choose someone of a different nationality to marry, which would you choose?

(5.2) Tourism and tourists   Reading

A1 This could be done as a whole-class activity. Noting down their ideas before reading helps everyone to approach the text with more interest – to find out if their ideas are mentioned in the text and what other ideas are mentioned in it.

Some ideas that might come up are:
- All-inclusive holidays are more expensive than 'normal' packages, especially if you have a small appetite and don't drink alcohol and don't want to take part in the organised activities
- You don't meet the people of the country, only fellow tourists
- The only local people you meet are the staff: waiters, sports organisers, chambermaids, etc.
- Mass-market tourism makes all countries seem the same, with the same international cuisine everywhere

2 There's plenty of 'meat' in the article, but this task focuses on scanning the text to find information. The questions are NOT in the order that the information appears in the article.

When native speakers scan a text like this, they tend to read it fast and disregard irrelevant information. However, students may need to read the whole passage through quickly first (disregarding unknown vocabulary) to get the gist. Then they should go back through looking for the required information (looking up or working out only the relevant unknown vocabulary).

ANSWERS

2 Dominica	**6** Dominica	**10** St Lucia
3 St Lucia	**7** Dominica	**11** St Lucia
4 Antigua	**8** Jamaica + Nevis	**12** Jamaica + Grenada
5 St Lucia	**9** Jamaica + Barbados	

> **CAE exam** The task in **5.2 A2** is similar to the kind of task candidates may have to do in the Reading paper, where they have to search a text to find specific information. (In the exam this kind of task is a multiple-matching exercise, but the reading skills are the same.)

B This can be done alone or in pairs. The 'synonyms' are not exact equivalents.

ANSWERS

¶ **1** zealous = over-keen   pass = permit

¶ **3** endorsed = supported   entrepreneurs = business people   élite = top people

¶ **5** settlement = village   rugged = wild

¶ **9** enclaves = enclosed grounds   disaffection = alienation

¶**10** gulf = division

¶**11** foundered = failed   antagonistic = hostile

C If anyone in the class has experienced an all-inclusive resort, encourage them to share their experiences.

(5.3) Making notes   Effective writing

A 1 Searching for the extra points will encourage everyone to read the notes, rather than just form a superficial impression.

The extra points in each example are:

1 *Even knowing a little about other places is better than being ignorant*

2 *Helps you see your own culture in context*

3 *Local people depend on tourism – adapt (their) way of life*

2 Which to prefer is a matter of taste. Allow enough time for everyone to see the pros and cons of each. In an exam, even though time may be short, notes are indispensable.

3 Two more points that might be added are: *Only the most adventurous travellers reach uncommercialised/unspoilt places* and *Many people only know their own country and family – travel extends their knowledge*

B It doesn't matter which topic students choose. Allow time for everyone to look at another student's notes at the end.

If it doesn't seem too burdensome with a Writing task coming up in 5.4, you could ask everyone to write an article, using their notes as the basis for this.

(5.4) A letter of complaint   Creative writing

A 1 There are quite a few improvements that can be made. The letter contains irrelevant information, which detracts from the seriousness of the situation, and it needs to be divided into paragraphs to make it clear where one point ends and the next begins. (And contractions aren't appropriate in this kind of letter.)

2 This can be done in pairs or alone.

SUGGESTED IMPROVEMENTS

> We have just returned from our visit to London, which you arranged for us. There were a number of problems that arose.
>
>   Firstly, the tickets you sent us had been completed incorrectly and as a result we missed our flight and had to travel on a later plane, not arriving in London till midnight.
>
>   When we arrived at the hotel you had booked for us, the rooms were no longer available, even though we had paid you for the accommodation in advance. The hotel staff found us a room in another hotel. Unfortunately, the other hotel was way out in the suburbs and it took us an hour to get into the centre the next day, which involved a long train journey.
>
>   Please send us a refund of the money we paid for the accommodation and also compensation for the inconvenience caused by your errors.
>
>   Looking forward to hearing from you,
> Yours sincerely,

B 1 Make sure everyone agrees what needs to be done before they start B2. Emphasise that they should make notes before they start writing – this could be done in class to make sure.

2 Homework.

3 Ask the readers to say what action they'd take after reading their partner's letter and note, if they were the hotel manager and the friend.

> **CAE exam** | Question 1 (Part 1) of the Writing paper is much more complicated than the task in **5.4 B**, with more information to take in. The task in **5.4 B** is a gentle introduction to this kind of exam task. Exam candidates will need further practice using *CAE Practice Tests 3* (or a later version).

(5.4) MODEL VERSION

Dear Ruth,

I was really upset to hear about your disappointing holiday, especially as I had recommended the hotel to you. It sounds as if the change of management has had a dreadful effect on all areas of hotel quality. I will write if you like but I'm not sure it will do much good given their current attitude.

Dear Sir/Madam,

I am writing to express my disappointment with your hotel's services on behalf of a friend of mine.

She and her family spent a week there from 21 to 28 June this year on my recommendation. They found the hotel brochure misleading on several counts and the attitude of the managerial staff most unhelpful.

The brochure claims that all rooms have en suite facilities whereas in fact one of their rooms had no toilet or shower. They were unable to get vegetarian food in spite of claims of a "cuisine to suit all tastes". Another major disappointment and inconvenience was the fact that the beach was a good five minutes away on foot – they had been relying on being able to reach the beach easily and without having to carry everything so far for their two young children. As it was, a trip to the beach was a major expedition and not the relaxed affair they had been expecting. The alternative would have been to stay beside the pool but it was far too cold for small children, or indeed for any normal warm-blooded adult.

It is dishonest to attract custom by making false claims in your brochure. I shall be reporting you to the Tourist Board and Trading Standards Authority and suggest that you make speedy compensation to Mr and Mrs Simpson for their spoilt holiday.

Yours faithfully,

© Cambridge University Press, 1998

5.5 Travel writers — Reading

Jonathan Raban was born in 1942. Among his most interesting books are:
Arabia – about his journey in different countries in the Arabian peninsula
Old Glory – about his journey by boat down the Mississippi River
Foreign Land – a novel about a man who buys an old sailing boat
~~around the coast of Britain in a sailing boat~~ el and literature from

Handwritten note: Module 2 — interested in doing a TEFL course in June?

...h students comparing answers
...e about and ask them to look

...has multiple-choice questions
...ves to choose between, not three

...ched differently from matching
...nate some of the incorrect
...the two most likely ones.

accumulation = collection
inherently = by nature
articulate = clear
trifles = unimportant things
inordinate = excessive
grouses = grumbles
languishes = loses vitality

D We finish with a follow-up discussion, focusing on memories of travelling.

5.6 *High, middle and low* — Idioms and collocations

ANSWERS

1 high and low
2 high season
3 highlights
4 highbrow lowbrow middlebrow
5 hi-fi high street
6 highlight them
7 high-rise low-rise
8 high-tech
9 in high spirits
10 at high tide at low tide
11 feeling low
12 middle-aged
13 middle-class
14 high school higher education
15 it's high time you *did* it

(6.1) What do they look like?　　Listening and Vocabulary

  A Pause the tape after each description for everyone (perhaps in pairs) to discuss which person they think was described.

> **CAE exam** | **6.1 A** reflects the format of the exam, where boxes have to be filled with the correct letter. However, the exam wouldn't have as many as 15 possible choices for each box.

ANSWERS

1 F　**2** C　**3** H　**4** B　**5** I　**6** K　**7** M

Transcript　3 minutes 20 seconds

1

MARCELLA: This person is about mid-fifties, I think. He looks like the kind of man who might be a bank manager or something like that, the sort of person who deals with money that you could trust, hopefully. He's got grey hair, slightly receding, he's got a rather nice smart suit on and a tie. Er…and a very content look on his face, quite tanned skin. A nice smile, nice teeth, and he's got a beard, a grey beard.

2

NICK: This person is a woman. She's sitting…er…in the sunshine, she looks very friendly, she looks like a granny, she looks like she could be a granny to some small children. Er…she's got…um…a top that has some red stripes on it and she's got a pair of glasses on her face.

3

ADAM: This person is in his late twenties or early thirties, I'd say. He's got a very neat haircut and he's got a very serious, distant, romantic expression on his face. He's wearing a flowery shirt. But he looks quite serious, he looks like he's in good physical shape.

4

MARCELLA: This person is about four or four and a half. Er…she's got long hair just down to her shoulders and a fringe and a lovely smiling face. She's wearing a blue top, she's got lovely blue eyes, um…nice brown skin and her hair is blonde.

5

SIMON: This man is…er…I would say elderly, he's in his seventies. Um…he's wearing glasses, he's sort of got a half smile, I would say, on his face, not quite showing his teeth. He's quite casually dressed in a shirt and rather nice cardigan. And…er…his hair is…er…is grey but…er…there's not much of it, it's sort of just at the sides and the top of his head is…er…is quite bald.

6

NICK: This person is…er…a young woman, she looks very relaxed, she's sort of resting her head on her hand. Um…she's wearing a…a sort of blue top…um… with a white-sleeved…er…blouse or jumper underneath. She's got very long hair and…um…she's also got a nice fringe hanging over her forehead.

7

SHARON: This person is a young boy, he's probably about 11 years old, he looks like he's sitting outside in the park, and he has a purple shirt on, he's got black hair and dark eyes and he looks very happy.

B1 While everyone is reading the examples answer any questions that arise. (The gaps are to be completed in B2.)

2 Arrange the class into an even number of pairs or small groups. Everyone tries to think of further similar words that could be used, filling the gaps with their own ideas. Ask them to think about the people they know – their family and friends and how they'd describe them.

3 Combine the pairs into larger groups for them to pool their ideas. Afterwards reassemble the class and answer any questions that arise. Point out that some words or phrases may cause offence – particularly if you're talking to someone about a person they like or admire, for example.

SUGGESTED ANSWERS

Age	youngish quite elderly about fifty over sixty
Face, hair, eyes and complexion	long hair shoulder-length hair a crew cut a moustache a beard brown/blue/hazel/dark eyes
Height and build or figure	tall short thin weak/wimpy/weedy
Clothes and footwear	jeans a skirt a sweatshirt a T-shirt trainers sandals
Family	has five grandchildren comes from a large family has two sisters has been married for five years
Job	is unemployed is between jobs at the moment is looking for work has just been made redundant has just been promoted
and interests	collects stamps loves skateboarding plays a lot of basketball

C If each person keeps the picture he or she's describing a secret, this activity is more enjoyable. Perhaps make it a rule that the speaker can't be interrupted until he or she has finished speaking.

D These activities may cause discomfort to some students if they feel sensitive about their appearance. If this might be the case in your class, this activity should be omitted. In any case, make sure everyone is aware of the *sensitivity* required when describing someone who is actually present, avoiding mention of such embarrassing features as obesity, spots, long noses, birthmarks or baldness.

1 Groups of four or five might be best here. This is only worth doing if the speaker closes his or her eyes, so insist on this.

2 Again, this is more fun as a guessing game and the speaker shouldn't be interrupted until he or she has finished speaking.

E In this Communication Activity, student A looks at **Activity 3** while B looks at **Activity 22**. Each has a different photograph to describe. (If you look at the photos beforehand you'll know what to expect – but don't allow the students to see each other's pictures!)

CAE exam   6.1 **E** is similar to Part 2 of the Speaking paper, where candidates have to describe, hypothesise and comment on two photographs on a common theme.

(6.2) Politically correct?   Reading

A 1 Give the students time to discuss various possible outcomes.

2 Student A sees the second part of the article in **Activity 12**, student B sees the first part in **Activity 32**. Make it clear that they should retell the story in their own words, not read it aloud.

B The article appeared about a month after the one the students read in A2. Some students may be sensitive to the mention of sexual harassment but in fact that is not the main subject of the article.

SUGGESTED ANSWERS

1 Vermont **2** New York **3** prisoners in the USA **4** Jerry Seinfeld* **5** TWA
6 Meg Greenfield

* An Apache is a member of one of the tribes of Native Americans (formerly known as *Indians*). A *cigar store Indian* is a wooden model of a Native American smoking a pipe,

which all American cigar stores used to put out on the sidewalk to show that they were open for business. This is similar to the cut-out cheery chef to be seen outside some restaurants, showing the day's menu.

C Make sure that the anti-PC tone of the lesson so far is redressed by considering the advantages of political correctness and the good intentions underlying it.

(6.3) Modal verbs   Grammar

A 1 & 2 SUGGESTED ANSWERS

1 *They might tell me but . . .*   *. . . I don't expect they will.*
= it's possible that they'll tell me (perhaps slightly less possible than *may* in the last example)
They might have told me but . . .   *. . . my memory is a little hazy about it.*
= it's possible that they told me (perhaps slightly less possible than *may have* in the next example)
They may have told me but . . .   *. . . I can't remember whether they did.*
= it's possible that they told me
They may tell me but . . .   *. . . they may not, it all depends.*
= it's possible that they'll tell me

2 *We could have tea early because . . .*   *. . . we're both going out later.*
= it's possible for us to have tea early today
We were able to have tea early because . . .   *. . . we had finished our work.*
= it was possible for us to have tea early (that day)

3 *You mustn't tell her that . . .*   *. . . she's putting on weight.*
= don't tell her
You needn't tell her that . . .   *. . . she has to do the washing-up.*
= it's not necessary to tell her
You don't have to tell her that . . .   *. . . she has to cook the dinner.*
= it's not necessary to tell her (same meaning as the previous example)
You oughtn't to tell her that . . .   *. . . she's overweight.*
= it's not advisable to tell her

4 *I should have trusted him but . . .*   *. . . I'm ashamed to say I didn't.*
= it would have been a good idea to trust him
I shouldn't have trusted him but . . .   *. . . I did, I'm afraid.*
= I trusted him, but I was wrong to do so
I needn't have trusted him but . . .   *. . . it seemed the only solution.*
= it wasn't necessary to trust him but I did trust him (same meaning as *I didn't have to . . .*)
I had to trust him but . . .   *. . . I had serious misgivings about doing so.*
= I trusted him: I had no choice
I didn't have to trust him but . . .   *. . . it seemed like a good idea at the time.*
= it wasn't necessary to trust him but I did (same meaning as *I needn't have . . .*)

5 *She can't have lunch because . . .*   *. . . she's got to catch a train at 12.30.*
= it's not possible for her to have lunch (in the future)
She couldn't have lunch because . . .   *. . . there wasn't time.*
= it wasn't possible for her to have lunch (in the past)
She can't be having lunch because . . .   *. . . it's only 11.15.*
= I'm sure she's not having lunch now
She can't have had lunch because . . .   *. . . she says she's starving.*
= I'm sure she hasn't had lunch

6 *He may not have seen her, so . . .*   *. . . you'd better ring up to find out if he did.*
= it's possible he didn't notice her / meet her
He may not be seeing her, so . . .   *. . . he may not be able to give her the present.*
= it's possible that he hasn't arranged to meet her / it's possible that they aren't going out together (as a couple)

He may not see her, so . . .   *. . . you'd better phone her to tell her about the party.*
= it's possible that he won't meet her / notice her
He can't have seen her, so . . .   *. . . that's why he walked right past her.*
= I'm sure he didn't meet her / notice her
He can't be seeing her, so . . .   *. . . it won't matter if he finds out what she was doing.*
= I'm sure they aren't going out together / going to meet
He can't see her, so . . .   *. . . she's arranged to go out with someone else tonight.*
= it's impossible for him to meet her / she isn't visible / she's hiding

B   **SUGGESTED ANSWERS**

1   We'll probably have lunch soon.   We might as well have lunch soon.
    Maybe we'll have lunch soon.   We might well have lunch soon.
    We'll possibly have lunch soon.   We've got nothing better to do, so
                                    let's have lunch soon.

2   You must be joking.   You've got to tell a joke.
    You have to tell a joke.   You can't be serious.

3   Can you speak English?   I'd like you to speak English.
    Do you know how to speak English?   Can you speak English, please?

4   You'd better tell him sooner or later.   You have to tell him sooner or later.
    You ought to tell him sooner or later.   You've got to tell him sooner or later.

5   You needn't tell him yet.   You can't tell him yet.
    You don't have to tell him yet.   You mustn't tell him yet.

6   It wasn't a good idea to tell her.   I didn't have to tell her.
    I shouldn't have told her.   It wasn't necessary to tell her.

7   You might have *told* me.   You may have told me.
    I'm not sure whether you told me.   You should have told me.

8   You probably won't take too long.   I advise you not to take too long.
    You shouldn't take too long.   It shouldn't take you too long.

C   **SUGGESTED ANSWERS**

> Dear Jane,
> As you **may** already know, we **had to** start looking for a new receptionist in our office last month. Mr Brown our boss, **could** have chosen someone who already worked in another department but he **wasn't** able to find anyone suitable so he **had** to advertise in the local paper. There ought **to** have been a lot of applicants but surprisingly only a couple of replies came in and only one of those was suitable. I told Mr Brown that he **ought to / should / had better** get in touch with her at once. He decided we **didn't need to / needn't** phone her as there was no hurry, and we **might** as well send her a card. Unfortunately we heard no more from her, so we've had to start advertising again – in vain so far.
>
>   For the moment, the job's being done by Mr Brown's son who **shouldn't / oughtn't** to be working really because he's unhelpful and sometimes he **can** be quite rude to visitors. I **needn't / don't** have to tell you that we're all pretty fed up with the situation. Well, as I don't **have** any more **to** say, I'll stop there.

D   Encourage everyone to use the modal verbs they've been revising so far as they use their imaginations. To start the ball rolling, perhaps brainstorm some ideas for the first situation before the pairs begin.

A Ask the pairs to report back to the class on their discussion.

B ANSWERS

clever ≠ stupid	prejudiced ≠ tolerant
generous ≠ mean/stingy	relaxed ≠ nervous
kind ≠ cruel	sensible ≠ silly/foolish
modest ≠ conceited	shy ≠ self-confident
narrow-minded ≠ open-minded	sophisticated ≠ naive

C Note that these are words with similar meanings – there is rarely such a thing as an exact synonym.

ANSWERS

clever = bright	jolly = cheerful
cunning = crafty	level-headed = sensible
excitable = highly-strung	reliable = trustworthy
fair = even-handed	self-confident = self-assured
forgetful = absent-minded	snobbish = stuck-up
frank = direct	surly = grumpy
glum = miserable	two-faced = insincere
good-natured = kind	

D ANSWERS

disagreeable	indiscreet	unkind	unpredictable
unapproachable	inefficient	unlikeable	unreasonable
inarticulate	unenthusiastic	illogical	unreliable
unbiased	inflexible	disloyal	disrespectful
incompetent	unfriendly	immature	insensitive
inconsiderate	unhelpful	disobedient	unsociable
discontented	inhospitable	disorganised	tactless
indecisive	unimaginative	impatient	thoughtless
undependable	unintelligent	impractical	intolerant

E 1 This activity encourages everyone to use the adjectives they've studied earlier.

2 An example of a fault turned into a virtue might be that someone is a perfectionist and never satisfied with what they have achieved.

If your students aren't taking the CAE exam, or if you don't want them to do written work in this unit, discuss with the class what qualities a suitable local rep would require – what sort of person would be best able to carry out each of the duties listed in the job ad?

CAE exam	6.4 E is similar to the kind of writing task candidates have to do in the Writing paper (Question 1), where they may have to read the information given in an advertisement or job description and then write a letter containing only relevant information. Here, each of the duties mentioned in the job description should be covered in the letter.
	A common reason for low marks in this part of the exam is failure to include all the relevant points specified – even in an otherwise good piece of writing.

Leo Jones *New Cambridge Advanced English*

6.4 MODEL VERSION

Dear Ms Watson,

I have known Michael Sharp in a professional and social capacity for 10 years and in all that time he has shown himself to be reliable, likeable and efficient.

His outgoing and friendly nature, allied to his organisational skills and his efficiency, mean that welcome parties would go with a swing. These qualities too would come into play when meeting clients at, and escorting them from and to the airport. He will take an imaginative approach to organising and escorting coach excursions and would fulfil this area of his duties with enthusiasm.

I have invariably found him to be discreet and tactful when dealing with others. His approachability and competence make him an ideal colleague as well as rep, so contact with head office should be a pleasure.

As far as I know he is not fluent in any foreign language, but as a resourceful young man he will make light work of language difficulties and will be able to offer assistance to those clients having problems with the local language.

He is practical and level-headed and should cope well with emergencies occurring at any time of the day or night.

I have no hesitation in recommending Michael Sharp to you as a local resort representative for Utopia Holidays.

© Cambridge University Press, 1998

6.5 Personalities

Reading

 A It may be interesting to find out how many members of the class start out as sceptics or believers and how many change their minds after doing this activity.

Ask the students to highlight the words which lead them to their answers (given as quotes in the suggested answers). This all depends on finding synonyms.

SUGGESTED ANSWERS   (With quotes from the text.)

1	Aquarius	resent criticism
2	Taurus	slow to anger
3	Libra	great entertainers
4	Sagittarius	optimistic, look on the bright side
5	Aries	overlook details
6	Pisces	compassionate, cry easily
7	Leo	like to be the centre of attention
8	Gemini	don't like monotony
9	Cancer	hate to throw things away
10	Scorpio	enjoy solving problems
11	Capricorn	suspicious of new ideas and inventions
12	Virgo	hate untidiness

B1 Besides doing this activity the students should highlight any new vocabulary they come across.

2 Even though your students may believe all this astrology stuff is far-fetched (or is it?) there's a lot of useful vocabulary in the personality descriptions.

EXTRA ACTIVITY

This is the only unit which doesn't contain a Verbs and idioms/collocations section. In case your students might suffer from withdrawal symptoms, there's an extra activity on the next page, which you can photocopy for them.

Ⓐ ANSWERS

MAKE collocations:
the most/best of a situation   a cake   mistakes   a plan   a habit of   arrangements   a suggestion   improvements   a decision   an effort   an excuse   your bed

DO collocations:
the shopping   your best   some painting   someone a good turn   someone a favour   an exam (also *take*)   some cooking   harm   some reading   good   the washing-up

Ⓑ ANSWERS

1 make room/way
2 make out
3 make up
4 made up
5 make do with
6 make out
7 make it up to you
8 makes out
9 make
10 make up to
11 do-it-yourself (DIY)
12 over and done with
13 dos and don'ts
14 do without
15 did away with
16 has something to do with
17 had nothing to do with
18 do up

Leo Jones   *New Cambridge Advanced English*

EXTRA ACTIVITY	UNIT 6

Make and *do*   Verbs and collocations

Which of these things or activities are MADE and which are DONE?

the most/best of a situation   the shopping   your best   a cake   mistakes
some painting   a plan   a habit of   arrangements   someone a good turn
someone a favour   a suggestion   an exam   some cooking   harm   improvements
some reading   a decision   an effort   good   an excuse   the washing-up   your bed

Replace the phrases *in italics* with suitable expressions from the list below.

MAKE
 1 Hundreds of homes will be destroyed to *provide space* for a new motorway.
 2 I could only just *understand* what he was trying to say.
 3 In section 6.1 B, we had to *invent* our own examples.
 4 They had a big row, but later they *became reconciled*.
 5 If there aren't enough pillows, you'll have to *manage with* cushions.
 6 As he's colour blind he can't *discern* the difference between red and green.
 7 Thanks for doing me a favour, I'll *return the favour* another time.
 8 She *pretends* that she's the only member of staff who does any work.
 9 They've got a brand new car, but I'm not sure what *brand* it is.
10 They're so well off that people are always trying to *gain favour with* them.

DO
11 One of the most popular adult hobbies nowadays is *home improvement*.
12 I'll be glad when this affair is *completely finished*.
13 When looking for a flat there are a number of *rules* you should be aware of.
14 You don't need to have a sofa to sit on, you can *manage without* one.
15 It's high time the government *abolished* nuclear weapons.
16 This newspaper cutting *is partly concerned with* modern architecture.
17 What he told me *was irrelevant to* the subject we were discussing.
18 He's put on such a lot of weight that he can't *fasten* his trousers any more.

make   make do with   make out   make out   make out   make room/way
make up   make up   make it up to someone   make up to someone

do away with   do up   do without   do-it-yourself (DIY)   dos and don'ts
over and done with   have something to do with   have nothing to do with

THIS DOCUMENT MAY BE PHOTOCOPIED.   © Cambridge University Press, 1998

(7.1) Handwriting
Speaking

A 1 Deducing personality from handwriting may seem as far-fetched as astrology, but it's a fact that some companies employ a graphologist to analyse job applicants' handwriting.

 2 Play the recording, perhaps pausing between each analysis.

SUGGESTED ANSWERS

1 intelligent inconsiderate gentle not aggressive tactless unreliable passive

2 shy fussy nervous insecure enthusiastic inconsistent unconventional eccentric

3 consistent confident sociable friendly independent logical impulsive adaptable

4 energetic mature objective versatile well-organised determined stubborn self-confident

Transcript   2 minutes 30 seconds

EXPERT: Now this person is quite intelligent. He, I think it's a man, um…is rather inconsiderate and I'd say likes to dominate other people. But he's a gentle sort of person, not at all aggressive. He…he can be quite tactless sometimes and he also tends to be unreliable. He probably lets things happen to him, rather than taking the initiative and tends to be passive.

Now this person, I would say, is rather shy and er…has a tendency to be fussy. She's probably somewhat nervous and insecure. But she can be enthusiastic too – she tends to be inconsistent, I guess is what I'm saying. She doesn't conform to um…to what's expected of her: she's unconventional and I'd say a bit eccentric.

This person is consistent and fairly confident…confident, yes. She likes the company of other people…um…she's sociable and friendly. She seems to be quite independent. And I'd say that although she's logical she does sometimes jump to conclusions and er…and can be impulsive, but also adaptable.

This person is quite energetic. He has a mature and objective attitude I'd say. He's versatile and well-organised. He wants to succeed and is quite determined and well sometimes even stubborn. You know, once his mind is made up, it's hard to change it. Yes, he's self-confident.

B 1 In this Communication Activity student A looks at **Activity 4**, while B looks at **Activity 23**. The Activities contain more information about the 'science' of graphology (handwriting analysis).

2 Begin this activity by asking everyone to write the same sentences on a slip of paper:

This is a sample of my handwriting. What sort of person do you think I am?

plus a pseudonym or phone number that only they know (Mickey Mouse, 776667, or whatever) so that in the end the students can identify their own and each other's work. Then collect up the slips of paper, shuffle them, and redistribute them among the pairs.

If some of your students are liable to get upset by this because they have extraordinary handwriting, or if everyone recognises everyone else's handwriting, you might prefer to collect some samples from members of your own family or circle of friends and bring them to class. Or ask the students to do the same and bring them to class.

(7.2) A professional writer

Listening

 A Before playing the recording ask everyone to read the sentences through – which answers can they guess before they even hear the interview? Looking at her handwriting sample, what kind of person do they think she is? Her star sign is Gemini – what kind of person should she be according to the information on pages 54–55?

ANSWERS

1 *Like* other writers she tries to put off the moment when she has to start work.

2 Self-discipline is ~~not~~ easier for her when she's working with a partner.

3 While she's working on a script she thinks about her characters *all* of the time.

4 Writing is *a safe* environment because you're working out your own fantasies.

5 The people who read her first script reacted in *two* different ways.

6 She thinks that rewriting a script is *necessary*.

7 She resents other people's criticisms and feels hurt by them for a *short* time.

8 Workshops for writers *can't* help you to become a better writer.

9 When writing dialogue you ~~don't~~ have to be able to hear what the characters are saying.

10 She *doesn't use* a word processor because she needs to see what she has crossed out.

11 She thinks that everyone needs food, and ~~not~~ everyone needs entertainment.

12 A television programme *can* enlighten people.

B This group discussion could be a whole-class activity, if you prefer.

Transcript 6 minutes 45 seconds

ISABELLE: My name is Isabelle Amyes and I'm a television scriptwriter.

INTERVIEWER: And how did you start?

ISABELLE: Well, I…I started off actually as an actress and having been…um…rather unhappy about the kind of work that I was getting, I thought I'd sit down and write something for myself…um…and it just kind of snowballed from there really.

INTERVIEWER: So what kind of things do you do on a typical day when you're writing?

ISABELLE: Well, um…I try and do it…er…as much in the morning as I can, and leave just things like typing to do in the afternoon. Um…and I just get up and try and force myself to do it, and I think in common with every other writer, I prevaricate, and I wash the kitchen floor and I phone up people I haven't spoken to in ten years – anything not to have to sit down and do it. Um…some days involve research, which is *wonderful* and you find out things that you never even thought of, let alone thought you would be writing about. But the hard graft I like to do between about 10 and 2.

INTERVIEWER: And you have to be quite disciplined?

ISABELLE: Yes, and that's quite tough, that…that really is quite hard. That's why sometimes to work with a partner, which I sometimes do, makes it easier because you have to discipline each other.

INTERVIEWER: And what do you enjoy about what you do?

ISABELLE: I love the people that I'm imagining and that I'm inventing. And I love living with them and I love the fact that I can take them through highs and lows. And I go to bed thinking about them, and I wake up thinking about them. And I miss them terribly when I'm…when I've finished with them, you know when I move on to something else.

INTERVIEWER: Yes, when does…um…er…reality become reality and not…er…fiction or not . . .?

ISABELLE: Well, I think, in a curious way, that's what…what's really nice about it is that it's a safe environment for you to sit down and…and work out your fantasies and your emotions and things like that. And you're not hurting anyone else or even affecting anyone else.

INTERVIEWER: And they may enjoy it at the end.

ISABELLE: And they may enjoy it. Let's hope they do.

INTERVIEWER: So what do you not like about what…what you're doing?

ISABELLE: Um…sometimes the solitude is a bit tough. Um…and people's reactions are…are very subjective. Um…the first thing that I wrote was a comedy and a lot of people, thankfully a lot of people would read it and say it made them laugh out loud, and other people would…would read it and hand it back and say, 'I'm sorry I don't get the joke.' And that can be very dispiriting. But I think really the hardest of all is the rewrites. You'll send something off to…to a television company and back will come the fax: 'Yes, we love it. Could you change this? Could you get rid of that character? Could you add another character? What about such and such? Couldn't the ending be this?' And then you, you know, you fling it across the room and you're furious, and then you've got to sit down, because you're being paid for it, you've got to sit down and…and…and do it. Or negotiate.

INTERVIEWER: And it could be your favourite character?

ISABELLE: Yes, and sadly quite often it is, and characters that you love and lines that you love sometimes, and lines that make you hoot with laughter. Um…but I think…I think probably everybody who writes would say that, that…that when you've spent a lot of time and effort and energy on something, um…you can't help but take it as a criticism. But interestingly when you then read something later on, having incorporated rewrites, somebody else's ideas, quite often when you're distanced from it you can look at it and think, 'Yes, actually they were right. Um…that does enhance it or it does improve it.'

INTERVIEWER: And if someone was to come up to you and say, 'Oh, I want to be a scriptwriter. What…what do I need to do?' What…what advice would you give them?

ISABELLE: I don't think that endless sort of courses and seminars and workshops and all of that…um…really do much good. I don't think there's any substitute for actually sitting down and…and doing it.

INTERVIEWER: What skills would you need?

ISABELLE: I think you would need…well, you'd obviously need imagination. And you'd need I think a fascination with character and what makes a character tick. Um…and you'd also need to be able, I think, to hear what you're writing in your head. And you'd need to hear the different people saying it. Do you see what I mean? You'd need to…you'd need to hear the flow of it. And you'd also…you'd absolutely need to know what is a good script and what is a bad script.

INTERVIEWER: But how do you…um…sit down and write a piece of…a script?

ISABELLE: You sit down and you look at a blank piece of paper and then you just hold your nose and jump into the icy water and you write rubbish quite often, embarrassing rubbish, and then you read it again and you think, 'Oh, it's absolute rubbish, I…I'm going to throw it away.' And then you think, 'Actually no, that line's all right, and actually that line's all right.' And then you can…you can build it from there. I write on scrap paper and it builds up on the floor beside me into a mountain. I mean I'm…I screw it up and throw it away, screw it up and throw it away endlessly. And I can't write on a…on a word processor at all, I have to write by hand. Um…it's something about being able to cross it out and still see it there. And I will, you know, I will end up with something several feet high on the table, and some pages will have two lines on and the rest is all crossed out. And I think that's the only way to do it.

INTERVIEWER: And why do you think what you do is important?

ISABELLE: Well, I don't suppose really in the great scheme of things that it is. I mean, I think it comes down to whether… whether you think that art and literature and culture is important…um . . .

INTERVIEWER: Well, entertainment . . .

ISABELLE: Well, e…exactly, I mean at its…at its lowest level it entertains and at its most elevated level I suppose it enlightens. Um…and I think, you know, I think it's 'bread and circuses' – everybody needs their circus. Everybody needs, even if what they do is come home and watch game shows, it's a variation of the same thing. It's…it's…it's entertainment and I hope that, you know, sometimes I make people laugh – and I think actually that's probably the most important thing of all.

7.3 Different styles **Reading**

A1 These are questions for discussion – students shouldn't feel inadequate if they can't guess the source of some of the extracts.

Write these phrases on the board, which the students can use to avoid sounding too dogmatic or even aggressive in their discussion:

It looks like . . . because . . .	It seems to me that it's . . . because . . .
I don't think it's . . . because . . .	It could either be . . . or . . .
It seems to be about . . . because . . .	I think this comes from . . . because . . .

SUGGESTED ANSWERS

1 Introduction to a 'simplified edition' of a novel (a Longman Simplified English Series Reader) – *as seen again in 7.4 D but don't let the students know this now.*
2 Weather forecast – printed in a newspaper or, perhaps, read aloud on the radio
3 Instructions packed with personal stereo headphones
4 Part of a personal description of a place, perhaps in a personal letter
5 Directions for use, from the back of a bottle of tablets
6 Description of a book and its plot (the blurb of *Empire of the Sun* by J.G. Ballard)
7 Part of a guidebook to Japan
8 Part of an advertisement persuading people to travel by train
9 Part of a book about running (*The Book of Running* by James Fixx)
10 The small print on an insurance form

▼ 2 Discuss this with the class when they have highlighted the 'clues'.

B This might be set for homework if not enough English texts are available in the classroom. Possible sources might be labels, books, newspapers, magazines, advertisements, notices, etc.

7.4 Long and short sentences **Effective writing**

A To save time in class, the text and the questions in A could be prepared as homework.

ANSWERS

1	N	7	N
2	HS	8	HS
3	N	9	HS
4	HS	10	AS
5	HS	11	HS
6	AS	12	N – the article itself is this long

B1 The 'synonyms' given here show the approximate meaning of the words in the contexts: they are not full-scale dictionary definitions. There is other vocabulary in the text that may cause problems, but this exercise picks out the more useful words.

ANSWERS

respectively = separately in the order mentioned   emulated = copied   futile = pointless
feats = achievements   entry = piece of information in a reference book
alerting = making aware of   freelance = self-employed   profounder = more serious
unabashedly = without shame   ramble = write/speak at great length   banal = unoriginal
ploy = tactic   superseded = replaced   constrained = limited   invariably = always

2 The same words are used in different contexts in this exercise.

ANSWERS

1 futile   feats
2 superseded   entries   respectively
3 rambled
4 invariably   rambling
5 profound/banal   banal/profound
6 ploy
7 constrained   alert

▼◉**1** This activity is intended to draw attention to some features of the article that students can use in their own writing. The examples in the article just go on and on – look at the article again to find them.

2 Other examples of participles in the article:

. . . but instead peppering it with dashes . . .
. . . a calendar detailing Guinness records on the date they were set . . .
. . . such as stating that the longest sentence . . .
. . . especially when, as expected, it appears in the next Guinness Book . . .

♟**ⓓ** This can be done in class or set for homework. The original paragraphs are shown below, but your students may have better ideas for splitting them into sentences – indeeed, the second one might be clearer if it was divided into shorter sentences.

THE ORIGINAL PARAGRAPHS

> Why does language provide such a fascinating object of study? Perhaps because of its unique role in capturing the breadth of human thought and endeavour. We look around us, and are awed by the variety of several thousand languages and dialects, expressing a multiplicity of world views, literatures and ways of life. We look back at the thoughts of our predecessors, and find we can see only as far as language lets us see. We look forward in time, and find we can plan only through language. We look outward in space, and send symbols of communication along with our spacecraft, to explain who we are, in case there is anyone there who wants to know.

from *The Cambridge Encyclopedia of Language* by David Crystal

> This book has been specially prepared to make it enjoyable reading for people to whom English is a second or foreign language. An English writer never thinks of avoiding unusual words, so that the learner, trying to read the book in its original form, has to turn frequently to the dictionary and so loses much of the pleasure that the book ought to give.

from the preface to a book in the Longman Simplified English Series – as already seen in 7.3 A1!

⑦.⑤ Living with a computer   Reading

Ⓐ**1** This discussion gives anti-computer people a chance to let off steam, and computer fans a chance to express their enthusiasm.

2 This should be done alone. Alternatives to the words that were in the original article may be possible (e.g. *flood* for *deluge* or *find* for *discover*).

3 Get everyone to compare their answers before dealing with questions.

ORIGINAL ARTICLE

Spammed

THE FIRST sign that something was *wrong* came Sunday afternoon, when I logged onto the Internet to check my weekend e-mail and found that someone had *enrolled* me in a Barry Manilow fan club, a Mercedes owners discussion *group*, a Fiji Islands appreciation society and 103 other Internet mailing lists I'd never heard of. I knew from *experience* that any one of these lists can generate 50 messages a day. To avoid a *deluge* of junk e-mail I painstakingly unsubscribed from all 106 – even Barry Manilow's – only to log on Monday morning and *discover* I'd been subscribed overnight to 1,700 more. My file of unread e-mail was growing by the *minute*.

I'd heard about "spam" – Internet jargon for machine-generated junk mail – and over the years I'd *received* my share of e-mail get-rich-quick pitches and cheesy magazine ads. But I had never experienced anything like this: a parade of mail that just got bigger and *bigger* . . . not only was I getting hundreds of subscription notices, but I was also receiving copies of every piece of mail posted to those lists. By Monday the e-mail was *pouring* in at the rate of four a minute, 240 an hour, 5,760 a day.

| **CAE exam** | The exercises in **7.5 A2** and **C1** are similar to the gap-filling task in Part 2 of the English in Use paper. Here, as in the exam, only one word must be written for each gap. So, in **A2**, *large amount* would not be an acceptable alternative for *deluge*, nor *find out* for *discover*. |

B1 Every language has its own keyboard layout. The purpose of this exercise is to encourage the students to say the names of the letters aloud as they GUESS which keys fit where. The missing ones include many that students confuse (G and J, A and R, E and I, etc.). Draw everyone's attention to the little dialogue in the speech balloons.

ANSWERS

2 This discussion is designed to encourage students to say letters and spell words aloud. If few students in your class use a keyboard, arrange the class into larger groups, each containing at least one computer-literate person.

C 1 This can be done alone or in pairs. There may be alternatives that make sense horizontally, but not diagonally!

ORIGINAL ADVERTISEMENT

Writing unlimited.

The freedom to write and think is for all of us. Now, there is a new word processor that's just **right** for us, too. It's called MacWrite® II, and it's made by Claris. MacWrite II makes it possible **to** share your ideas and thoughts with other computers and word processors. You'll be **free** to open documents from over 50 word processors, on all kinds of computers, with all kinds of **speech** , and work on them without reformatting.

But there's more you can do. (The feature is called XTND.) You can import graphics, not **only** from Macs, but many computers, guaranteed. And you can scale and crop them, **one** and all, in your MacWrite® II document. In short, MacWrite® II with XTND is a powerful word processor that lets you freely exchange text and graphics. You'll find also that your MacWrite® II **lets** you change fonts, styles, sizes and colors, as well as text with its find/change feature. And **you** can create custom styles and save them as stationery – with all formats preset. You'll **share** your reports and letters quickly.

But what good is freedom of expression if you find **your** editing to be a hassle? That's why the page layout and editing is fully WYSIWYG: the **thoughts** you see are the thoughts you get. This WYSIWYG feature, by the way, is found only with MacWrite® II. It's another way Claris simplifies word processing for you, whether you're 52, 22, or 72.

Called upon daily MacWrite® II smooths your writing assignments and other chores. There's MacWrite II spell checking, for example, and foreign dictionary programs that are optional, **and** a host of other features that come standard. (Like a thesaurus, and a mail merge feature **you'll** discover saves lots of time.)

What it adds up to, you'll **find** is a simple and powerful tool designed for people. All the people. It is for writers, and **it** is for business people. And it is for those of us in between. The freedom to write is **liberating**. Now technology is, too.

CLARIS™

2 Question 10 isn't answered in the passage, but many students are likely to know the answer anyway. Features 1 to 8 are not mentioned in the same order in the ad as in the list of questions.

ANSWERS

The features that are mentioned are: 1   3   6   7   8

9 XTND

10 What you see is what you get

3 Computer buffs may find the text more interesting than others – but they may know most of the vocabulary already, so might highlight fewer words.

(7.6) Formal letters and personal letters
Reading and Effective writing

A This is a warm-up discussion. If your students are doing the CAE exam, remind them that they'll have to write at least one letter in the exam, maybe more.

B1 Preparation If you can get everyone to read this before the lesson, it'll save a lot of time.

2 The idea of this exercise is to encourage students not to depend on dictionaries or the teacher (or despair) when they come across unfamiliar words. All the meanings can be deduced from their context.

SUGGESTED ANSWERS

remorse = regret
whodunit = who is responsible (a whodunit /huːdʌnɪt/ is a detective story)
suspect = not to be trusted
deadwood = unnecessary/superfluous text
sap the strength = take away the force
credibility = being believed and trusted
wimpy = weak and timid
cover-up = attempt to conceal a problem
vented his fury = expressed his anger
upbeat = positive, hopeful
tenfold = ten times
hat-in-hand = humble, self-effacing
regimen = plan or system
heavy-duty = large and complicated

(In this context a word processor refers to a computer program or application, not a dedicated word processor.)

3 The ad appeared in an American computer magazine (it could have been a business magazine) and the intended reader is a business person who has to write a lot of routine letters.

C1 The first letterhead is suitable for a personal letter and the third is suitable for a business letter – this should be well-known to everyone, but it's probably a good idea to remind everyone of the standard formats shown here. The middle one isn't suitable for either.

2 SUGGESTED ANSWERS

Dear Mrs Simpson,	B	Marge!	✗?
Dear Ms Simpson,	B	Dear Marge,	P
Dear Margaret Simpson,	✗	Dear Friend,	✗
Darling Marge,	P?	Dear Mrs M B Simpson,	✗
Dear Madam,	B	Hi Marge!	P

It's a very long time since I last wrote to you and I feel quite . . .   P
I'm pleased to inform you that . . .   ✗ – *I'm* isn't suitable
            in a business letter, *pleased to inform you* isn't suitable in a personal letter
I'm sorry not to have written earlier, but I've been very busy with . . . P
I hope your new job is going well . . .   P (+ B ?)
How are you? I'm fine.   P
Thank you for your enquiry about . . .   B
The reason I'm writing this letter is to let you know that . . .   P
I hope you enjoyed your visit to . . .   P + B

3 SUGGESTED ANSWERS (Some are more typically British or American English.)

Good luck with your new job.	P
I'm off to lunch now, so I'll post this on the way.	P
I have to stop now because lunch is nearly ready.	P
I hope you enjoy your holiday.	P + B
I look forward to meeting you next month.	B
Well, I must stop now so as to catch the post.	P
Give my regards to your husband and the family.	B
Again, thank you for doing business with us.	✗ – according to 7.6 B
Remember me to Homer and the kids.	P
Assuring you of our best attention at all times,	B? – too old-fashioned

Yours,	P
Best,	B (US)
All the best,	P
Kind regards,	P
Your loving friend,	P ? – sounds too effusive
Yours faithfully,	B (GB)
Yours sincerely,	B (GB)
Best wishes,	P + B
Sincerely,	B (US)

4 Two more opening phrases:

I've been meaning to write to you for ages, but . . .	P
Thank you very much for your letter, which I received today.	B

Two more closing phrases:

Do write back soon if you can.	P
I am looking forward to hearing from you.	B

CAE exam

In the exam it's important to use appropriate style or register, and this is rewarded in the assessment. Either British or American usage are equally acceptable in the exam – but not a mixture of the two.

For more information about the way the Writing paper is marked, and sample graded compositions, please refer to the Teacher's Book for *CAE Practice Tests 3* (or later).

7.7 The differences between spoken and written English

Listening

  A This is the first part of a lecture. Although the 'silent language' used by the lecturer in his talk would only be observable on video, the listener can easily imagine what he's doing as he demonstrates.

SUGGESTED ANSWERS

Speech: 'rapid conversational English'
– happens face-to-face, it's *unplanned*, *interactive*
Writing: 'formal written English'
– happens alone, it's *planned*

Main differences between speech and writing:

1 Hesitation
  – in speech we hesitate to give us time to think while we're speaking
  – in writing hesitation not apparent because the writer *stops to think, rests pen or stops typing* – but the *reader* doesn't notice the pause

2 Listener contact
  – the people in a conversation are always *interacting*
  – question tags (rather like a *tennis match*!)
  – *eye* contact
  – *questions* at end of lecture

3 'Silent language'
  – body language e.g. *scratching your head*
  – gestures e.g. *thumbs up, pointing, waving your arms for emphasis*
  – invisible in a *recording* or on the *phone*

4 Tone of voice

CAE exam **7.7A** is similar to a task type in the Listening paper where candidates have to complete notes as they listen to a talk. This is different from the sentence-completion tasks we've done earlier because the students have to understand the overall meaning of the talk, rather than concentrating hard on catching relevant details.

B 1 First everyone starts discussing their reactions to what the lecturer said.

2 Then the discussion continues, with more ideas from the Communication Activities: student A looks at **Activity 10** and B at **29**. They should use the notes in their Activity as prompts for making more points in the discussion – not read the notes aloud to each other.

Transcript 6 minutes 15 seconds

LECTURER: OK, what I'm going to do is to compare two very common styles of English. There's 'rapid conversational style', which is conversation with friends or colleagues, and 'formal written style', that's business letters, reports, textbooks, etc. I'm going to refer to the former as 'Speech' in this lecture, and o...of course there are other kinds of speech as well, obviously – and the latter as 'Writing', although obviously there are other kinds of writing as well, er...many many other styles.

So, first: Speech. Rapid conversational English is face-to-face – you can see each other, and each other's reactions. It...it's unplanned: you don't know what *you're* going to say until you say it, and it's interactive: what the other person says influences what *you're* going to say next.

OK, now second: Writing. Formal written English happens alone, if you could actually see someone you wouldn't bother to write to them. It...it's...um...it's planned: you don't write something until you've thought what you're going to write.

So, what are the main features of Speech that you don't get in Writing? First...um...well...um...w...what I'm doing now a lot...um...is hesitating! Now, hesitation happens all the time in conversation but in writing it's not that apparent. Now, that doesn't mean to say, of course, that in Writing we write and write and write j...just non-stop. Of course not, because when we're writing if we need to stop and think, if we need to find the right word or to look something up, or find some information, what we do is we stop writing, and we put the pen down, and we stop typing, whatever. Er...now, the reader of course doesn't notice the pause when we rest our pen or stop typing for a little while – or even if we leave the desk for several hours. In other words, although hesitation in Writing is invisible, hesitation in conversation is always...um...audible, and some people hesitate more than others. Now, what I was doing just now was hesitating more than I would normally do, just to illustrate the point.

Now the second feature of Speech is what I could call 'listener contact'. Er... listener contact is the way in which... um...in a conversation the people involved are always interacting. Um...a typical example of this is the use of what are called 'question tags', er...such as... er...'isn't it?' and...er...'don't you?'... er... 'can't you?' And I often think that this is something like a...a tennis match where someone is serving the ball to the o...t...t...to the other person, you know, it...so it goes:

'It's a lovely day, isn't it?'

'Oh, yes, it's wonderful too. It was nice yesterday too, wasn't it?'

'Oh, yes, yes I think it's going to be nice tomorrow, don't you?'

And, you see, so the 'ball' goes to and fro, backwards and forwards in the conversation. In other words, er...the people are always allowing each other to speak or react. And...er...listener contact goes on in other ways. Er...in this lecture that I'm giving you now I'm keeping in contact with you while I'm lecturing, I...I'm not looking at my notes (not all the time anyway) reading word for word what it says down here, I'm looking at the

reactions that I'm getting from you, you see, we're keeping in touch with our eyes. Now, in a lecture you can't interrupt me and...er...talk back to me but when I've finished at the end, you'll probably have some questions and that's your way of contacting me about the communication that's gone on between us.

Um...eye contact is something we could also describe as 'silent language'. An important part of Speech is communication that you can't actually hear. So if you're listening to a recording of...um...people speaking (or a recording of this lecture), um...there are many things that you can't see which are important in the communication that's going on. Look, if I do this . . . you see, or this . . . – well, *you* can see that I'm scratching my head and...er...giving a thumbs up sign. But a listener wouldn't be able to see that and wouldn't know that I meant...um...'I'm puzzled' or 'Everything's OK'. And...um...if I point at something and say 'Now, look at this!' then *you* can see what I'm pointing at, you know what it is, but someone just hearing a recording wouldn't know what I'm indicating. In other words, Speech, even in a lecture like this, depends on your being able to see each other, for us being able to see each other, and not just hear each other.

And gestures are invisible on the phone too. Wh...when you're on the phone to someone if you want to draw attention to something it's no good pointing at it and saying 'Now, look at this'. It's no...it's no good waving your arms and saying 'This is very important' because the person at the other end of the line can't see what you're doing. Er...if you've ever looked at people in telephone boxes you often see them waving their arms about and...and pointing at things because they can't help it, it's part of what we do when we're talking and so we don't stop even though we're just talking down the phone.

Another feature of Speech is tone of voice: we show our feelings by the *way* we say something. Um...if I say to you: 'That's interesting!' or 'That's interesting!!' or 'That's interesting . . .', each way of saying that phrase has a different meaning, so you could see that . . .

(7.8) A tactful letter   Creative writing

 A To start things off, it might be best to brainstorm some ideas in class. Has anyone had to write a letter like one of these (in their own language)? What did they say in their letter?

B1 If there's a group of three rather than a pair, make sure there's a three-way exchange of letters (A→B, B→C, C→A).

2 This can be done in class, or set for homework.

CAE exam	Writing a postcard (as in **7.8 B2**) is similar to writing a note to someone, which candidates may well have to do in the Writing paper. Students need to get a feel for how much they can write in 50 words, as well as in 250 words. Other word lengths (200, 150, 100 words, etc.) are also specified for various tasks in Question 1 of the Writing paper.

Leo Jones *New Cambridge Advanced English*

(7.8) A & B MODEL VERSIONS FOR BOTH TOPICS

Dear Mr and Mrs Brown,

I wonder how you are. It seems ages since we've been in touch. How is Sam? How did he get on in his exams? I really had a great time with you last summer and the visit certainly helped my English.

As you may remember I was about to start my university course on my return from England and got very involved in looking for accommodation and a job, as well as actually starting the academic work. Well, I found a rented room in a house only about 10 minutes from the university by bike and I'm working at a bar four evenings a week and some weekends. My course is quite interesting but the amount of work we're expected to do is enormous. Consequently when I'm not studying, working or travelling I'm asleep!

I'm really sorry I didn't write to you when I got back but, as you can imagine, there just don't seem to be enough hours in the day.

I'm coming to England again in August and will be spending four weeks in York working as a tourist guide. I'd love to see you all again and wonder if you'd be able to put me up for a few days towards the end of August, after I've finished working.

I look forward to hearing from you.

All the best,

Steve

PS Tell Sam that he's welcome to come and stay with me if he wants to practise his _____.

Dear Steve,

How nice to hear from you after all this time. We'd love to have you to stay in August but it really depends on the dates you want to come. We're going on holiday on 27 August and will be away for five days. Let us know as soon as possible.

Regards,

Chris Brown

Dear Uncle Peter,

How are you? We're all fine as I expect Mum has told you. She said you'd just been to a conference in Hawaii. Lucky you!

Actually I'm hoping to travel in the near future. As you probably know, I'm taking a year out between school and university and travelling is going to take up the major part of that year. As soon as school finishes I'm going to start work at the local brewery and plan to do that for about three months. The idea is to earn a substantial sum to fund myself on my travels. Dad and Mum have said they will give me half of the cost of a round-the-world ticket but I have to find the rest and also earn enough for food and accommodation while I'm abroad. I hope to be able to work at some places during my trip, particularly in _____ -speaking areas.

I wonder if you'd be able to help me out at all during this year, either with a job or a loan of money. I'd be willing to do any kind of work in one of your factories or offices in the States. If this isn't possible I wonder if you might be able to give me a loan of about $1000.

I have been meaning to write and thank you for the $50 you sent for my birthday. The reason I haven't done so earlier was that it came during my school exams and I was so preoccupied at the time that it slipped my mind. Anyway, thanks a lot. The money is in the travel fund!

I hope you will be able to help me with my year off . . . it means a lot to me and will be good experience for my future career.

Love,

Val

Dear Val,

No problem about a loan and/or a job. Just keep in touch and let me know when you will need the cash and when you will be arriving in the States. Mike, Gene and Mary Lou are looking forward to seeing more of their cousin.

Love,

Uncle Peter

                    © Cambridge University Press, 1998

7.9 *In . . . and *out of* . . .*   **Idioms and collocations**

A ANSWERS

   1 in tears   in a whisper
   2 in doubt
   3 In comparison with
   4 in public   in the circumstances   in private
   5 in pencil   in ink
   6 in person   in cash
   7 In view of   in addition to
   8 in difficulty / in trouble   in   trouble/difficulty
   9 in   detail   in brief
   10 in return   in fun

B ANSWERS

   1 in   danger   in control
   2 out of fashion   in love
   3 in contact/touch   out of touch
   4 out of focus   out of practice
   5 in   pain   out of hospital
   6 in season   in stock
   7 out of luck   out of work   in debt   in prison
   8 out of tune   out of doors

➡ Here are some more expressions, not introduced in the Student's Book, with their
   opposites in some cases:

   in action
   in secret – in public
   in short

   out of breath
   out of date – up to date
   out of earshot – within earshot
   out of the ordinary – normal
   out of reach – within reach
   out of order – working

Eight | Past times

8.1 The good old days?

Reading

A The pictures are 'Baby's Birthday' by George Hardy (19th century), 'A Woman Scraping Parsnips' by N. Maes, a pupil of Rembrandt (1655), and a photo of nursery children queuing for a mouth spray (1944).

B1 The correct sequence of paragraphs was: C   F   B   E   D   A – but other arrangements may be possible.

> **CAE exam** | Although not an exam-style exercise, **B1** will help to prepare candidates for the so-called 'gapped text' – the second text in the Reading paper. Here, looking at the linking devices used between the paragraphs helps the students to decide on the correct sequence.
>
> There's more practice in doing this kind of exercise in **9.4**, **11.5** and **12.6** – plus an extra activity for exam candidates at the end of **Unit 11**.

2 This task requires students to find the relevant information in the text, but it's also designed to encourage them to discuss this.

SUGGESTED ANSWERS

- Events are reported 'as they happened' as if on TV
- German, French and American editions
- It reflects a British perspective on world events – presumably including events that affected Britain but not other countries

➡ Ask the class this extra question about the Chronicle blurb:

- *How many women are mentioned in the blurb?*

The answer is 'None at all, apart from Queen Victoria' (see also 8.2 D). Perhaps this is because female achievements are not considered newsworthy in the same way as male achievements: women are rarely responsible for starting wars, for example. Moreover, female historical figures are often less well-known internationally than they are within their own countries.

Ask the members of the class to name some female historical figures who are well-known in their country – e.g. Emmeline Pankhurst in Britain, La Pasionaria in Spain, Rosa Luxemburg in Germany, Joan of Arc in France, Susan B. Anthony in the USA, etc.

3 This can be prepared in class but done as homework. As paragraphs B and D are about 60 words long, your students' paragraphs should be about the same length.

C Again the questions are designed to stimulate discussion as well as encourage the students to find information in the text.

SUGGESTED ANSWERS (Only the answers to Question 1 are explicitly stated in the text.)

1 Film, fashion, design, the media, popular music, sport, advertising

2 Politics, wars, power struggles, etc. (i.e. none of the above)

3 to 5 *are a matter of opinion*

D If some of your students might be embarrassed by revealing their age, or if your students have a very hazy knowledge of recent history, you might prefer them to talk about the decade they were born in, rather than the year.

8.2 ## The past – 2   **Grammar**

The ideas in this section are intended as revision, but as this is a notorious 'problem area' of English grammar, there may be some unexpected difficulties.

A 1 & 2 SUGGESTED ANSWERS

1 ... *we would spend our holidays at the coast and* . . . . . . *play on the sand every day.*
= we used to do so, this happened usually or repeatedly
... *we spent our holidays at the coast and* . . . . . . *stayed in an old-fashioned seafront hotel.*
= straightforward narrative
... *we had to spend our holidays at the coast and* . . . . . . *were sorry we couldn't stay at home.*
= we were obliged to do it

2 ... *I didn't use to stay in hotels so* . . . . . . *the first time I went to a hotel as an adult was quite a treat.*
= this didn't usually happen
... *I wasn't used to staying in hotels so* . . . . . . *I didn't know how to behave there.*
= I wasn't accustomed to it
... *I wouldn't stay in hotels so* . . . . . . *my parents had to go on holiday without me.*
= I refused to stay

3 *I was going to tell him what had happened but* . . . . . . *I didn't have the nerve.*
= I intended to tell him but something stopped me
I was telling him what had happened but . . . . . . *he stopped me and said he already knew.*
= I was in the middle of telling him
I told him what had happened but . . . . . . *he didn't believe me.*
= straightforward narrative or report
I had told him what had happened but . . . . . . *he said he didn't remember me telling him.*
= I told him earlier
I was about to tell him what had happened but . . . . . . *then I realised that he already knew.*
= I was on the point of telling him

4 ... *they had been doing some research because* . . . . . . *their books were open on the desk.*
= they had done some of it and they still had more to do
... *they had done some research because* . . . . . . *they had already finished their report.*
= they had completed all of it
... *they were doing some research because* . . . . . . *they were busily looking things up.*
= they were in the middle of doing it.
... *they were going to do some research because* . . . . . . *they had a long list of books they were going to consult.*
= they hadn't started but they were planning to start soon

5 *I used to be interested in reading history books* . . . . . . *but I've gone off it now.*

= a habit or activity that I have now dropped or grown out of.
I was interested in reading about history . . . . . . *because it was my favourite subject at school.*
= straightforward report or narrative
I was used to reading history books . . . . . . *so reading another one was easy for me.*
= I was accustomed to it

B ANSWERS

1 I didn't *know* that you *were coming* to stay with me next weekend.

2 In the 1970s people *used to be / were* less well-off than they are now.

3 In the nineteenth century people *didn't (use to) watch* TV – they *had to* make their own entertainment.

4 I *had just written / was just writing* a letter to her when she *phoned* me.

5 *no errors*

6 He *studied / has studied / has been studying* history for three years.

7 It was the first time I *had been / gone* abroad and I was feeling very excited.

8 He arrived late because he had *forgotten* what time the train *would be leaving / was leaving / left*.

C ANSWERS

1 lay	had stung	**5** laid	swept	**9** rode	led
2 rewound		**6** arose	chose	**10** wept	shrunk
3 awoke		**7** swore	trod		
4 flown	clung	**8** foresaw	rewritten		

➡ Some other verbs with tricky past simple and past participle forms are:

bind   deal   draw   forego   grind   mistake   overcome   overhear   overthrow   seek
spread   stride   swing   weave   withhold

D ANSWERS

VICTORIAN BRITAIN

When Queen Victoria *died* in 1901 she *had reigned* for 63 years. During her reign many great scientific discoveries *were made* and the population of Britain *rose / had risen* from 18 million to 40 million. The British Empire *had grown* to become the largest empire the world *had* ever *known* and by then it *included* a quarter of the world's people. During her reign Britain *enjoyed* a time of peace and prosperity and *had* not *fought* in any major war since the battle of Waterloo in 1815. No one *suspected* that the First World War, in which so many young men *would be killed*, *was going to / would break out* some 13 years later.

THE DARKER SIDE

During the reign of Queen Victoria (1837–1901) life for the middle classes and the aristocracy *had* never *been* better: the Industrial Revolution and the Empire *provided* them with undreamed-of luxury, convenience and wealth – but at the expense of the lower classes. Although slavery *had been abolished* in the British Empire in 1834, the working classes in the slums of Britain's industrial cities *were treated* almost as badly as slaves, and even young children *were forced / were being forced* to work long hours in factories and coal mines. During this period over 10 million people *escaped* from these appalling conditions and *emigrated* to America and Australia. The magnificent Empire which *brought* vast profits to Britain's manufacturers *exploited* the people of the colonies, who *produced* cheap raw materials for British factories, and *created* nations of clients who *came* to depend on a supply of British products.

CAE exam   The exercise in **8.2 D** is similar to Part 4 in the English in Use paper, where the gaps in the second text have to be filled with suitable information without using the same words given in the first text. In other words, synonyms have to be used, as here. But the gaps wouldn't all be irregular verbs, as here.

E Here is the correct arrangement in chronological order of people, events and dates:

William the Conqueror	Battle of Hastings	1066
Christopher Columbus	Atlantic Ocean	1492
Ferdinand Magellan	Pacific Ocean	1521
Napoleon	Waterloo	1815
Wilbur and Orville Wright	Dayton, Ohio	1903
Archduke Franz Ferdinand	Sarajevo	1914
October Revolution	Russia	1917
Charles Lindbergh	Atlantic Ocean	1927
John F. Kennedy	Dallas, Texas	1963
Neil Armstrong	Moon	1969

Some other significant historical events might be:

Berlin Wall (1961–1989)   World War II (1939–1945)   French Revolution (1789–1799)

Leo Jones   *New Cambridge Advanced English*

EXTRA ACTIVITY   UNIT 8

Special uses of the Past   Grammar

Ⓐ *Work in pairs*   **Discuss the difference in meaning or emphasis (if any) between these sentences:**

1   I was hoping we could have a talk today.   I hope we can have a talk today.
    I had hoped we could have a talk today.   I'm hoping we can have a talk today.

2   I wonder if you could help me.   I wondered if you could help me
    I was wondering if you could help me.

3   Were you wanting to see the manager?   Did you want to see the manager?
    Do you want to see the manager?   Didn't you want to see the manager?
    Don't you want to see the manager?   Would you like to see the manager?

4   I wish there was more time.   I wish there were more time.
    I wish there had been more time.   If only there were more time.

Ⓑ **Fill the gaps in these sentences. The first is done as an example.**

1   He always talks to us as if we ....*were*........ children.

2   I'd rather you .... smoke in here, if you don't mind.

3   It's time you .... to the station to catch your train.

4   I wish I .... better at putting a name to a face.

5   If only I .... the solution to the problem.

Ⓒ1 **In these sentences most of the continuations are grammatically correct, but some are wrong. Mark the ones that are correct with a tick ✓ .**

1   It's past midnight and I think it's time . . .
    . . . I went to bed.   . . . for me to turn in.   . . . I call it a day.

2   It's terrible, he behaves as if . . .
    . . . he owned the place.   . . . he weren't a guest.   . . . it was his own home.

3   He spoke to me as if . . .
    . . . I were a half-wit.   . . . I was simple-minded.   . . . I have no brains.

4   I wish . . .
    . . . she wouldn't speak her mind so frankly.   . . . she were less outspoken.
    . . . I can tolerate criticism better.   . . . I was less sensitive to disapproval.

5   I'd rather . . .
    . . . you didn't tell me off.   . . . you don't scold me.   . . . not to blame me.

6   I wouldn't mind if . . .
    . . . he isn't such a daydreamer.   . . . he was less absent-minded.
    . . . he weren't so forgetful.

7   If only . . .
    . . . the world is a better place.   . . . the world were a better place.
    . . . the world be a better place.   . . . the world should be a better place.

2 Now use your own ideas to continue these sentences:

1 It's high time . . .

2 I'd much rather you . . .

3 He looked at me as if . . .

4 I'd like to suggest that . . .

5 It'd be much better if you . . .

6 I do wish . . .

D1 *Work in pairs* **Here are some ideas that can be expressed by using different structures. Put a tick ✓ beside the continuations that 'feel' suitable to you. Again several are correct. The first is done as an example.**

1 It is absolutely essential that these letters . . .
 . . . are posted today. ✓   . . . were posted today. ✗
 . . . should be posted today. ✓   . . . be posted today. ✓

2 If any unforeseen problems . . .
 . . . should arise, let me know.   . . . were to arise, keep me in the picture.
 . . . arise, don't keep me in the dark.   . . . are to arise, tell me at once.

3 I insist . . .
 . . . that he should be informed.   . . . that he is given the information.
 . . . he be informed.   . . . to inform him.

4 It's important . . .
 . . . that we were on our guard.   . . . that we are as careful as can be.
 . . . to be extremely careful.   . . . that we should show the utmost care.

5 I propose that . . .
 . . . we take a vote on it.   . . . we should ask for a show of hands.
 . . . the matter be put to a vote.   . . . we held a ballot.

6 We demand . . .
 . . . that payment is made at once.   . . . that payment be made at once.
 . . . to be paid at once.   . . . that payment was made at once.

▼ 2 Highlight ONE continuation for each sentence that you feel most 'comfortable' with. Which of the continuations would you use in a more formal style?

Ⓐ SUGGESTED ANSWERS

1 *I was hoping we could have a talk today.*
= slightly pessimistic about the chances of talking, perhaps trying to persuade someone
I had hoped we could have a talk today.
= pessimistic about the chances OR regretting the impossibility of it
I hope we can have a talk today.
= straightforward expression of hope OR more forceful request for time to talk
I'm hoping we can have a talk today.
= straightforward expression of hope, perhaps emphasising that I've got this constantly in my mind

2 *I wonder if you could help me.*
= straightforward request
I was wondering if you could help me.
= rather tentative request
I wondered if you could help me.
= very tentative request

3 *Were you wanting to see the manager?*
= very indirect enquiry, possibly deferential or maybe slightly sarcastic
Do you want to see the manager?
= straightforward enquiry
Don't you want to see the manager?
= surprised tone, perhaps suggesting that you seem to have changed your mind
Did you want to see the manager?
= slightly indirect enquiry, possibly deferential
Didn't you want to see the manager?
= surprised tone, perhaps suggesting that you should be in there talking to him or her now
Would you like to see the manager?
= inviting someone to meet the manager

4 *I wish there was more time.*
= regretting the shortage of time now or always
I wish there had been more time.
= regretting the shortage of time in the past
I wish there were more time.
= regretting the shortage of time now or always (as first example)
If only there were more time.
= regretting the shortage of time now or always (as first example)

Ⓑ ANSWERS

2 didn't   **3** went   **4** were/was/had been
5 knew/had known/could work out/could have worked out, etc.

Ⓒ**1** Correct continuations with ✓ – incorrect ones with ✗.

1 It's past midnight and I think it's time . . .
. . . I went to bed. ✓   . . . for me to turn in. ✓   . . . I call it a day. ✗

2 It's terrible, he behaves as if . . .
. . . he owned the place. ✓   . . . he weren't a guest. ✗   . . . it was his own home. ✓

3 He spoke to me as if . . .
. . . I were a half-wit. ✓   . . . I was simple-minded. ✓   . . . I have no brains. ✗

4 I wish . . .
. . . she wouldn't speak her mind so frankly. ✓   . . . she were less outspoken. ✓
. . . I can tolerate criticism better. ✗   . . . I was less sensitive to disapproval. ✓

5 I'd rather . . .
. . . you didn't tell me off. ✓   . . . you don't scold me. ✗   . . . not to blame me. ✗

6 I wouldn't mind if . . .   . . . he isn't such a daydreamer. ✗
. . . he weren't so forgetful. ✓   . . . he was less absent-minded. ✓

7 If only . . .

. . . the world is a better place. ✗ . . . the world were a better place. ✓
. . . the world be a better place. ✗ . . . the world should be a better place. ✗

2 Some suggested continuations . . .

1 It's high time . . .   you had your hair cut.
2 I'd much rather you . . .   smoked out in the garden.
3 He looked at me as if . . .   I was crazy.
4 I'd like to suggest that . . .   we all go out together after the lesson.
5 It'd be much better if you . . .   wrote to her.
6 I do wish . . .   I had worked harder before the exam.

D1 Correct continuations with ✓ – incorrect ones with ✗.

2 If any unforeseen problems . . .
. . . should arise, let me know. ✓   . . . were to arise, keep me in the picture. ✗
. . . arise, don't keep me in the dark. ✓ . . . are to arise, tell me at once. ✗

3 I insist . . .
. . . that he should be informed. ✓   . . . that he is given the information. ✓
. . . he be informed. ✓   . . . to inform him. ✗

4 It's important . . .
. . . that we were on our guard. ✗   . . . that we are as careful as can be. ✓
. . . to be extremely careful. ✓   . . . that we should show the utmost care. ✓

5 I propose that . . .
. . . we take a vote on it. ✓   . . . we should ask for a show of hands. ✓
. . . the matter be put to a vote. ✓   . . . we held a ballot. ✗

6 We demand . . .
. . . that payment is made at once. ✓   . . . that payment be made at once. ✓
. . . to be paid at once. ✓   . . . that payment was made at once. ✗

(8.3) Fourteen ninety-nine   **Listening**

A Before playing the recording allow everyone time to look at the questions and see if they can guess any of the missing information. What do they already know about the two explorers?

> *Vasco da Gama* left Lisbon on *8* July 1497 with *170* men and provisions for three years. Out of sight of land for *93* days between Cape Verde Islands and Cape of Good Hope (*6,000* km). Finally arrived at Calicut in India on 22 May *1498* after *23*-day voyage across *Arabian* Sea.
>
> Left India in *August* 1498 with cargo of spices, *drugs*, silk and *precious stones*. Arrived back in September *1499* with only *55* survivors – the rest died of scurvy (a disease caused by lack of vitamin C).

> **Christopher Columbus**'s first voyage was financed by King Ferdinand and Queen *Isabella* of Spain. Left Spain on *2* August 1492 with *three* ships and *90* men to travel west via the *Canary* Islands. Out of sight of land for *36* days (*4,000* km). Reached other side of Atlantic Ocean on *12* October 1492.
>
> Returned to Spain in *March* 1493 with cargo of a small amount of *gold*, *six* 'Indians' and some parrots.
>
> His second voyage began in *September* 1493 with *1,200* men – set up first permanent European *settlement* on other side of Atlantic.
>
> His third voyage began on 30 May *1498*: didn't find *through* route to the Indies.

Transcript   5 minutes 45 seconds

PRESENTER: Good evening, we have with us in the studio two people who have recently come back from Asia: Mr Vasco da Gama . . .

VASCO DA GAMA: Hello.

PRESENTER: . . . who has just returned from India and Mr Christopher Columbus . . .

COLUMBUS: Hello, everyone.

PRESENTER: . . . who has just returned from his third voyage to the east coast of Asia. Mr da Gama, you set off from Lisbon in July 1497, didn't you?

VASCO DA GAMA: Yes, July 8th it was, July 8th, if I remember rightly. Now, I set off and I took with me 170 crew and also provisions for approximately three years, just to make sure, you see. Now, the longest leg of the journey was a 6,000 km stretch between Cape…the Cape Verde Islands and the Cape of Good Hope. We were out of sight of land for 93 days – a long time! Anyway, now on the way I managed to deal with some rather unfriendly Muslim rulers on the East coast of Africa and then another long sea voyage of about 23 days across the Arabian Sea. Well, we arrived in India on May 22nd last year, and thanks to my skills as a diplomat we got on good terms with the ruler of Calicut.

COLUMBUS: Er…could I just come in here for a minute, Robyn?

PRESENTER: Oh yes, certainly, Mr Columbus, yes.

COLUMBUS: Isn't it true, Vasco, that Bartolomeu Dias first sailed round the southern tip of the African continent in 1488, ten years earlier than you – and if his crew hadn't refused to carry on further a…a…across the Indian Ocean that he'd have got there first?

VASCO DA GAMA: But he didn't and that's the point. Anyway, we left Calicut late August 1498, loaded with lots of spices, drugs, silk and precious stones . . .

PRESENTER: You didn't get back till this September, did you? Er…why did it take so long?

VASCO DA GAMA: Well…um…in fact we were delayed by contrary winds and difficulties en route, you see. Unfortunately only 55 members of my crew survived.

PRESENTER: Oh! Why was that?

VASCO DA GAMA: Because of scurvy.

PRESENTER: Oh. Still, it is a fantastic achievement and it looks as though you've opened up an important new trading route with the Orient.

VASCO DA GAMA: Yes.

PRESENTER: Now, Christopher Columbus, you've just returned from your third voyage, I think?

COLUMBUS: Yes, that's right, Rob…er…and I think that in the long run…er…my discovery of the east coast of Asia will be more significant than Vasco's little trip.

PRESENTER: Perhaps you could remind our listeners about your previous trips.

COLUMBUS: Yes, certainly Robyn, well, most educated people believe the earth is round, of course. You do too, don't you, Vasco? And…er…so you just have to keep going west to reach Japan and the Indies. Well, I couldn't persuade the King of Portugal to finance the trip in 1484, so in the end I had to go next door to…er…Spain and…er…get the money from King Ferdinand and Queen Isabella. That was eight years later and I have to tell you that I had to do a big selling job on them because they hesitated quite a lot before deciding they would finance my incredible voyage.

So I left Spain on 2nd August…er…in '92. Er…a lot of people were leaving Spain that day, you may remember it was the same time that all the Jews were driven out of Spain. Anyway, we left… 2nd August…er…1492, we had three ships and 90 men. Well, I decided to go…er…via the Canary Islands so that I could pick up the winds to carry us off to the west. Now, on this first voyage we were out of sight of land for 36 days from the Canary Islands to the Indieth… to the Indies, sorry. That…that's a distance of 4,000 kilometres, Robyn. Er…we reached the other side of the Ocean on October 12th of that year and…er…we explored one or two of the islands. Obviously these are islands off the coast of China or Japan.

PRESENTER: Now, you arrived back in Spain on… in March 1493, yes? With a small amount of gold, six local residents from the island – um…er…you call them 'Indians', yes?

COLUMBUS: Indians is…is right, Robyn, yes.

PRESENTER: Yes, and some parrots. Not quite the gold mine you had promised, uh?

COLUMBUS: Er…n…not…that…that may be true. Maybe not, but that was early days, remember. I…I'd proved it could be done, and that is the main point, if I may say so, Robyn. Now, my…my second voyage began six months later. This time I had 1,200 men and I set up the first permanent European settlement on the other side of Atlantic, do not forget that! My third voyage began on 30th May last year . . .

PRESENTER: Yeah, and what was the purpose of this third voyage?

COLUMBUS: To discover a sea passage through to the Indies.

PRESENTER: And did you?

COLUMBUS: W...well, to be quite frank with you, no, no. But we did discover a huge river and we sailed all along the coast of Asia looking for a route through it or around it. Now, the...the trouble is that land appears t...to block the through route to the Indies but I am convinced that if we can find a route then it's only a few days' sailing to...er...to get to the Indies.

PRESENTER: So what are your plans for the future?

COLUMBUS: Well, of course, I've already started organising a...a fourth voyage and this time I'll sail through to India. I'll see you there, Vasco!

VASCO DA GAMA: I rather doubt it, Chris.

PRESENTER: Mr Da Gama, Mr Columbus, thank you.

COLUMBUS: Yeah, thank you, Rob.

VASCO DA GAMA: Thank you.

B If the last question catches your students' imaginations, they might perhaps role-play some historical interviews.

C This should be prepared in class before being done for homework. Students may well have to do some research from reference books particularly to check dates.

(An alternative task might be to write a report of an interview with a historical figure, either in dialogue form or as a newspaper article.)

Leo Jones *New Cambridge Advanced English*

(8.3) MODEL VERSION

Florence Nightingale (1820–1910) was an English nurse and the founder of modern nursing. Her life was dedicated to the sick and the war-wounded. In 1854 she took 38 women nurses to Turkey during the Crimean War and by the war's end she had become a legend. The death rate at her hospital in Scutari fell from 42% to 2% in the year of her arrival due to her excellent care and insistence on hygiene. In 1860 she established a nursing school at St Thomas's Hospital, London and under her guidance nursing developed from a rather suspect and haphazard affair into a respected profession. She was famously known as 'The Lady with the Lamp' because she walked around the rows of wounded at night to comfort and treat them.

Horatio, Lord Nelson (1758–1805) was the English naval hero of the French Revolutionary Wars. He destroyed Napoleon's fleet at Aboukir thereby crippling his Egyptian expedition. In 1801 Nelson defeated the Danes at Copenhagen and in 1805 achieved his greatest victory, defeating the combined fleets of France and Spain at Trafalgar. He was mortally wounded in the action. His statue now stands on a column in London's Trafalgar Square. He was rather a small man and due to battle wounds had lost an eye and an arm. Nevertheless he was attractive to women and conducted a celebrated affair with Emma, Lady Hamilton, which started in Naples and caused Nelson to stay there longer than duty required. He is said to have died on deck at the Battle of Trafalgar in the arms of Captain Hardy, with the words "Kiss me Hardy."

     © Cambridge University Press, 1998

8.4 **Forming adjectives**   **Word study**

A **ANSWERS**

-ous	ambitious courageous dangerous mountainous synonymous
-ic	artistic catastrophic dramatic energetic Islamic magnetic metallic optimistic pessimistic sarcastic scientific symbolic sympathetic systematic tragic
-ical	ecological grammatical logical philosophical political theatrical theoretical
-al	commercial emotional financial functional intentional national professional regional sensational social traditional

B **ANSWERS**

-able	enjoyable forgettable knowledgeable memorable obtainable preferable reasonable regrettable reliable
-ive	communicative competitive decorative descriptive destructive explosive informative possessive productive repetitive
-y	dusty gloomy guilty hasty itchy jumpy lucky moody sandy satisfactory shiny slippery stripy supplementary sweaty tasty
-ly	daily fortnightly monthly neighbourly quarterly yearly

C **1 & 2** Arrange the class into an even number of pairs. Alternatively, each student could work individually and then pass his or her exercise to a partner.

 8.5 **In other words ...**   **Listening and Effective writing**

 A Play the recording, pausing as necessary for students to note down their answers or to discuss them one by one. The tone of voice is all-important here.

It may be helpful to play the complete recording again afterwards and ask the class to say what clues they gathered from each clip to help them make their decision.

Transcript with Answers 4 minutes

NARRATOR: You'll hear 15 short clips of spoken English. Follow the instructions in your book. The first is done for you as an example.

1 . . . Yeah, I know it doesn't look very good but…um…I…I mean, I spent literally hours on it honestly, and…and then I…I…asked Mr Brown and he said it was perfectly all right so I mean if you're happy . . .   LIE

2 . . . you know Tony? Well, listen to this: apparently he and Tracey are going on holiday together, which is incredible because everyone thinks he's about to get engaged to . . .   RUMOUR

3 . . . Right, er…the deadline for handing in the assignments is July 7th – but if any of you want to give them in…er…ahead of that date, please don't hesitate. So has everyone got that? July 7th.   ANNOUNCEMENT

4 . . . and so Ferdinand Magellan set sail in 1519 with a crew of 150 men, sailed round the world and was the first European to circumnavigate the earth . . .   LECTURE

5 . . . sorry, if…if I could come in here, in fact Ferdinand Magellan didn't actually get all round the world, because he was killed by hostile natives in the Philippines. Er…he *was* the first European to sail across the Pacific Ocean but it was his second-in-command…er…Delcano with just 18 men out of the original 150 who were the first Europeans to actually sail all round the world, I think you'll find . . .   CONTRADICTION

6 . . . you see the normal practice, when we refer to historical figures is to talk about the leader or…or the captain or whatever. I mean if you're talking about Napoleon marching on Moscow, it's understood that he had thousands of anonymous soldiers under his command and . . .   EXPLANATION

7 . . . if you get the facts wrong in an essay you're sure to lose marks, so you need to be especially careful about dates and so forth . . .   WARNING

8 . . . might be a good idea to check your facts before you start writing, especially the dates. It's easy enough to look them up in a reference book . . .   FRIENDLY ADVICE

9 . . . so after waiting for a very long time I started to feel rather uncomfortable so I knocked at the door and this strange young woman opened it! Well, you can imagine how embarrassed I felt! I mean there was I . . .   ANECDOTE

10 . . . but I'm sure I set it right. Anyway, that meant I got stuck in rush-hour traffic so that's why I'm . . .   EXCUSE

11 . . . sure I said I'd do it but I just forgot. Er…I know you were relying on me and all that but, sorry I just couldn't… couldn't be helped. Still I…I'm really . . .   APOLOGY

12 . . . mm, well yeah, I thought it was a very good film. Oh, by the way, how's your work going ? Last time we met you were feeling a bit fed up and thinking of leaving. Do you remember?   SMALL TALK

13 . . . and about your present job? Why are you thinking of leaving? Er, what are your reasons for leaving . . .   INTERVIEW

14 . . . happy about it. I think it'd be better for all of us if you spent a little less time . . .   COMPLAINT

15 . . . the fat man said to the thin man, 'Why did you jump so high?' And the thin man said to him, 'Well, if I hadn't done that, you'd be . . .'   JOKE

B ANSWERS

1	(an) enjoyable	**5**	likeable
2	complimentary	**6**	pleasant
3	thoughtful	**7**	friendly
4	smart	**8**	generous

C ANSWERS

In **informal** writing, such as a personal letter, fax or note (I) :   2   5   6   9   10   13

In a **formal** letter, article or essay (F) :   1   3   4   7   8   11   12

D This exercise can be done alone or in pairs. Make sure everyone is aware of the contrast between the informal and informal styles. Some variations may be possible from the suggested answers below – discuss these with the class, if necessary.

SUGGESTED ANSWERS

1 lecture   **2** kind/generous   **3** spare   **4** appreciated   **5** discussed/debated   **6** following   **7** disappointed   **8** reassure   **9** reticent/subdued/silent/unresponsive   **10** concentrating   **11** failed   **12** opposite/contrary   **13** welcoming/seeing/having   **14** long

---

CAE exam | **8.5 D** is very similar to Part 4 in the English in Use paper, where the number of words to be filled in is always specified. Usually in the exam two words are required, not one as here.

Some words don't fit because of the surrounding context – for example, *enjoyed* is wrong in 4 because you'd say *greatly enjoyed*, not *much enjoyed*. Others don't fit because the instructions specify one word only – so, for example, *talked about* is wrong in 5. Others are, for exam purposes, too similar to the informal letter – so *talk* is not acceptable in 1.

8.6 *Get*

Verbs and idioms

A ANSWERS

1 have
2 persuaded
3 become
4 fetch
5 earn
6 manage
7 understand
8 receive
9 prepare
10 arrive
11 obtain
12 attain
13 start
14 annoys

B Sentences 3 and 5 need to be completely rewritten to show the change in word order.

ANSWERS

2 get through
3 It may be difficult to get these ideas over/across to everyone.
4 getting at
5 Try not to let it get you down if someone gets at you.
6 get down
7 get out of
8 get over
9 get together   got round to (it)
10 get into
11 get away
12 get ahead
13 get going   getting on for
14 get back to you
15 getting nowhere
16 got his own back

Some other idioms with **GET** are:

get at = reach
get through to = reach
What's got into her? = what's the matter with her?
get on = become old
get over a setback/illness = recover from

9.1 The Third Age
Reading and Listening

A1 Some words that might spring to mind are:

nostalgia wisdom elderly pension rest home retirement grandchildren
maturity financial security grey hair wrinkles Zimmer frame senior citizen
senile funeral memories leisure no exams

– but this unit tries to emphasise the plus side!

2 Another factor that might be added is:

keeping your health / staying fit and healthy

> **CAE exam** The activity in **A2** relates to Parts 3 and 4 of the Speaking paper, where students may have to rank points and discuss their reasons. The examiners will expect an extended response to questions about their reasons, rather than just a list of numbers.

B According to the article, there are four ages of man. Shakespeare, rather more unkindly, chronicled seven ages of man in Jaques' famous speech in *As You Like It*.

Perhaps your class might like to see this speech – you may photocopy it.

FROM *AS YOU LIKE IT* BY WILLIAM SHAKESPEARE

Jaques:
                    All the world's a stage,
And all the men and women merely players:
They have their exits and their entrances;
And one man in his time plays many parts,
His acts being seven ages. At first the infant,
Mewling and puking in the nurse's arms.
And then the whining school-boy, with his satchel
And shining morning face, creeping like a snail
Unwillingly to school. And then the lover,
Sighing like a furnace with a woeful ballad
Made to his mistress' eyebrow. Then a soldier,
Full of strange oaths and bearded like the pard,
Jealous in honour, sudden and quick in quarrel,
Seeking the bubble reputation
Even in the cannon's mouth. And then the justice,
In fair round belly with good capon lined,
With eyes severe, and beard of formal cut,
Full of wise saws and modern instances,
And so he plays his part. The sixth age shifts
Into the lean and slippered pantaloon
With spectacles on nose and pouch on side,
His youthful hose well saved, a world too wide
For his shrunk shank; and his big manly voice,
Turning again toward childish treble, pipes
And whistles in his sound. Last scene of all
That ends this strange eventful history,
Is second childishness and mere oblivion,
Sans teeth, sans eyes, sans taste, sans everything.

Act II Scene VII

SUGGESTED ANSWERS

1 The students are older; the new one is younger; anyone can be a student there

2 bored, lonely, useless

3 To postpone the Fourth Age of weakness and death by filling the Third Age, which may last 30 years, with activities and stimulation

C Even if you suspect that your students might find this 'stylistic analysis' beyond them, I suggest you let them try doing it in pairs – or, if you prefer, as a whole-class activity.

SUGGESTED ANSWERS

- By using short verbless clauses, repeating *the* at the beginning of each one.

- By using *you* in the description: *your friends, you may not notice it*.

- By using comparative forms in the second sentence: *cheerier, more intense, more avid, more grey hairs* – and by prefacing most of these with an understated *little*.

 D Play the recording. The students will probably need to hear it two or three times to get all the answers.

ANSWERS

1 Latin   German   play

2 gardening   literature

3 thick   posh

4 learning   paces   tolerant

5 55   72   nothing

6 amiable   friendly   concerned   opportunity

7 best   understand

8 have   get

Transcript   4 minutes 45 seconds

GEOFFREY: I'm Geoffrey Smerden, I'm a retired general practitioner. Er…I started the University of the Third Age here in Colchester. Well, the University of the Third Age is an organisation which started in France and which has now spread worldwide, and it consists of people who have skills and knowledge which they're willing to give to other people and the other people voluntarily come and…and join in, in…in…in classes and in lectures. It's very informal, each branch is aun… autonomous and…um…it has a very wide spread of…er…of…interests of all kinds. And it simply means that … I teach Latin and German in it because I speak German and I speak Latin and I do play-readings because I'm interested in play-reading. My wife does…er…gardening groups and also does…takes a literature g…group and does embroidery. But we do all kinds of things, people who've never learnt languages before suddenly find themselves learning languages at 67 and 70.

Well, er…I…one knows a lot of people who left school at 14 who had no academic education at all and always felt the miss of it and who now learn foreign languages, go to sociology groups, er…learn to play instruments and so on and so forth. I think it's…the motto really is: 'If you can do it, do it.' People once upon a time believed (a) 'I'm old therefore I'm thick,' (b) 'I'm…this is for posh people and not for the likes of me,' and I think U3A has demolished that.

It's open to anybody who isn't working. Technically it's really for s… retired people but we do have some younger people who've joined because they're unemployed and so on and so forth. But it's really for retired persons, it's for persons who have time on their hands *theoretically*.

INTERVIEWER: Is the attitude of the students of the University of the Third Age different to, say, the attitude of students in general?

GEOFFREY: Well, it is, because we're not studying for a degree, I mean there are persons who say…try to say we should do A levels and so on and so forth. We don't want to do that, we do it because we like learning, we learn at different paces and we're all very tolerant of each other. I mean, some people, as I say, in either of the groups that I take are never going to be very good at it, and some are already very good at it. But we're all there together, we...we just enjoy it, we like doing it, it's gone on for...the German group's gone on for four years now, and so...and it shows no sign of diminishing.

INTERVIEWER: Do you think the role of retired people in Britain has changed over the years?

GEOFFREY: Oh, in...incalculably! I told you the story, my mother was a very great reader. My mother was a suburban housewife, and my father died aged 58 and my mother was 55. And for the rest of her life till she was 72 she sat and did nothing. Whereas she'd love U3A, she would just adore it. But i...all kinds of people who've never had an opportunity to get at...at learning in their lives. Either they were in the wrong sort of place or the wrong sort of job, or some of them alas, you know 'It's not for the likes of us' and they suddenly discovered that they could *learn*, and they want to learn and I think this is super, I mean it's...er...excellent, it opens their lives up.

INTERVIEWER: Do you think young people have a...a better attitude towards older people now than ... ?

GEOFFREY: Oh, I'm quite sure. I was talking to my...my granddaughter, who is 16, and...er...and saying, 'Well, I'm always hearing people saying how dreadful the young are.' And of course some young are dreadful but then some old are dreadful too. But I said, 'When I was young it was assumed that the old are always right and the young are always wrong. The fact is some young are right and some young are wrong.' And I said, 'I find today's young v...very amiable, they're very friendly, and they're very concerned. Er...the sad thing is they don't have opportuni...the opportunity they ought to have.' But my granddaughter said, 'Do you think perhaps your atti...attitude has changed to the young from what your parents had?' And I said, 'I think it probably has. My parents w...were doing the best they could for me but they didn't.' Perhaps everybody says, 'My parents don't understand me', but I don't think they did. I think we make more effort to...to meet the young than they...than our parents did.

INTERVIEWER: There isn't such a big gulf, is there, between young and old now?

GEOFFREY: I don't think there is. Er...I find that ...er...most of the young people I meet are much more tolerant of the old.

I had a friend who was a GP, whose wife sits there groaning and he...he...he died of Alzheimer's recently, but he sat... he drank whisky and he played golf, that's all he ever did, and his wife said to Mary, 'Oh, I do envy you your interesting life, Mary.' And so she said, 'Cathy, you don't have an interesting life, you *get* an interesting life.' And I think this is true, I think...I like to feel that i...if I can do a thing I like to have a go. And if I can't do it, I've just got to say, 'No.' But I think you've got to try.

E It might be worth pointing out that in many cultures there is no 'problem' of old people – they have an acknowledged part to play in society and remain active, valued members of the community throughout their lives. It may only be a 'Western' or 'Northern' problem.

(9.2) Paragraphs   Reading and Effective writing

A This may be debatable: basically the reason is that each new paragraph contains a new idea. And shorter paragraphs make it easier for the reader to make his or her way through the article.

The original article was laid out like this, though other arrangements may be possible:

> "We need cooperation and not polarisation," Professor Lehr said. Both the economy and society had to face the enormous challenge of adjusting to the demographic changes caused by a drastic fall in birth rates, she said.
>
> But she added that a minimum pension would not solve the problems linked to ageing. "The Greys have opted for the wrong path."

> At present, some 90 per cent of the two million Germans who need care are looked after by their families, and 600,000 people live in homes. But staffing problems in hospitals and in the care sector have reached alarming proportions, and reports of "scandalous conditions" in old people's homes make headlines almost every week.
>
> The anger of those involved in caring for the old has recently been fuelled by a decision of a Mannheim court which, in response to a complaint from residents in a small town in Baden-Württemberg, ruled that old people's homes should not be situated in "high-quality residential areas".
>
> The plaintiffs argued that they were "disturbed at night by the sound of ambulances and occasional screams from home inmates".
>
> It was high time, Mrs Unruh said, that those in power realised that Germany was fast becoming a society hostile not only to children, but also to the aged.
>
> She said her proposals for greater integration of the old and reduced dependence on the state welfare system had exposed the serious gap between private care provided by the family and the official welfare system in hospitals, homes and other institutions.

C This is best done in pairs, so that the students can compare their work and offer each other advice.

(9.3) Granny power   Listening and Speaking

A 1 This short discussion enables everyone to get ready for the listening exercise.

2 Play the recording, perhaps pausing it after each topic (shown by ★★★ in the Transcript).

ANSWERS   (Four answers are given for Questions 4–6 but the students only have to note three.)

In 2025:

1 41%   27%

2 10%

3 20%

4 Japan   USA   Germany   + other European countries

5 Brazil   Korea   Egypt   Thailand

6 productive   adaptable   inventive   flexible

7 skill   judgement   speed   flexibility

8 cheaper   wages

In China:

9 20%

10 60   55   payroll

11 450,000   half/50%   two-thirds/$\frac{2}{3}$

12 35   four

13 widows   widowers   immoral

The main problems facing the West are:

14 support   unproductive

15 competitive   innovators

➡ Afterwards, perhaps ask everyone to summarise the whole broadcast in a single sentence.

SUGGESTED ANSWER

In the 21st century, Western countries will find it increasingly difficult to support their older populations and compete with 'younger' countries.

Transcript   4 minutes

PRESENTER: . . . for both old people and young people. Nowadays, in industrialised countries, old people are living longer and fewer babies are being born. According to Susan Harris, this is having a worrying effect on the profile of the population.

SUSAN HARRIS: If we look ahead to the year 2025, we can see that the profile of the population in many countries will be very different. In Germany, for example, it's estimated that 41% of the population will be over 50 in 2025 – the figure is now 27%. And one in ten Germans will be over 75 years old – and that will also be the case in Japan. By 2025 in most Western countries one in five people will be over 65. Today's young adults are tomorrow's over-sixties.

PRESENTER: But why should this be regarded as a 'problem'?

SUSAN HARRIS: The reason is that the major industrial nations, like Japan, the USA and European countries will be 'elderly'. Countries like…er…Brazil, Korea, Egypt, Thailand will be 'young'. Young workers are more productive, more adaptable, more inventive – they're more flexible. It's true that old workers acquire skill and judgement, but they tend to lose speed and flexibility with constant changing technology. It's the more adaptable workers who are going to succeed, and they are more likely to be the younger ones, you see. And younger workers are cheaper to employ than older ones – they don't expect such high wages.

★★★

PRESENTER: It's not only in the West that this trend is visible. Tony Green has travelled widely in China.

TONY GREEN: China has had a 'one-child' policy for a very long time now: married couples are only allowed to have one child. So this means that the population is getting older all the time. By the year 2025, 20% of Chinese people will be over 60 years of age. In China the official retirement age is 60 for men and 55 for women, but many workers stay on the payroll. For example, Shanghai's textile mills employ 450,000 people, but only half of these are workers – the rest are former workers, retired workers who continue to draw two-thirds of a working employee's wages.

Before 1949 life expectancy for the Chinese was 35. Those old people who did live to a ripe old age were looked after in traditional large family units. Now couples, who these days are often the only child of their parents, face sole responsibility for all four parents. Widows and widowers are officially encouraged to marry – in fact they're often unwilling to live with their married children because apartments are so cramped – but in some parts of China where people still believe that widows who remarry are immoral, there this policy is not popular.

★★★

PRESENTER: According to Susan Harris, there are two problems facing Western countries in the future.

SUSAN HARRIS: There are two big problems facing Western countries:

The first is that a relatively small working population is going to have to support a growing number of unproductive retired people. Even if they can support themselves by contributing to pension schemes that enable them to retain their financial independence, they will still need health care that taxpayers will be paying for.

And the second problem is that the countries I've called the 'younger' countries will be more competitive in the world market – because a young workforce is cheaper to employ than an experienced workforce, but also because their inventiveness and flexibility will mean that they will be the innovators and that they will be able to adapt more easily to the demands of the market.

PRESENTER: So what can we do about this? What should we be doing to find out . . .

B1 & 2 There are no correct solutions to these case studies!

9.4 **Family life**   Reading

A If you fear that this exercise might take too long in class, it could be done for homework. In class, it could be done in pairs or alone.

ANSWERS
2 C   4 D   7 A   9 E   11 B (or possibly F?)

| **CAE exam** | The task in **9.4 A** is similar to the task candidates have to do with the second text in the Reading paper. As in the exam, if you get the first two wrong then your chances of getting the rest right are drastically diminished.

There's more practice in doing this kind of very tricky exercise in **11.5** and **12.6** – plus an extra activity for exam candidates at the end of **Unit 11**.

In the exam this would be the only task candidates would have to do with the text – here, in **B** and **C**, there are further tasks which depend on the text having been reassembled correctly. |
| --- | --- |

B1 The original headline was: **Big is beautiful** but **The more the merrier** might also be all right.

2 To find the answers the students need to have reassembled the text with the missing paragraphs placed in the right places.

ANSWERS   (+ paragraph where the answer was)

1 Sarah and Hannah	¶ D = 4
2 Sarah	¶ 3
3 John	¶ C = 2
4 Eleanor	¶ 1
5 Hannah	¶ D = 4
6 Rowena	¶ 10
7 Colin and Neil	¶ D = 4
8 John and Jacob	¶ 8

C This can be done alone or in pairs.

ANSWERS
¶ 3   reproduce = have children   trainee = not-yet-qualified
      apprentice = learning a skilled trade
¶ 8   bulk = majority   bungalow = house with one storey
¶ C   daring = brave   foolhardy = reckless   boundaries = limits   ribbed = teased
      snap = photo
¶ D   chores = household jobs   a baker's dozen = 13
¶ E   clutter = mess   odd = 1, 3, 5, 7, etc. (*Strange* doesn't mean the same as *odd* in this
      context.)

D Are large families the exception or the norm in your students' country/countries? If any of your students come from recently-broken homes, or have no families, this may be a sensitive area for them, and if so perhaps these questions should be skipped.

A The article reads more like an advertisement, and this is one of the things the students may object to. Reassemble the class so that the pairs can hear other students' reactions.

B1 If possible, show the students a Letters page from a magazine (or newspaper) so that they can see what such letters are like.

2 Feedback from a fellow student is always valuable. Allow everyone time to make minor improvements to their work before handing it in to you. When *you* look at everyone's work, pay attention to their use of paragraphs.

Leo Jones *New Cambridge Advanced English*

9.5 MODEL VERSION

Dear Editor,

I am writing to express my reactions to the article about pension plans published in this month's issue of "Globus" magazine.

What were you thinking of? Do you think your readership is really interested in planning their retirement? For most of us, our working lives have barely started, either because we're not qualified yet or we can't get work. Thoughts of retirement and pensions are a million miles away, both in terms of age and resources. Did you get paid by some insurance company to publish it?

Most of us don't have any spare cash anyway but if we did it would not be spent on a pension. Going out, music, clothes, holidays are more the theme as I'm sure you know. I might begin to find it hard to afford your magazine if this boring trend continues.

If you have to write about money and work, far better use your expertise to give us some relevant advice, such as where to find cheap eating places, how to do well in interviews, how to produce an impressive CV, where to get vacation jobs, the best areas nationally and locally to find particular types of work, etc.

"Globus" is supposedly aimed at a young audience and if you want such people to continue to buy your magazine, I suggest you rethink including articles like this. A real turn-off! Ugh!

Yours faithfully,

9.6 **Ages**   Idioms and collocations

A ANSWERS

1 under age = too young (to drink, vote, etc.)
2 Old World   New World
3 new blood = new, young members of a group
4 old flame = someone you used to be in love with   for ages
5 newcomer   old hands = experienced members of staff
6 old friends   old times
7 freshwater
8 fresh start = begin again
9 old masters = famous painters of the past
10 come of age

11 old wives' tale = belief handed down as traditional wisdom   fresh air = pure, cool air

12 Stone Age   space age   young at heart   as old as you feel

➡ A few more idioms, not included in the exercise:
for old times' sake = because of happy times in the past
brand new = completely new
fresh out of = just sold the last

B This exercise depends on finding words that fit in the contexts and are suitable collocations. The words that appeared in the original piece come first in the suggested answers. Further variations may be possible.

SUGGESTED ANSWERS
1 face   **2** before   **3** friends   **4** felt   **5** old   **6** acquaintances/colleagues   **7** remember
8 times   **9** expression/look   **10** inside/still/nevertheless   **11** shame/pity
12 opposite/different

CAE exam   **9.6 B** is similar to Part 2 in the English in Use paper.

(10.1) An ideal home?   Vocabulary and Listening

A1 Some words that might come up are:

flat   block of flats   suburbs   living room   rent   mortgage   porch   verandah
conservatory   balcony   garden   park   amenities   parking   trams   metro
underground   entertainments

2 Make sure that everyone makes notes of vocabulary that comes up, or that they want to ask you about, during this discussion.

B1 Play the recording, perhaps pausing after each speaker.

ANSWERS

Catherine	My home isn't in the country, but it seems like it.
Melinda	My ideal home would be an old house in the country.
Blain	American houses take up more land than British houses.
Kate	American houses have screen doors to keep the flies out.
Richard	My house is very isolated.
Karen	My ideal home would have a large living room, with a bed.

CAE exam | In the Listening paper candidates have to do a rather similar multiple-matching exercise. In the exam there are likely to be one or two statements that nobody made, as distractors – and there would be two tasks on the same set of extracts. The exam tasks are more difficult than the one here but similar skills have to be applied: matching each clip to an identifying phrase, summary or label in a list.

---

2 After reacting to the speakers' ideas, the students talk about their own homes. If they don't know anything about British homes, ask them to think about British (or American) films they've seen.

Transcript   2 minutes 30 seconds

NARRATOR: Listen to six people talking about their houses. First we hear from Catherine.

CATHERINE: I like my present home because it's in the suburbs, in that there are a lot of trees around it but it's only about half an hour's ride from the centre of town. And it's got this ridiculous patch at the end of the garden that's owned by my next-door neighbour that has ducks and…er… chickens and…and geese, w…who are like guard geese and who quack in the night if there are strangers about. I like that.

NARRATOR: Now Melinda.

MELINDA: I wouldn't mind moving home if I had enough money to move into the country and live in the sort of house I'd really like to live in…um…something really old, with lots of land…um…preferably a beach to wander on in the mornings. Er…yes, I'd move home for that!

NARRATOR: Now Blain.

BLAIN: The main differences between homes in North America and Britain are really two: size and height. Er…homes in North America tend to be a little bigger, I suppose because they don't cost quite so much in most places, and secondly they don't go 'up' quite so frequently, they spread out, whereas homes in Britain tend to be built on one, two, three storeys perhaps.

NARRATOR: Now Kate.

KATE: The main differences between homes in North America and Britain are…you've got screen doors in North America to keep the flies out and it's not warm enough in Britain usually to have flies. Um…the heating in Britain is terribly important – it's less so in America, we use underfloor heating there.

NARRATOR: Now Richard.

RICHARD: Um…I like my present home

because…because it's in the country to start with and surrounded by fields and because it's sort of the end of a no-through road so very few people drive past, it's on an old dirt track. Mind you, you hear them when they do. And because it's an old cottage and I like…it's got an open fire and things like that and I'm a bit of a romantic.

NARRATOR: Finally Karen.

KAREN: My ideal living room would contain absolutely everything that you need for everyday life. In fact it would even have the bed in it because I cannot stand having to go upstairs and downstairs having left something that I needed upstairs to bring back down. So I'd have all mod cons and every single thing you could imagine that you n…you might need throughout the day there.

(10.2) The perfect society?
Reading and Listening

If necessary, point out to the students that although taking notes is not a skill that is required for the CAE exam, it is something that is vital for anyone who attends academic or business lectures, seminars or workshops. They'll be practising this skill in A and in B2 – and again in 10.3 A1.

> **Aldous Huxley** (1894–1963) described a more nightmarish 'utopia' in *Brave New World* (1932), his most influential work.
>
> **Plato** (427–348 BC), the Greek philosopher, was a pupil and friend of Socrates. His own most famous pupil was Aristotle. The Republic was described in one of his 'dialogues' – conversations with Socrates that illustrate his ideas.
>
> Sir/Saint **Thomas More** (1478–1535) became Lord Chancellor of England under Henry VIII, but was imprisoned and executed when he refused to give up his Roman Catholic faith.
>
> **H.G. Wells** (1866–1946) was one of the founding fathers of science fiction: *The Time Machine* (1895), *The Island of Doctor Moreau* (1896) and *The War of the Worlds* (1898) are still widely read.
>
> **James Hilton** (1900–1954) also wrote *Goodbye, Mr Chips* (1934) and *Random Harvest* (1941).

A1 As what constitutes 'good points' and 'bad points' is a matter of opinion, there are no 'correct answers' here. However, it might be a good idea to highlight what YOU consider to be good and bad about Pala in your copy of the Student's Book. Similarly, you could highlight the good and bad aspects of the other utopias described in B in the transcript below.

2 Give everyone time to compare their ideas. Have they noted down all the important points?

If there's time . . .

The article contains a lot of useful vocabulary – ask everyone to highlight ONE or TWO words in each paragraph that they would like to remember, and use a dictionary to look up the meanings and see further examples.

Here are some of the more useful words and phrases in each paragraph:

¶ 1 venerating   at the expense of

¶ 2 status symbols   weapons

¶ 3 sane   short on

¶ 4 siege economy   out of bounds

¶ 5 radical changes   swapped jobs   rounded person   integration

¶ 6 constraining   polarise   camps   concocts   amalgam

¶ 7 idealists   holistic health care

¶ 8 snag   cooperatively

¶ 9 evolved   the material world

¶10 dangerous waters   forestall   infused   does the trick

¶11 muzak   consciously

B 1 Play the recording after everyone has looked through the 13 questions.

2 Play the recording again, pausing between each speaker for everyone to complete their notes.

ANSWERS

1 P **2** M **3** H **4** W **5** M **6** P **7** H **8** M **9** W + P(?) **10** P **11** M **12** P + W **13** P

Transcript   5 minutes 30 seconds

PRESENTER: I suppose everyone wishes the world could be a perfect place, where everyone lives in happy harmony. Well, we're going to hear about four people's visions of the perfect society. Going back to Ancient Greece first, Plato called his imaginary perfect society 'The Republic'. Mandy . . .

MANDY: Plato's Republic has only 5,040 citizens – that's the number that can be addressed by a single orator. In Plato's Republic marriage is controlled by the state and only the best are allowed to marry the best. Only superior children are allowed to survive and all the rest are killed at birth. They aren't brought up by their parents, but collectively as a group.

The children go to school until they're twenty years old and then they do tests. The ones who fail these tests become businessmen, workers, farmers – they are permitted to own property and to use money.

The ones who pass the tests are educated for ten more years, then they take more tests, and the ones who fail these tests become soldiers and they live in a communist society and they own no property and they don't have any money, they share everything.

The ones who pass these further tests go on to study philosophy for another five years, and then they live practical lives in the real world for another fifteen years. And then, when they're 50, they enter the ruling class – these are…er… political leaders or 'guardians'. They have no possessions but they do have power. There are 360 'guardians' and each month 30 of these rule over the Republic.

PRESENTER: Now, Thomas More invented the term Utopia, didn't he, Terry?

TERRY: Yes, it means 'nowhere' in Greek. Thomas More's *Utopia* is on an island somewhere in the Pacific, ruled by a king, with slaves doing menial work, and women are inferior to men. Well, no money changes hands because there's no monetary system at all. There's no private property, so there is no envy and no theft.

Every adult male works…ooh…six hours a day at a job he likes to do, and a job which helps to serve the needs of the community. You see, he doesn't receive payment in money, as such. He gets what he needs from a common store: food, drink, clothes – everything he needs for his family.

Now, the way it's made up: each group of thirty families elect a leader, and every ten leaders elect a chief and the chiefs are members of the national council. The national council elects one king, who rules for life – a democratically elected king, mm?

Education emphasises vocational subjects, subjects which will be useful to the people who work, for the benefit of the community.

And war: war is only acceptable if the island is attacked by another army.

PRESENTER: H. G. Wells also had a vision of Utopia. Polly . . .

POLLY: H.G. Wells's *Modern Utopia* is a world state – that means one government for the whole world. The state owns all the land and all the sources of power and food. But individuals *can* earn money – the more they produce the more they earn – and they can own and inherit property and personal things.

Now, Wells has visions of amazing electric trains that go at 300 kilometres per hour, with their own libraries and sofas and reading rooms. Most work is done by machines, so people have a lot of free time.

The world is governed by a special ruling class and you have to take a test to qualify, and if you qualify you're not allowed to smoke, drink or gamble, but you *can* tell the rest of the world what to do!

Personal details of every person on the planet are stored in Paris, and this information is used to control population and labour. If you want to have children, you have to prove that you are healthy, and you have enough money and you're the right age. But the state takes the children away to special estates where they are educated and taught to live useful lives.

PRESENTER: Finally, Shangri-La. James Hilton wrote about this magic land in his novel *Lost Horizon*, which was made into a film in 1937 and I believe remade in 1973, wasn't it, Tony?

TONY: Er...yes, that's right. Shangri-La is high in Tibet. It's an idyllic land surrounded by mountains and inaccessible to the rest of the world. In Shangri-La people live to be at least 200 years old. There's a special magic berry they eat, which keeps them young. At the age of 100 they start to *look* old, but their minds are still young. Then they devote the rest of their lives to contemplation, research and the pursuit of wisdom.

Many of the people are travellers who have lost their way in the mountains. First they spend...er...five years forgetting their past lives. Then they start eating the magic berries, er...practising yoga and following the teachings of Buddha.

Everyone is good-mannered, honest and sober – and very happy.

(10.3) The best of all possible worlds   Reading and Speaking

 A1 Play the recording. It's a reading of an authentic letter from James M. Rodengen in Costa Rica. The students should make notes and then compare their notes with a partner, so they'll need to hear the reading a couple of times.

Transcript   1 minute 30 seconds

Dear Friend,

Most of us have dreamed at one time or another of finding a place where we can be truly happy… a Shangri-La with an ideal climate, remote from turmoil and confusion; where the air is fresh and free from pollution and the only noise we hear is that of the wind in the trees, the roar of the sea and the song of the birds – but still close enough to civilization to enjoy the benefits of a thriving, metropolitan city.

There is such a Paradise, and you can reserve your own special corner for only $150 down-payment and interest-free monthly payments of $150 at absolutely no risk. If you examine your property any time within one year and are not completely satisfied, **every cent you paid will be refunded** with no questions asked.

We are talking about the Beaches of Nosara on the West Coast of Costa Rica, a country known throughout the world for its peace, tranquility and solid, democratic government.

First, let me emphasize that Costa Rica is not threatened by the conflict in Central America and most definitely **IS NOT** what is generally known as a "Banana Republic".

But to assure your dream for tomorrow, it's up to you to take action today. I hope to hear from you soon.

Sincerely,   James M. Rodengen

▼2 This should be done individually.

3 Perhaps reassemble the class afterwards for an exchange of views. Has anyone noticed that sportfishing in ¶6 includes catching dolphin – surely a slip of the pen?!

If there's time . . .

▼ The text on page 85 contains a lot of useful vocabulary – as well as some that is less useful: e.g. ¶5 *pecary* (a small pig-like mammal), ¶6 *marlin*, *wahoo* and *snapper* (types of fish). Ask everyone to highlight ONE or TWO words in each paragraph that they would like to remember, and use a dictionary to look up the meanings and see further examples.

To start everyone off, look at the letter on page 84 and discuss which TWO 'new' words or phrases seem the most useful. These might include two of these:

turmoil   confusion   thriving

Here are some of the more useful words and phrases in each paragraph of the text on page 85:

¶1 tucked away   secluded cove   afforded protection

¶2 dreams come true

¶3 subdivided   ecologically sound

¶4 full title   down-payment   interest charge   no questions asked   a trade (= exchange)

¶5 wildlife refuges   without equal

¶6 amenities   crave   cosmopolitan city

B 1 Another view of Utopia!

2 Arrange the class into teams of four to six for this discussion, which needs a good 15–20 minutes – or even longer.

If there's time . . .

Ask each team to give a presentation of their Utopia to the rest of the class – each member of the team should participate in the presentation, perhaps covering different aspects of the topic.

C This may be based on the team's ideas – or be an independent production – and is probably best done as homework.

(Perhaps explain to everyone that the readers of 'a student magazine' are people of the same age as themselves. They should include content that will be of interest to other students who haven't taken part in the discussions, and should be written in a fairly informal style.)

(10.4) Articles   Grammar

> **CAE exam** The correct use of articles is an important aspect of completing open cloze passages, error correction/proofreading and in the English in Use paper.

A SUGGESTED ANSWERS

1 *She has some grey hairs.*   *She has some grey hair.*
  = just a few grey hairs   = more than just a few
  She has grey hair.   *She has a grey hair.*
  = all her hair is grey   = just one grey hair

2 *There's a hair in my soup!*   *There's hair in my soup!*
  = one hair   = quite a lot of hair
  There's the hair – in my soup!   *There's some hair in my soup!*
  = the hair that was mentioned earlier = one hair or several hairs

3 *Ask a teacher if you have a question.*   *Ask the teacher if you have a question.*
  = it doesn't have to be a particular teacher   = your own teacher, or a particular one
  Ask any teacher if you have a question.   we have in mind
  = every teacher will be willing and able
    to answer the question

4 *After leaving school he went to sea.*   *After leaving the school he went to the sea.*
  = he worked as a seaman after finishing   = he went out of the school building and
    his education   down to the sea shore, perhaps for a swim

5 *I'm going to buy a paper.*   *I'm going to buy some paper.*
  = a newspaper   = writing, typing or wrapping paper
  I'm going to buy the paper.   *I'm going to buy paper.*
  = the newspaper I usually take, or the   = writing, typing or wrapping paper – not
    writing paper that was mentioned earlier   another product

B ANSWERS

air U · breath C	gadget C · equipment U	poetry U · poem C
architecture U · plan C	harm U · injury C	progress U · exam C
behaviour U · reaction C	job C · work U	report C · news U
bridge C · engineering U	joke C · fun U	safety U · guard C
cash U · coin C	journey C · travel U	thunderstorm C · lightning U
clothing U · garment C	laughter U · smile C	traffic U · vehicle C
cooking U · kitchen C	luck U · accident C	tune C · music U
experiment C · research U	luggage U · suitcase C	university C · education U
fact C · information U	peace U · ceasefire C	water U · drop C
flu U · cough C	permit C · permission U	weather U · shower C

C This can be done in pairs or alone. Refer to a dictionary for examples of the two uses of these words, if necessary.

D ANSWERS

1 If there has been *a* robbery you should call *the* police.

2 Her brothers were all *in bed* asleep when she left home in *the* morning.

3 Most houses in *the* South of England are built of brick.

4 He's *in hospital* having *an* operation.

5 *no errors*

6 What wonderful news about Henry's sister getting *a/the* scholarship!

7 How *much luggage* are you going to take on *the* plane?

8 I'd like *some information* on holidays in *the* USA. Can you give me *some* advice?

9 What *a* magnificent view of *the* mountains in *the* distance!

10 He has beautiful brown eyes and *a* moustache.

E SUGGESTED ANSWERS

2 First of all make sure you disconnect the computer from the mains before you lift the cover. Then to replace the battery you have to use a screwdriver to loosen the screws shown as A and B on the diagram and then lift the cover. Take out the old battery from the socket labelled Z and replace it with a fresh battery.

3 Is a building like a work of art or is it a piece of engineering? Should it be designed for the people in the street and also for the people inside? Is a building a 'machine for living in' where every part of it has a function? Or can some of the parts be for decoration, so that it is a 'pleasure to the eye'?

4 When you're in the supermarket, could you get a kilo of potatoes, some ketchup, a loaf of bread, a bottle of wine, and some food for the cat – he only eats the sort with the blue label, remember.

5 Could you send us the instruction manual for the machine we ordered at the end of the month? The Production Manager would also like a copy of the specification sheet, please.

ANSWERS

> 60% of families in *the* UK own *their* own homes after borrowing money (known as *a* mortgage) from *a* building society or bank. They have to make Ø monthly repayments of *the* total sum (plus interest) for 20–25 years. People can usually borrow *a* sum equivalent to three times *their* annual salary, but need to put down *a* cash deposit of 10% of *the* purchase price. Ø people in Britain tend to move Ø house several times in *their* lives. *The* typical pattern is for *a* young couple to start as 'first-time buyers' in *a* small flat or house, then move to *a* larger house when they have *a* family and, when *the* children have left Ø home, to move into *a* smaller house or bungalow. Usually they move into Ø other people's houses or into *a* new home that has been built on *a* new estate by *a* builder. Families in Ø/*the* lower income groups are more likely to live in Ø rented accommodation, for example in *a* council house or flat.

Moving home can be *a* stressful experience, only slightly less traumatic than *a* bereavement or divorce. Often *the* buyer and seller of *a* house are part of *a* 'chain', where *the* sale of one house depends on *a* whole series of strangers doing *the* same thing at *the* same time. If one deal falls through at *the* last moment, *the* whole chain breaks down and no one is able to move.

(10.5) Describing a place   Speaking and Creative writing

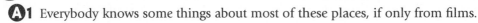

A1 Everybody knows some things about most of these places, if only from films.

2 Pause after each speaker for everyone to catch up with their notes. The speakers are talking about favourite places, so there are mostly likes. Perhaps mention that although the speakers don't actually say, 'I like so and so,' their tone of voice shows enthusiasm.

3 Afterwards give everyone time to compare notes with a partner.

SUGGESTED ANSWERS

City	Likes
Rome	1 wonderful heat 2 the area north of the Circus Maximus – green, beautiful, cool 3 museums, galleries 4 walking 5 restaurants, cafés
New York	1 the classic clichés: yellow cabs, skyscrapers, etc. 2 not as dangerous as he expected 3 the people: friendly, cosmopolitan
Amsterdam	1 narrow streets – bicycles, slow pace 2 outdoor activity 5 nightlife 3 friendly people 6 beautiful architecture 4 culture: museums 7 canals
Austin	1 green 2 young people 3 lots of things happen at night 4 people strolling on summer nights 5 live music 6 water sports 8 culture: theatres 7 safe drivers 9 music

Transcript   6 minutes

ISHIA: I always love going back to Rome. It's a city I've visited quite often and it's al…a great source of joy to me. I love flying in over the Mediterranean, seeing the sea, arriving in the plane, the doors open and that *wonderful* heat hits you. Driving through the city in order to get to wherever you're going to stay is not always the most fun part…um…the driving is…er…something to behold, but I love the area north of the Circus Maximus, which is…which is really the kind of… er…the Hampstead I suppose of Rome, which is very beautiful and very green, and full of palm trees and absolutely beautiful buildings. Um…there…it isn't sort of in the centre of Rome, which is awfully nice, and it's much cooler there of course. Er…I…I suppose I like *all* aspects of Rome…er…particularly visiting the museums and the galleries which are really quite stunning, but to actually walk round the streets, see those beautiful buildings, sit in a restaurant, sit outside, have a cup of coffee, is a delight and I would recommend it to anybody.

TIM: As far as big cities go, I think New York's my favourite place. When I arrived there I felt as though I'd arrived in a movie, I came in a cab from the airport, and there were all the skyscrapers and the heat and the dirt and the yellow cabs and all the classic clichés that you think about America – they were all there. Um...I worked in a...a...in the PanAm building in the centre of New York. That meant travelling by subway every day, which was one of the hottest experience... experiences I've ever had! Because it was in the summer and it is very very hot in New York, so much so you arrive at your workplace and you have to change your clothes. The people of New York are terrific. I've got...was very frightened I was going to be mugged, in fact I thought that if you stepped out of your hotel at night you'd be shot, but it's proved not to be true. Um...I find the people very friendly, very cosmopolitan, nobody was worried about the fact that I was English because they...everybody talks with funny accents there. Um...I find it a really wonderful place – a bit dangerous but really fast and really fun.

JULIET: I've been to Amsterdam many times now...er...it almost feels like my second home. Erm...there's something about being in a city where there's a...there's a lot of water which is...seems to have a very...erm...gentle effect on people and also the fact that there's no...um...th... the roads are very narrow, so car transport is quite limited and people tend to get around by bicycles. Um...that again just seems to slow down the pace of the city. Um...it's...it's a very very lively place, there's a lot of...a lot of outdoor activity, a lot of people sitting outside cafés and...er...drinking. Um...there's...there's...people are very friendly as well. There's also a lot of cultural activity, there's the van Gogh Museum and there's...um...Rembrandt's House and...erm...the wonderful museum called the Rijksmuseum, so there's plenty to see as well. And...er... there's a lot of nightlife too: the infamous red light district of course and...er...a lot of theatre and events like that. Um...it's just a...a beautiful city architecturally, lots of the...very tall, slender houses. Um...and...er...it's...it's

lovely to take a...a w...a ride along the canals as well, you can get in boats and things. It's just a...a really pretty place to go, and a really nice city.

MICHAEL: I suppose one of the first things that would strike anybody going to Austin in Texas...er...specially coming from Europe would be how green it is – in Austin and around it because the image people have of Texas is of course a sort of dry, dust-blown prairie, but around Austin in that part of Central Texas there are hills and lakes and forests. And I think that's my first impression of Austin going back there after a long time away was just how green it was. Um...Austin is the capital of Texas and also...er...it's the home of the University of Texas, which means that there are lots of...er...young people in Austin and it's full of young people and full of nightlife for them and so, as a result, there's a lot of things that happen at night in Austin and, like a lot of Southern towns, what happens is that... er...specially on summer nights people just walk up and down the streets – families, er...groups of boys or girls, and there are bars up and down the centre of town where they play live music all the time. And...er...it's really a lot of fun. Course there's lots of water sport and a lot of outdoor things to do, as you might imagine, being Texas. Um...I guess one thing that also struck me...er... coming from...er...Europe to America is that the way people drive in Au...in America, it's all so very disciplined, everybody sticks to the lines that are painted on the roads and...er...you don't see so many people...um...driving recklessly. Um...I guess the...the main thing about Austin that I like is the...er... the culture that the kids bring to the...to the city...er...from the University. There's lots of fringe theatre, there's not so much professional theatre, but...er...a lot of fringe theatre, and a lot of local music that's made, not just country and western as you might expect but folk music and rock music of all kinds – and classical music as well. There's a brilliant auditorium in downtown Austin. All in all it's a...I think it's an atypical place...er...for Texas, which is one of the reasons I like it.

B As the purpose of this exercise is to explore the many ways we can describe a place, a large number of variations are possible. No more than three possible answers are given below, and your students may have ideas for more, equally appropriate adjectives.

The exercise can be done alone or in pairs, but afterwards discuss the possible answers with the whole class.

SUGGESTED ANSWERS

1 futuristic/new/modern **2** great/famous/renowned **3** sweeping/wide/broad
4 beautiful/impressive/huge **5** fantastic/glorious/amazing **6** leafy/green/comfortable
7 spectacular/concrete/modern **8** main/new/astonishing **9** squalid/depressing/awful
10 magnificent/efficient/wonderful **11** chaotic/appalling/inadequate **12** empty
13 frequent/regular

C 1 Begin by asking everyone which place they'd like to discuss – if they live in a large city, they could describe just the district they live in. Try to arrange the groups so that people from the same place are together. If each group can discuss a different place, all the better.

2 Rearrange the students into pairs with each partner from a different group.

If everyone has been talking about the same town/city/district so far, turn this into a role-play with one student playing the role of newcomer.

D Instead of writing this letter your students might prefer to write a **leaflet** describing their town, city, village or district.

Note that the model version is rather longer than the 250 words required.

Leo Jones *New Cambridge Advanced English*

10.5 MODEL VERSION

Dear Students,

The first thing you'll notice about Bournemouth is its spaciousness. The broad tree-lined residential avenues of the classier parts of town give it an elegant air but even in the less elegant areas there are parks and gardens everywhere.

Then of course there is the sea and the beach: Bournemouth developed in the late 19th century as a resort for the new Victorian pursuit of sea-bathing. There are seven miles of golden sandy beach protected by heather- and pine-covered cliffs. You'd love the beach in all seasons, but especially in summer when it's bustling with visitors.

You can walk to the beach through the central gardens from the town centre where there are plenty of shops and department stores, cinemas, pubs and clubs. In fact, it is said that there are more nightclubs here proportionately than in London. Although London is very easy to reach for a day out, under two hours by train, you'll be glad to return to the clean unpolluted sea air of Bournemouth.

Despite its history Bournemouth is a modern town with lots to do and lots of young people to meet: shopping, entertainments, beach, museums, sports centres. It has its own symphony orchestra and its own university.

It's easy to find accommodation in host families or at B & Bs or in hotels. There are many grades of hotel from small family-run ones right up to 5-star ones.

Transportation by bus round the town is pretty good although a bit expensive and there are no student reductions.

Within very easy reach are many sites of historic and natural interest, e.g. Poole, Winchester, Salisbury, Stonehenge, the New Forest, etc.

As a place to have your first taste of a foreign country it's ideal, and the town is designed to welcome visitors.

Best wishes,

Jill

10.6 Synonyms and opposites – 3   Word study

The exercises in this section are quite time-consuming. They're best done in pairs, so that the students can compare ideas, but if time is short they could be done at home and then checked in class afterwards. To save time, different groups could be assigned different groups of words in section B to deal with.

A 1 SUGGESTED ANSWERS

VERY LARGE		large	small	very small
gigantic	tremendous	extensive	insignificant	minuscule
immense	vast	roomy		minute
majestic		spacious		tiny
		wide		

2 The students might need to look up *minuscule* /ˈmɪnɪskjuːl/ and *minute* /maɪˈnjuːt/.

3 SUGGESTED ANSWERS (Further variations are possible.)

a(n)   gigantic city   majestic/big mountain   wide/vast lake   tremendous fortune
     immense crowd   tiny/spacious hotel room   majestic/vast ballroom
     vast/majestic palace   roomy luxury car   extensive/minute car park
     tiny/miniature toy gun   big/insignificant mistake   wide avenue   vast/big city square

B

Here the students have to use their judgement and feelings for appropriateness. Encourage the use of dictionaries during these exercises – if possible, have a number of English-English dictionaries available for consultation in class.

SUGGESTED ANSWERS

No 'correct answers' for which adjectives collocate with which nouns are given below, and you may not agree with some of the categorisation. There are no 'rules' – this kind of thing is largely a matter of feeling and opinion. If necessary, check any words you are yourself unsure of before the lesson.

1 very pleasant	**pleasant**	**unpleasant**	**very unpleasant**
charming	agreeable	annoying	appalling
delicious		awful	atrocious
delightful		dreadful	disgusting
picturesque		frightful	
spectacular			
splendid			
wonderful			

2 very beautiful	**beautiful**	**ugly**	**very ugly**
enchanting	attractive	unpleasant	grotesque
glamorous	good-looking	(plain?)	hideous
graceful	handsome		
	lovely		
	pretty		

3 very old	**old**	**new**	**very new**
ancient	disused	fresh	all the rage
dilapidated	traditional	up-to-date	the latest
historical	unfashionable		ultra-modern
obsolete	worn-out		
run-down			

4 very safe	**safe**	**dangerous**	**very dangerous**
guarded	harmless	harmful	deadly
secure	protected	hazardous	fatal
	reliable	insecure	
		precarious	
		risky	
		unsafe	
		vulnerable	

5 **very far**	**far**	**near**	**very near**
faraway	distant	accessible	next door
isolated	a long way away	close	opposite
out-of-the-way		convenient	
remote		handy	
		nearby	

6 **very quiet**	**quiet**	**noisy**	**very noisy**
peaceful	calm	loud	deafening
silent	restful		ear-splitting
sleepy	unobtrusive		

C 1 The discussion is preparation for the writing task. There are many other aspects that may come up besides the ones covered in A and B.

2 This should be set as homework. If preferred, the article could be shorter (say 150 words).

(10.7) *Hard, soft, difficult* and *easy*　　　Idioms and collocations

ANSWERS

1 *hard*-hearted = without compassion　give someone a *hard* time = make it difficult for them　make life *difficult* = create problems

2 *hard*ware = computer equipment　*soft*ware = computer programs

3 *hard* copy = printed material produced by computer

4 *hard* disk = not a floppy disk

5 *hard*-wearing = durable

6 *hard*ware store = ironmonger's

7 un*easy* = anxious, not relaxed　he's being *difficult* = obstinate　*soft*-hearted = compassionate　*easy*-going = not getting worried or angry　have a *soft* spot for = feel affectionate

8 *hard/difficult*　*soft*-spoken = have a quiet, gentle voice

9 *Hard* drugs = addictive, dangerous drugs　*soft* drugs = marijuana, etc.

10 *soft/easy*　*hard* line = uncompromising attitude

11 *hard*-and-fast rule = fixed rule

12 *hard*back = not a paperback

13 take it *easy* = don't get excited/worried　*hard* up = short of money

14 *soft* drink = non-alcoholic cold drink

15 I'm *easy* = I don't mind

16 *hard* sell = aggressive selling techniques　*soft* sell = using gentle persuasion to sell

17 *hard* currency = dollars, etc.

18 take it *easy* = relax

Some other related idioms:

hard cash = notes and coins (not cheque or cards)
hard drink = whisky and other spirits
hard-headed = tough and shrewd
hardwood = wood from deciduous trees

a soft option = less difficult alternative
softwood = wood from coniferous trees

a difficult person = unpredictable, hard to deal with or please

(11.1) Role models

Listening and Vocabulary

Pause the tape after each person has spoken, for students to make notes. As each speaker gives more than one reason, there should be plenty to discuss when the students compare notes afterwards.

SUGGESTED ANSWERS (More than one reason is given here, but the students only have to note down one.)

Nelson Mandela   *united blacks and whites in South Africa*
    ability to see the 'big picture'

Oprah Winfrey   *natural touch*
    honesty
    strong, fine woman after her suffering

Bill Gates   *remained down-to-earth*
    still excited about what he does

Transcript   2 minutes

MARCELLA: Oh, the person I most admire is Nelson Mandela, er…prime minister of South Africa after the first free elections. He was imprisoned until 1990. He's a man of great charisma, an…and dignity, I think, and a very entertaining speaker, a…and very attractive to normal people and to sort of world statesmen as well. Er…and main thing: he's…he's united the blacks and whites in South Africa against all odds, er…extraordinary feat of achievement. He has a sort of natural leadership, I think, and an ability to see the 'big picture', which is s…so important.

★

GABRIELLA: Somebody that I admire greatly is…um…Oprah Winfrey. Um…she's a…I…I just think she is such a wonderful chat show hostess. Um…she's got a really natural touch, she can talk to anybody. She's charming, she's sincere, she's got a…an honesty about her that…that really shines through. Um… she comes from a very…er…poor background, in fact. She was…um…she grew up in…er…in the South of the United States and suffered…er…a… abuse from her father when she was a little girl. Um…and I think through her suffering she's…she's learnt and…and… and become this…this very strong, very fine woman…um…and…and I really…really do admire her a lot.

★

DEBORAH: I admire Bill Gates, he's the chairman of the Microsoft Corporation. Not because he has invented an amazing product, but…um…because although he's so wealthy, and he's obviously so amazingly clever, he's still down-to-earth and kind of grounded and like a real person. He's still really excited about what he does and he's a youthful enthusiast. Um…he…he's approachable, people can contact him by e-mail and he replies personally, he's a really down-to-earth person and that's really why I admire him.

B ANSWERS

1 awarded   shared   right   outstanding

2 billionaires   profitable   publicity   profile   admired/respected

3 rules   subjects   standards   reserves   respectively   palace   shy   appearances

4 charismatic   runs   brand   hands-on   appears   headlines

(*executive* and *respectfully* are not used)

C Perhaps tell the class about some people YOU admire, to start their discussions going.

(11.2) Emphasísing the ríght sýllable   Pronunciátion

A 1 The stresses are marked but in case some students haven't spotted this, draw their attention to the stress mark on the y in syllable and before the s in /ˈsɪləbl/.

 2 ANSWERS   (Recorded on the cassette – 1 minute 40 seconds)

acádemy académic	lécture lécturer
árt artístic	líterature líterary
biólogy biológical	máths mathemátics mathemátical
bótany botánical	phýsics phýsical
chémist chémistry chémical	pólitics polítical
consúlt consultátion	sécond sécondary
económics económical ecónomy	sécretary secretárial
éducate educátional	socíety sociólogy
exámine examinátion	spécial spécialise specialisátion speciálity
geógraphy geográphical	statístics statístical
grámmar grammátical	zoólogy zoológical
hístory histórical	

 B   ANSWERS   (Recorded on the cassette – 1 minute 30 seconds)

1 She's stúdying pólitics at univérsity and hópes to becóme a politícian.

2 Máths is an ínteresting súbject but I dón't wánt to be subjécted to a lóng lécture about it, thánk you very múch!

3 Whát a lóvely présent! I was présent when they presénted her with the awárd.

4 Wáit a mínute – I just néed to máke a minúte adjústment to this machíne.

5 Whén are you permítted to úse the emérgency éxit?

6 You néed a spécial pérmit to úse this éntrance.

7 I've réad the cóntents of the bóok and nów I féel quíte contént.

8 Áfter our dessért, we wátched a fílm abóut some sóldiers who desérted and escáped into the désert and jóined a gróup of rébels.

9 Whén a métal óbject cóols dówn it contrácts.

10 This cóntract is inválid becaúse it hásn't been sígned.

11 The péople rebélled becaúse they objécted to the góvernment's pólicies.

12 I dón't nórmally mínd being insúlted – but I dó when such dréadful ínsults are úsed.

C   Play the recording, pausing between each group of sentences (after 1–7, 8–12, 13–18 and 19–24).

ANSWERS

1 to 7: 'Terry had a stomach ache because the plums he ate were unripe.'

not the *apples* 1 3		not a *headache* 4	not *over*ripe 5
not *Sally* 2		it *is* really true 7	not the ones *you* ate 6

8 to 12: 'I need more time if I'm going to take up a new sport.'

not *money* 8 12	not *less* time 11
not a new *hobby* 10	not if *you* are going to 9

13 to 18: 'Most people like Helen because she has a friendly personality.'

not an *unfriendly* one 15 17	not *everyone* 16
they don't like *another* person 13 14	not a friendly *smile* 18

19 to 24: 'Ted has a cough because he smokes thirty cigarettes a day.'

not a *sore throat* 22 24	not *Helen* 21	not *thirteen* 23
not *cigars* 19	not per *week* 20	

Transcript   2 minutes 45 seconds

1 No, Terry had a stomach ache because the *plums* he ate were unripe.

2 No, *Terry* had a stomach ache because the plums he ate were unripe.

3 No, it was the *plums* that were unripe.

4 No, Terry had a *stomach ache* because the plums he ate were unripe.

5 No, Terry had a stomach ache because the plums he ate were *un*ripe.

6 Terry had a stomach ache because the plums *he* ate were unripe.

7 Terry *did* have a stomach ache because the plums he ate were unripe.

8 No, it's more *time* I need if I'm going to take up a new sport.

9 No, I need more time if *I'm* going to take up a new sport.

10 No, I need more time if I'm going to take up a new *sport*.

11 No, I need *more* time if I'm going to take up a new sport.

12 No, I need more *time* if I'm going to take up a new sport.

13 No, most people like *Helen* because she has a friendly personality.

14 No, most people like Helen because *she* has a friendly personality.

15 No, the reason why most people like Helen is because she has a *friendly* personality.

16 No, *most* people like Helen because she has a friendly personality.

17 No, most people like Helen because she has a *friendly* personality.

18 No, most people like Helen because she has a friendly *personality*.

19 No, Ted has a cough because he smokes 30 *cigarettes* a day.

20 No, Ted has a cough because he smokes 30 cigarettes a *day*.

21 No, it's *Ted* who has a cough because he smokes 30 cigarettes a day.

22 No, Ted has a *cough* because he smokes 30 cigarettes a day.

23 No, Ted has a cough because he smokes *30* cigarettes a day.

24 No, what Ted has is a *cough* because he smokes too much.

(11.3) Charlie Chaplin   Reading

As this is a particularly long text, it should be prepared for homework, if possible.

A1 Possible questions one might want to find the answers to:
Where was he popular?
How did he start in the movies?
What kind of personal life did he have?
Who thought he was funny?

2 Thinking of questions gives everyone a purpose for reading the continuation of the article.

B **ANSWERS**
1 B 2 D 3 B 4 C 5 A 6 C

C **ANSWERS**

¶1 subversive = undermining authority   resilience = ability to recover from setbacks

¶4 headache = problem   postponed = put off

¶6 gags = visual jokes   inanimate = not living   bust = broken   adroitness = skill
charged = filled

¶7 corresponding = matching   reconcile = harmonise and resolve
cynicism = lack of trust   misogyny = hatred of women

¶8 stable = secure   effaced = erased   ominous = threatening   prudently = wisely
turbulent = violent   unfounded charges = allegations

¶9 macabre = horrifying   bequeathed = leave after one's death

D This is a follow-up discussion.

E1 Arrange the class into an even number of pairs. This activity requires students to make notes and not actually write the article. The purpose of this is to encourage everyone to think about how they'd plan an article.

They should select what is relevant for a relatively short article – they can't get all the information from the 950-word text into a 250-word article.

2 Combine the pairs into groups.

If there's time, and if your students have got interested in the topic, ask them to write the article for homework – but note that there is another writing task coming up in 11.5, as well as in 11.6.

(11.4) Style, tone and content   Effective writing

A This is a warm-up discussion in groups.

B Student A has some facts about the short life of Marilyn Monroe in **Activity 14**, student B has some facts about the life of James Dean in **Activity 37**. They should spend some time studying the information before beginning their conversation, to avoid the temptation of reading it aloud to each other.

C1 All four paragraphs have features that you might consider more or less effective. Perhaps point out that clumsy or inelegant style is also ineffective – it may make people focus on the style instead of the content. The fourth paragraph is probably too chatty for a magazine article – though this too may be a matter of taste, I guess!

Perhaps ask everyone to 'vote' on which of the four paragraphs they think is the best.

2 The highlighting should not just focus on the style – engaging turns of phrase or apt expressions – but also on the information that each writer has chosen to include.

> **CAE exam**   Style is particularly important in Part 2 of the Writing paper: candidates are rewarded for writing clear, stylish prose which is a pleasure to read.

D1 This should be done in small groups of three or four students, so that everyone gets a look at two or three other people's paragraphs later.

2 This is best done in class, with each student working alone. Set a time limit.

3 The students compare their work . . . and then rewrite it, probably for homework.

(11.5) Sharing opinions   Speaking, Listening and Reading

 A1 Pause the tape after each speaker to allow time for students to decide how they might reply – this can be done as a class or in pairs. Encourage everyone to trust their feelings for what sounds appropriate.

 2 Play the recording again, pausing it from time to time as necessary.

Transcript   (The introductory gambits are in **_bold italics_**.)   2 minutes

NARRATOR: How would you reply to each of these people?

MAN: Well, *as I see it*, millions of people in the world are worse off than us, but there's nothing we can do about it.

WOMAN: *I'd say that* if you do have plenty of money, there's no point in spending it on private education for your children.

MAN: *It seems to me that* the only way to help the poor in the world is to find ways of helping them to help themselves…er… not by…er…giving them free food.

WOMAN: *If you ask me*, taxes for rich people should be really high – 95% or something – so that everyone is at the same economic level.

WOMAN: *It's quite obvious that* in a capitalist society anyone who is intelligent can become rich – all they have to do is work hard and use the system.

MAN: Er…*in my view* i…it's worth making a lot of money…er…so that you can leave it to your children when you die.

WOMAN: *I can't help thinking that* the reason why poor people are poor is that they don't work hard enough.

MAN: *Don't you agree that* if people are starving or have nowhere to live, it's the duty of better-off people to give them food and shelter?

WOMAN: Look, *let's face it*, there's only one reason why people work and that's to make as much money as possible.

MAN: *Surely*, as long as you've got enough to live on, there's no point in making more and more money.

WOMAN: If you're earning a good salary, *surely* you should save as much as you can for a rainy day.

MAN: *I must that say that* one thing is certain: money doesn't buy happiness.

B In this case the tone of voice, as well as the actual words used, expresses agreement or disagreement. Again, pause the tape after each conversation for everyone to comment on what they have heard.

Transcript and ANSWERS   1 minute 30 seconds

NARRATOR: You'll hear ten people reacting to various opinions – decide if they are agreeing or disagreeing with the opinions expressed. Pay attention to the tone of voice they use.

1
WOMAN: Aren't you glad you're not a millionaire?
MAN: Sure!   ✓ sincere tone = agreement

2
MAN: Don't you wish you could afford to spend your holidays
     in the Caribbean?
WOMAN: Mm, ye-es.   ✗ doubtful tone = disagreement

3
WOMAN: It's not worth saving your money, it's better to spend it.
MAN: Oh, sure!   ✗ sarcastic tone = disagreement

4
MAN: It's better to be happy than rich.
WOMAN: Hmm.   ✗ doubtful tone = disagreement

5
WOMAN: Well, basically, in a job the most important thing is how
     much you earn.
MAN: Oh yes!   ✓ sincere tone = agreement

6
MAN: It's really important to save a little money every month –
     you never know when you might need it.
WOMAN: I don't know about that.   ✗ sceptical tone = disagreement

7
MAN: The only way to survive on a tight budget is to keep a
     record of all your expenses.
MAN: I didn't know about that!   ✓ surprised tone = agreement

8
WOMAN: Children these days get far too much pocket money.
WOMAN: Mmm!   ✓ sincere tone = agreement

9
WOMAN: In a family it should be the mother that controls
     the budget.
WOMAN: Yes!   ✓ emphatic tone = agreement

10
MAN: If I inherited a lot of money it wouldn't change my life
     at all.
MAN: Oh yes!   ✗ sarcastic tone = disagreement

C Try to structure this discussion exercise fairly rigidly, following the guidelines in the Student's Book instructions. Maybe practise the first couple of questions as a whole-class activity, encouraging everyone to experiment with using the expressions listed in A1.

CAE exam	In Parts 3 and 4 of the Speaking paper, in which candidates work in pairs, they're involved in a discussion, as in **11.5 C** and **D1**. They are given credit for good interactive communication, and they shouldn't try to dominate the conversation so that the other candidate has no chance to speak. Indeed, they should encourage each other to give their views.

D1 This discussion helps to set the scene for the text the students have to read in D2.

2 Begin by explaining that Camelot is the name of the company that runs the National Lottery in Britain, and that Blackburn is in the north of England, whilst Hastings is in the south.

This task is quite tricky, and other arrangements may be equally plausible.

ANSWERS

2 A **4** C **6** B **8** F **12** E (D nowhere)

> **CAE exam** | **11.5 D2** is similar to the 'gapped text' exercise in the Reading paper – there is more advice for candidates in an extra activity on this tricky kind of exercise at the end of this unit (page 139).

E1 Maybe brainstorm some ideas in class before everyone does this for homework.

2 The target reader's reaction is important.

Leo Jones   *New Cambridge Advanced English*

(11.5) MODEL VERSION

Dear Sharon,

What a stroke of luck, winning all that lovely money! Well done!

You may think this is a bit of a cheek but I'd like to give you some advice on how to deal with it. You may remember I had a similar win myself about three years ago and made a few mistakes that I bitterly regretted afterwards.

Well, first of all, you have to spend some of it on something you've been wanting for ages, maybe a better car or a really luxurious holiday in the sun or a whole new wardrobe. You'd probably like to give some to charity as well. I was far too careful with my winnings and thought that I had to get the most out of them and not waste anything; so I didn't even have a minor spending spree.

Once you've got that out of your system then with what's left, let's say about £40,000, make a plan of how to get the most advantage from it. Obviously what you do depends on your circumstances. I know that you and Colin have been wanting to buy a flat; why not use £20,000 as a deposit on a property, then your monthly mortgage repayments would not be so hefty and could be confined to 10 rather than 20 years. With the remaining £20,000 you ought to make some provision for the future in terms of investment. You could invest in a pension fund or some other tax-free fund or maybe buy a holiday cottage or flat that you could rent out as a source of income and of course use as a holiday home for yourselves.

Good luck with your spending!

Love,

Mel

11.6 Household names   Listening and Creative writing

A1 In case some students haven't heard of The Body Shop, this gives them a chance to find out more from those who have.

2 Before you play the recording, warn everyone that Anita Roddick speaks VERY fast. They should NOT expect to understand everything she says on the first listening. They should just concentrate on answering the questions, which cover the main points she makes. The task is relatively easy in order to HELP the students to understand, rather than to test their understanding. Pause the recording at the places marked with ★★★ in the Transcript below.

Anita Roddick uses quite a lot of difficult (and sometimes idiosyncratic) words and phrases – these are printed **in bold type** in the Transcript below [*and explained in italics*].

If there's time . . .

Photocopy the Transcript and let your students read it while they listen to the recording.

ANSWERS

The points that should have crosses (✗) are:

1 a   (untrue)

2 f   (untrue)   + h (not mentioned)

3 b   (untrue)

4 d   (untrue)

5 d   (untrue)

6 c   (not mentioned)

– all the others should have ticks

Transcript   10 minutes 45 seconds

ANITA: My name is Anita Roddick and I'm founder of The Body Shop.

INTERVIEWER: And how did your career start?

ANITA: I was trained as a teacher, English and history. And like most teachers in the sixties…er…er…the world was big and you…you moved out of your career really fast. So I had a…a lot of…a lot of the experiences I had that formed my thinking for when I started The Body Shop were formed by the ability to travel, because in the sixties students suddenly, you know, had the ability to travel. Um…I worked with the United Nations in Geneva for the Women's Department. I lived with…er… communities, fishing communities, farming communities, in Indian Ocean islands, in the Pacific islands, and it's there that I got the idea for skin care from natural ingredients.

★★★

INTERVIEWER: And why do you think The Body Shop has been so successful?

ANITA: I think we have a **covert** [*hidden*] understanding of women, I think…er… um…we have an amazing sense of not feeling when you go into the shops that you're going into a female **fortress** [*castle*], everything is…it's very much like going into a supermarket, there's information that you can take or not take, there's…um…samples that you can try or not try, there isn't that **heavy-duty** [*strong*] pressure, and th…you don't feel that you're less than the products, coming in. Um…so I think, and…the…there's a very strong female identity in The Body Shop and that's a lot to do with language and…er…the visual images.

There's never a celebration of a perfect type, a perfect Caucasian type: very **passive** [*allowing others to be in control*] um…very **flawless** [*without imperfections*]. In fact the images are never that, the images are very much multicultural, very real. There's that, and then the language is almost profoundly **puritanist** [*puritanical/ simple*]. You never get…er: 'This product will do this for you' it…outside of the function of cleaning, protecting and polishing the skin and the hair. We never espouse and support this absolute obsession with youth, youthful looks. Er…we **celebrate** [*show admiration for*] wrinkles, we celebrate the ageing process, we celebrate women and social justice, rather than women and passivity. And I think that's…that's been a real bonding with women…er…in many ways.

Plus we have a great smell! You know, go into the stores and it smells like, er…you know, whatever, you know, a **pantry** [*room where food is stored*], it smells like, you know, a fruit bowl and that's very **tangible** [*real – you can feel it*] in there. And I think the other success to The Body Shop is because we stand…we turn our shops into social action stations, you know, we campaign on human rights issues, we campaign on social justice issues, environmental issues, and we **leverage** [*try to influence*] the customer as they come into the shops or they're in the shops on these actions, so it's not only selling skin and hair care it's, you know, it's the ability to campaign in those shops as well.

INTERVIEWER: I must say I always feel that your customers can feel that they are doing something positive: trade not aid for…er…Third World countries, so…

ANITA: Yes, I think there's a…it's a very difficult thing for us because there's a whole, you know, behind the scenes there's a whole…er…market of thoughtfulness and it's really hard to describe thoughtfulness in a very very busy shop: how we **source** [*obtain*] our ingredients, how we determine our re…relationships with small and fragile communities in the majority world, how we…er…make sure that we audit the process towards **sustainability** [*not causing environmental damage*], how we don't do excessive packaging, how we make sure no ingredient is tested on animals. I mean, I'm amazed, really amazed that we get any products on the shelf because there's a **minefield** [*dangerous area*] of things you can't do, cannot say, um …

INTERVIEWER: And that must have changed tremendously since you started?

ANITA: Yeah, I think…er…where people are looking at everything we do through a microscope, everything, everything we said twenty years ago, every **aspirational statement** [*declaration of what we aim to achieve*], so that's quite…that's quite constraining. But it's…um…it's the nature of the company, because when you act in a very very radical way, when you challenge the system and challenge a very powerful beauty industry and, you know, accuse it of racism, accuse it of not celebrating real women…you know…you, you know, it's, as Helena Rubinstein said, 'It's the nastiest business in the world'.

★★★

INTERVIEWER: What do you really enjoy about your life?

ANITA: I love my life because it's a **thumbprint** [*version?*] of who I am. If…you know, if one had to describe The Body Shop, being active and being socially concerned and having a sense of humour and a sense of **counter-culture** [*personal freedom and anti-materialism – cf hippy*] and being…guerrilla tactics, that's exactly my personality so I think a lot of what I like about it is I constantly, you know, reinvent it and thumbprint it. I love, because it's again, it's my…the fact that there are so many **planks** [*different aspects*] in my job: the planks of, you know, creation, creativity, looking at the style and image, looking at the product development. And then the amazing stuff which, you know, if I packed it in tomorrow, which I'm not prepared to do, the work I would do on human rights, you know, the…the profits that we make, the way we choose to channel them into supporting activists, human rights activists, or…um…social justice activists, so…and one minute I can be, you know, **knocking my head on** [*racking my brains over*] looking at product or redesigning the store and then I'm rushing to a meeting in Bosnia about what we can do in the orphanages there. And I think that…that is really what women are good at, they **juggle** [*do several tasks simultaneously*], they won't be boxed into…um…a style that says 'This is who we are.' You know, you know, we have relationships that we have to deal with, we have issues that we have to deal with, we have style that we have to deal with and that very much is what I love about the job, its multiplicity of…er…of involvements.

INTERVIEWER: And it allows you to use your…your potential fully.

ANITA: Yeah. I mean it's… I think what's…certainly at my age, in my mid-50s, for me everything is about continuous education, you know, and education of the human spirit. That's why I spend so much time travelling because it's like a university without walls, and pushing myself into **arenas** [*fields?*] and areas and situations that are very very uncomfortable. Because when you run a company as popular as this and when you have wealth, which I have, the great and worst things it can give you sus…the great thing it gives you is spontaneity but at the worst is it **corrodes** [*damages*] your sense of empathy, you know, your sense of understanding the human condition.

And putting myself into situations where I'm either for ex…like, travelling with a **vagabond** [*person with no home*] and living in some of the worst areas of black rural America or working in…er… **majority world** [*Third World*] countries makes for a very uncomfortable existence, but gives you a sense of human connection and I would be **bereft** [*lacking a great deal*] without it and the company would be bereft without that type of stuff.

★★★

INTERVIEWER: What…what do you *not* enjoy so much about . . . ?

ANITA: You know, I think it's the dark side of this company and the dark side of any entrepreneur is that sense of huge, onerous responsibility. You cannot be **dilettante** [*partially involved – normally **a dilettante***], you can't say, 'Oh, I'm going to go off for six months, and laze around on an island in some, you know, Caribbean. You've got thousands and thousands and thousands of people that depend on you for their livelihood, and their life. And I'm not dilettante about the 150 people that are working in a project in Kathmandu, most of them 'untouchables', who depend on our relationship, our trading relationship with them. So it gives you…er…the dark side is that you never have time for nourishing yourself in terms of what you want to do, you end up being so bloody selfless that you're…that selflessness is…um…counter-productive. So that's the dark side. The other dark side is that I hate, loathe, fight against structure and…er…hierarchy. And women are not good at **hierarchy** [*a system where people are put at different levels according to their importance*], we're much more inclusive, we want all the world to sit round a table and work things out. We want to talk feelings and we want to talk how… how…emotions in the workplace, and…er…when you have a company as big as ours you yearn for intimacy. Where are those intimate relationships that you had 20 years ago, when you went into somebody's home and you…er, you know, you sat in the

televis…watched television with them? And so I constantly have to try and **regenerate** [*create again*] that. So the lack of intimacy, the hierarchy, um…the…the anguish of people in the workplace, um…which is **a constant** [*never changes*], I think are the things I don't like.

★★★

INTERVIEWER: Well, how do you then relax when you have a. . . ?

ANITA: I have a very very strong family life. I'm Italian and the Italians always have a strong sense of extended family. I have a wonderful granddaughter and, you know, I'm much more reflective and playful with my granddaughter than I ever was with my kids when it was survival and you just got out and worked. I'm a great one for…um…er…for the movies, the theatre, so it's all performing arts stuff. Er…long walks is another way, you know, I'll do great six-hour, five-hour walks. Um…and I think being in the company of people I love, a…and being a *housewife* in the best sense, you know, where you…people come and you eat, you cook them dinner, you walk, I mean it's the way I fashion my home, it's four sinks in the kitchen, a great jukebox, we all cook together, we all clean up together, we all rock 'n' roll. So it's very much around the…the…the **haven** [*safe place*] of the house.

★★★

INTERVIEWER: What do you think you're proudest of having done?

ANITA: I think I'm proudest that…a couple of things: one is that really challenging the beauty industry, really challenging it, and…er…hopefully redefining beauty. Really defining it as not as some manipulation of…er, you know, bone structure but about vivaciousness and energy and action and…er…the… the essential qualities of what women are, and…and the self-esteem that goes with that. And I think the second thing has to be, we will go down in the books in terms of how we've reinvented business, giving it a kinder and gentler face, er…um…giving it a social agenda that…er…and a responsibility again for which there are no books for.

B It sometimes requires a surprising effort of the imagination for students to realise that the rest of the world may not share their cultural background. These activities draw attention to the fact that one of the tasks that they may sometimes have to do is to act as 'cultural interpreter' – explaining aspects of their country to foreigners.

In a multinational class perhaps arrange the groups so that there is a mix of nationalities in each group. Then there can be a genuine exchange of information about each country's household names.

1 If you anticipate that this might take a long time, it could be set for homework, which would also give everyone a chance to do some research if they wish.

2 The pairs should, as far as possible, consist of people from different groups.

C1 The example is about 80 words and is intended as a model for what the students will have to do in C2.

2 This is probably best done as homework.

3 Encourage feedback on the style and tone as well as the content.

Leo Jones *New Cambridge Advanced English*

11.6 MODEL VERSION

Edwina Currie 50-something, talented, energetic, Jewish female Conservative ex-Member of Parliament for Derbyshire South. She is well-known for her sensational books, her outspoken opinions, and her criticism of her own party, particularly of Margaret Thatcher. She is still famous for the egg scandal in the 80s, when, as junior minister for health, she authorised the destruction of thousands of battery hens because their eggs were infected with salmonella, which cost the taxpayer millions in compensation. She has a talent for saying the wrong thing at the wrong time and frequently hits the headlines.

Eddie Izzard 35-year-old stand-up comedian. Always appears in visible make-up, including nail-varnish, lipstick, mascara and eye-liner. He often dresses as a woman and came out as a transvestite at the age of 21 when he was at university studying accountancy. He dropped out after a year and took his show to the Edinburgh Festival but success didn't come until years later. In 1993 he brought his show to the West End and won the British Comedy Award for Top Stand-up Comedian. His fame and success have spread to the States and he is now attempting to get into Europe – even doing some of his act in bad French. His humour depends on developing a series of surreal ideas and taking them to hilarious conclusions, as if he's just thinking aloud in front of a group of friends. He rarely appears on TV because he likes to improvise and develop his act in front of a live audience and use the same jokes, rather than come up with fresh material for each performance.

Ian Wright British footballer, born in Woolwich, London in 1963 to Afro-Caribbean parents. He started with Crystal Palace and then moved to Arsenal where he has become their top goal scorer ever – 301 goals to date. His speed off the mark and superb reflexes as well as ability in the air have secured him a place in the England team on many occasions since 1991. His quick temper and frankness often get him into trouble but he is dear to the hearts of many fans and is a great role model for young blacks.

(11.7) *For* and *on*   Idioms and collocations

Ⓐ ANSWERS

1	on the menu on a diet	**7**	on average
2	on purpose	**8**	on television
3	on behalf of	**9**	on the hour
4	on condition that	**10**	on foot
5	for a long time for a walk	**11**	on the contrary
6	on the way	**12**	for a change

Ⓑ ANSWERS

2	on account of	**9**	insisted on waiting
3	searching for last have it on	**10**	wind the tape on
4	apologise for being	**11**	fell for it
5	feel sorry for me	**12**	grew on me
6	depends on	**13**	rely on him count on me
7	walked on	**14**	comment on
8	is an expert on cars		

➡ Some more related expressions:

later on   on duty   on business   on display   on fire   on no account   on toast
on the phone   on time

for sale   wait for   ready for   vote for

Extra advice and an Extra activity for CAE exam candidates (only)

The 'gapped text' exercise in the Reading paper requires special techniques that are not normally required in real life. Even if your students have done similar exercises in an FCE course it's still likely to be one of their least favourite activities. This part of the exam tests candidates' understanding of the organisation of a text and the way in which cohesive devices and structures operate to link paragraphs together.

However, even intelligent native speakers, who *can* understand every word and idiom in the text, find this kind of exercise confusing – so it's no wonder that foreign students find it baffling, particularly if the text is about an unfamiliar or unappealing topic. Although, surprisingly, some candidates take this kind of exercise in their stride, most find it intimidating. It also seems unfair, because if you get one answer wrong you automatically get another wrong too.

Exam candidates need to do several tests from *CAE Practice Tests* to familiarise themselves with the techniques suggested in the extra advice below, and to help them lessen their fears.

ANSWERS (For page 141.)

1 B
2 E
3 F
4 D
5 A

EXTRA ACTIVITY   UNIT 11

The 'gapped text' exercise in the Reading paper is very tricky — even educated British people find it hard to do.

Here are some techniques that will help to get you started:

1 Skim the whole text and the missing paragraphs to get a feel for the topic of the text. Don't make any hasty decisions yet about what fits where.

2 Put a pencil ring around the words that may refer back to ideas in a previous paragraph. Do this in the first sentence of each paragraph of the main text AND in the paragraphs to be fitted in.

   Look for PRONOUNS which may refer back to things, people, events and ideas mentioned in the previous paragraph, such as:

   it this that he she him her them one

   Look for CONNECTING WORDS which may refer back to the previous paragraph, such as:

   However In spite of this Consequently But Moreover So A few days later
   After this/that

3 Read the beginning of the text and the paragraph after the first gap. Then see if you can find one of the extra paragraphs that may fit in the first gap – if you can't, or if you are unsure, move on to read the paragraphs before and after the second gap. Then see if you can decide which of the extra paragraphs may fit there – if you're unsure, move on to the third gap. Cross out each extra paragraph when you've fitted it in somewhere.

   Remember that if you get the first two answers wrong, you'll be lucky to get the rest right – this isn't fair, but it's how the exam works.

4 When you've reached the end and filled some of the gaps, go back to the ones you missed and try to work out which of the extra paragraphs you haven't crossed out will fit in.

5 If there's time, go back through all the gaps and see if the extra paragraph you haven't used might fit better in any of the gaps you've already filled.

6 Don't leave any blanks. If in doubt, guess!

© Cambridge University Press, 1998

Leo Jones *New Cambridge Advanced English*

EXTRA ACTIVITY   UNIT 11

Read this article and decide where paragraphs A to F below fit in the numbered gaps 1–5. There is one extra paragraph that doesn't fit anywhere.

Britain's busiest thief takes secrets to grave

The man who could claim to have been Britain's most active thief died yesterday, taking to the grave the secrets of some of this century's most spectacular robberies.

He stole the Duke of Wellington's swords from the Victoria and Albert Museum, got away with what was the biggest armed robbery of his era and is estimated to have stolen and gambled away more than £100 million.

1 [ ]

"He was the Attila the Hun of the pillaging game," said an old friend, Peter Scott, yesterday. "He was undoubtedly the most prodigious thief this century. He was still at it at the age of 81."

During his final theft, Chatham fell badly while trying to get into an art gallery and was in great pain during his last years.

2 [ ]

Works of art were his speciality and he broke into a total of 26 art galleries, selling off the paintings, including a Renoir and a Matisse, and gambling away the proceeds.

3 [ ]

In the former, he broke in through a window, stole the swords and removed the precious stones, giving some to girlfriends and using some to gamble with. In the latter, he and his team escaped with £287,000 in a robbery which led to questions in the Commons and heralded the arrival of organised armed robbery in Britain.

4 [ ]

Great train robber Bruce Reynolds described him as a "legendary climber who stole

and spent several million pounds". Young criminals liked to drop his name and regarded it as a privilege to work with him.

5 [ ]

Born in London to middle-class parents, his last home was a tiny flat in sheltered accommodation in Fulham.

A But despite his abilities at climbing into the buildings of the rich and famous he ended up with nothing. He had no regrets about his victims: "They were usually very, very rich people, millionaires. Some of them regarded it as a nice thing to talk about at dinner parties."

B George "Taters" Chatham, who died aged 85 in a nursing home in Battersea, south London, yesterday, was a legendary figure in criminal circles. But although he spent a total of 35 years in prison, he got clean away with some of his more exotic crimes.

C He died at work: while attempting to steal a painting by Magritte worth over £2 million from the Tate Gallery he suffered a fatal heart attack.

D He was also proud of having cat-burgled the Maharajah of Jaipur of £80,000 at his manor house in East Grinstead, West Sussex. He described how he had used a foot-long key to get into the safe. He was not caught.

E His first conviction was in 1931 and he was regularly back in court throughout his career. At one stage, he was jailed so frequently that one cell at Chelmsford prison was known as "Chatham's cell".

F His two most spectacular crimes, for neither of which he was caught, were the 1948 theft of the Duke of Wellington's swords from the V&A and the 1952 Eastcastle mail van robbery.

(12.1) Science and technology

Listening and Vocabulary

A1 Make sure everyone reads the questions through before you play the recording.

SUGGESTED ANSWERS

1 communicate with each other **2** revolutionised
3 something new/something she's never seen before **4** stained/coloured
5 open-plan lab **6** training students **7** cutbacks **8** healthier and happier
9 practical work **10** animal testing

2 Even if everyone comes from the same country, it's important to discuss all the questions so that the necessary vocabulary is used.

Transcript 6 minutes 15 seconds

WENDY: My name is Wendy Fielder and I'm a research scientist for the University of Nottingham. I'm doing food microbiology, which is basically food bacteriology. This is…um…dealing with the food poisoning organisms like…um…salmonella, listeria, the…the organism in cheese that can cause problems with pregnant women, and any other type of…er…bacteria which can cause a problem to the food industry.

INTERVIEWER: What…what kind of things do you do on a typical day?

WENDY: On a typical day…um…I…well, I have a rolling programme. To be a scientist you've got to be thinking of…as you're doing one thing you've got to be thinking of the next thing. So…um…it…it would vary. It's very important that you talk to your colleagues, and I don't just mean within your own institute, um… sort of collaboration and…um… the gaining of knowledge and pooling of knowledge is extremely important in…in this…in this type of work because… um…it's very very very fast rolling.

INTERVIEWER: And…so computers have made a huge difference to science?

WENDY: Com…computers in the last five years have totally revolutionised science. Now you have things like the World Wide Web, a lot of scientists put information on the Web so that other scientists can retrieve this information and use it. You can contact people easily now all over the world electronically and so information is very very fast.

INTERVIEWER: What do you particularly enjoy about what you do?

WENDY: Oh, I just love it. It's so interesting. There's always something new. I find it exciting, if I didn't find it exciting I couldn't do it and it would be amazingly boring if you didn't find it exciting because it's repetitive and it…um…so I just find the fact that you can see something new, you look down a microscope…um…you…you see something you haven't seen before. It's… it's rather like making a product, to…to produce a really good slide and have stained it really well, um…it…it's like an…a work of art, it's wonderful.

INTERVIEWER: When you say 'look down a microscope at a slide', what's on the slide?

WENDY: A bacteria is very small and to see it you have to use a microscope. Um…on…you can…er…you can put your bacteria onto your slide and…um…you…you cannot normally see it unless you stain it, so staining is colouring…um . . .

INTERVIEWER: It's quite a solitary job, isn't it?

WENDY: Um…it is and it isn't. I actually work in a fairly large open-plan lab so there are people around me. I also interact a lot with students, this is part of my job, part of my job is to train students on a one-to-one basis, so that when…when they go home they've made the most of their time here. So quite often I have a lot of dealings with students, so it's actually very busy. Um…but yes, when…when I'm actually working…um…on the bacteria themselves it's…it's actually quite important to be quiet because you need to concentrate, otherwise you…you might miss something.

INTERVIEWER: Why is what you do so important, do you think?

WENDY: Oh, I think the health of the nation is paramount and I think because the population of the world in general is growing, um…that really we have a duty and responsibility to try and feed the world…um…decently and efficiently and I think modern agriculture is certainly the way forward.

INTERVIEWER: And is that why you think research is so important?

WENDY: I think research is very important. Um…I think I…these days it's…a lot of it's funded by industry, um…there are cutbacks in government funding… um…because it…it has become very expensive. But I think it would be a very sad day when we stop putting money into research and I…I think the world as a whole has benefited because of it.

INTERVIEWER: Where's it going from here?

WENDY: I think bacteriology, I think molecular…molecular microbiology is the…the way forward and I think that so much information is being…um…learnt and used, I think that we will have designer vaccines, designer medicines, and I think we should have a much healthier, much happier population.

INTERVIEWER: How would you like to see science taught in schools?

WENDY: You could widen science, I think you should do engineering in schools, I think the wide…and biotechnology, because that's the way forward, biotechnology, using science for the good of everybody. I'm sure that's the way forwards, I think if you can…once you motivate the young then I…I…I think that's the way forward.

INTERVIEWER: And make it accessible to them?

WENDY: Oh, definitely. I would like to see more practical work done in schools…um… because I feel that hands-on practical skills, trying things out, seeing things happen is the way you learn and…er… I'm very sorry that these days there isn't so much practical work done within the school system. I also think the fact that they do science now in primary schools is absolutely excellent and I'm sure at that age…that is the age to fire the enthusiasm and to get…get people thinking.

INTERVIEWER: Is there, finally, a field or a project that you would really like to work on?

WENDY: There is a…a unit in Nottingham called 'FRAME'. Um…FRAME is basically… um…using tissue culture to replace animals for animal testing, so you don't have to use live animals. I can sanction the use of animal testing when it's used for medical research, when something positive and good comes out of it, um…but I'm very unwilling to use animals unless I absolutely have to and I have to satisfy myself that…um…it's absolutely necessary. I would love to work on this project which is there to exclude animals from the system and so we could work entirely in a…an artificial cell culture situation.

B **SUGGESTED ANSWERS**

1 screw/woodscrew nut bolt washer nail drawing pin paper clip hook bracket hinge

2 push-button lever handle dial/gauge knob switch

3 hammer mallet chisel screwdriver pliers spanner saw electric drill

4 *Some more tools:* plane pincers awl file hacksaw scissors axe monkey wrench spirit level *etc.*

C This is a very challenging activity – and it needs time to do justice to it. It is an ideal activity for showing students how useful an English-to-English dictionary is – even for looking up words they already think they know, as most of the ones here are likely to be.

The activity could be prepared at home and then done as a paired activity in class.

D Play the recording, pausing it between each speaker to give everyone time to write their answers. Some of the answers are debatable, particularly the 'Who's (s)he talking to?' ones.

| **CAE exam** | In the Listening paper candidates hear clips like the ones in **12.1 D** and may have to identify who the speakers are or what topic they're talking about. They may have to identify the speakers' intentions: trying to persuade, giving advice, criticising, etc. |

SUGGESTED ANSWERS

	SUBJECT	TONE OF VOICE	TALKING TO
2	gravity/gravitation	superior, condescending	an adult
3	lightning	patronising, talking down to	a child or an adult
4	X-rays	enthusiastic, not talking down	children
5	lasers	bored, uninspiring	children or students
6	yeast	friendly, intimate	one person in private/secret
7	encyclopedias	good-humoured, slightly sarcastic	small group or individual child or adult
8	friction	loud, neutral	a large group of adults
9	recycling	very patient	an adult or maybe a child
10	acids	impatient	a class of children or students

Transcript   4 minutes 30 seconds

NARRATOR: What are they talking about? Listen carefully to each of these ten extracts and make notes according to the instructions in your book.

1

WOMAN: . . . as you all know it's quite hard to use one at first because it feels very strange and unstable, quite frightening, especially for an adult, but they say that, once you've learned, you never forget. In fact once you've got the knack it's easy, isn't it? Did you know that when they were first introduced in the 19th century, there was a law that you had to ring the bell all the time to warn people you were coming . . .

2

MAN: . . . Yes, you see, it's the force of attraction between any two objects. The strength of the force depends on the mass of the objects and the distance between them. Er...the most obvious effect is the way objects on the surface of the earth are attracted towards the centre of the earth. . . .

3

WOMAN: . . . as it comes down it goes relatively slowly: 100 to 1,000 miles per hour and you can't see it, but the return stroke goes up from the earth to the cloud and it goes at over 87,000 miles per hour and that's the one you can see, you see, the one that goes back up, mm? It's really just a very large, powerful spark. The distance in miles you are away from it is the time in seconds between it and the sound you hear. . . .

4

MAN: . . . Well, they were first discovered in 1895 and they can penetrate matter that is opaque to light. Some matter is more transparent to them than others, which means you can see inside somebody. They are actually quite dangerous and people who work with them wear special protective clothing . . .

5

MAN: . . . ordinary light consists of electromagnetic waves of different frequencies and phase. This is a bundle of waves of the same frequency and phase. You can create the beams from a ruby rod or a tube of carbon dioxide that's stimulated with flashes of ordinary light. The word is an acronym for Light Amplification by the Stimulated Emission of Radiation. Now, does anybody . . .

6

MAN: . . . they're all types of fungus. There are many different kinds of them but the best known are the ones used in cooking and brewing. When they're mixed with sugar they cause the sugar to ferment and two things happen: first carbon dioxide is given off and second alcohol is formed, but when the proportion reaches 12% it's all killed off naturally. . . .

7

WOMAN: . . . Well, it *might* be useful to have them with you but usually they're too heavy to carry around so you have to go to a special place to consult it. They don't have an index or even a table of contents but they do have cross-references, but still it's relatively easy to use them . . .

8

MAN: . . . two bodies are in contact with each other, there's a resistance to movement between them. The main reason why we use ball bearings and lubricating oil is to counteract this: the main reason why rubber is used in tyres and shoes is to increase the effect of it . . .

9

MAN: . . . No, it's the process whereby materials are used again. Normally it's cheaper to do this because it's more energy-efficient. On the other hand, one

material that's hard to deal with in this way is plastic – there are so many types that it's very difficult to separate . . .

10

WOMAN: . . . and their molecules all contain hydrogen atoms some of which separate from the molecules when dissolved in water. The hydrogen atoms become electrically charged and they have a strong tendency to react with other substances. Vinegar? Yes, that's right, yes, that is one, yes. Another one that's used in all kinds of industrial processes is . . .

(12.2) First day at school

Listening and Speaking

Laurie Lee was born in 1914 and died in 1997. His best-known book is *Cider with Rosie*, an account of his childhood in rural Gloucestershire. He is well known as a poet and for two autobiographical works about his travels round Spain: *As I Walked Out One Midsummer Morning* and *A Rose for Winter*.

Evelyn Waugh (1903–1966) is one of the foremost English novelists of the 20th century. His most enjoyable satirical novels are: *Scoop, Brideshead Revisited, A Handful of Dust* and *Black Mischief*.

A1 First the students read the extract and try to guess what happened next.

 2 Play the recording – it's a straightforward reading from the book, which is quite amusing.

Transcript   1 minute 15 seconds

The morning came, without any warning, when my sisters surrounded me, wrapped me in scarves, tied up my bootlaces, thrust a cap on my head, and stuffed a baked potato in my pocket.
'What's this?' I said.
'You're starting school today.'
'I ain't. I'm stopping 'ome.'
'Now, come on, Laurie. You're a big boy now.'
'I ain't.'
'You are.'
'Boo-hoo.'
They picked me up bodily, kicking and bawling, and carried me up to the road.
'Boys who don't go to school, get put in boxes, and turn into rabbits and get chopped up Sundays.'
I felt this was overdoing it rather, but I said no more after that.

I spent that first day picking holes in paper, then went home in a smouldering temper.
'What's the matter, Laurie? Didn't you like it at school then?'
'They never gave me the present!'
'Present? What present?'
'They said they'd give me a present.'
'Well, now, I'm sure they didn't.'
'They did! They said: "You're Laurie Lee, ain't you? Well, you just sit there for the present." I sat there all day but I never got it. I ain't going back there again!'

3 Again, the students guess what might happen next.

 4 Play the recording – it's a hilarious scene which gives lots of people the giggles when they think about it.

Transcript 1 minute 30 seconds

The masters went upstairs.

'That's your little mob in there,' said Grimes; 'you let them out at eleven.'

'But what am I to teach them?' said Paul in a sudden panic.

'Oh, I shouldn't try to teach them anything, not just yet, anyway. Just keep them quiet.'

'Now that's a thing I've never learned to do,' sighed Mr Prendergast.

Paul watched him amble into his classroom at the end of the passage, where a burst of applause greeted his arrival. Dumb with terror he went into his own classroom.

Ten boys sat before him, their hands folded, their eyes bright with expectation.

'Good morning, sir,' said the one nearest to him.

'Good morning,' said Paul.

'Good morning, sir,' said the next.

'Good morning,' said Paul.

'Good morning, sir,' said the next.

'Oh, shut up,' said Paul.

At this the boy took out a handkerchief and began to cry quietly.

'Oh, sir,' came a chorus of reproach, 'you've hurt his feelings. He's very sensitive; it's his Welsh blood, you know; it makes people very emotional. Say "Good morning" to him, sir, or he won't be happy all day. After all, it is a good morning, isn't it, sir?'

'Silence!' shouted Paul above the uproar, and for a few moments things were quieter.

B 1 Combine the pairs into groups.

✒ 2 This could be prepared in class (in the same groups as B1) before being written for homework.

Here are some reassuring phrases that could be written on the board if your students need some guidance:

There's no need to worry because . . .
I'm sure things will turn out all right.
Everyone feels like that at first . . .
After a few days you'll make friends and feel at home.

(12.3) Education systems Reading

A ANSWERS

A British university year is divided into three *terms*. Students are known as *undergraduates*. At the end of a university course, graduates are awarded a *degree* – probably a BA (*Bachelor of Arts*), BSc (*Bachelor of Science*) or BEd (*Bachelor of Education*). After graduating, if they wish to continue at university, *postgraduates* can take a further course or do *research* and write a *dissertation/thesis** in the hope of becoming an MA (*Master of Arts*) or a PhD (*Doctor of Philosophy*).

In America, first-year students are known as *freshmen* and second-year students are called *sophomores*. Their year is divided into two *semesters*. A university is often called a *college*.

* a *dissertation* is shorter than a *thesis*

B ANSWERS

2 H **3** L **4** H **5** G **6** G **7** C **8** F **9** H **10** L
11 F **12** D **13** D **14** L **15** J **16** L **17** E **18** D **19** I **20** N

> **CAE exam** In the Reading paper there's often a task which requires candidates to state in which section of a text particular points are mentioned. **12.3 B** helps to develop this skill, but it's not in the same format as an exam task.

C **ANSWERS**

¶D fuming = very angry   pernicious = harmful   nurture = cultivate

¶F A-student = bright pupil   utilitarian = practical   quantification= measurement

¶G continuous assessment = evaluation throughout the course   grades = marks

¶H aspirants = hoping to be admitted

¶J idiosyncrasy = unconventional behaviour   fast stream = top class

¶M efficacy = effectiveness

¶N much-vaunted = over-praised

D1 Make sure everyone asks each other to give their reasons – 'because it's interesting' isn't an explanation!

2 There's a lot to talk about here – tell everyone to choose the ones that seem most provocative: there's no need to start with the first topic.

3 Note the different tasks for multinational and single nationality classes.

12.4 The sixth form   Reading and Creative writing

A **ANSWERS**

1 F   2 H   3 B   4 G   5 D   6 A   7 E   8 C

> **CAE exam**   **12.4 A** is similar to one of the tasks in the English in Use paper. In the exam there are also some phrases or sentences which don't fit anywhere.

B1 Further questions for discussion:
- How old is the writer of the article?
- Why is he not looking forward to his next year at school?
- What does he think he *will* enjoy about next year?

2 Decide with the class which task they're going to do. (The first is probably better CAE exam practice.)

Leo Jones   *New Cambridge Advanced English*

12.4 MODEL VERSION

Dear Tom,

I was interested to read your article but I can't say that I share your feelings entirely. I am one of those who is moving on, in my case to work in Leeds. I have absolutely no sentimental feelings about leaving those companions who we have spent the last twelve years with. I am relieved to finally be able to move out of the tight-knit circle, where privacy was impossible, where everyone knew everything about you: who you'd broken up with, who you were seeing, what you'd done at the weekend, where your dad worked, where you had your hair cut, etc. etc. I am really looking forward to meeting some new people and at long last to being anonymous!

I feel only elation at leaving school and pleasure at never having to face those crabby old teachers again. I know I shall be in a learning situation in my new job but at least I will be a paid employee and have the right to stay or go if I don't like it, unlike at school.

You are right to say though that the friendships we made were forged through geography and shared experience of good and bad times. And I suppose those friends and our home environment will always provide a stable base wherever we go in the future.

Best of luck with your A-levels and say hello to all those mates I am happy to leave behind.

Yours,

Sam

12.5 Comparing and contrasting   Grammar

A1 This exercise may take some time and requires a fair amount of thinking. Allow enough time for this. It could be prepared at home and then discussed in pairs in class. Be prepared for some debate on the interpretation of the chart, particularly the questions about the length of the 'days' and 'years'.

Note that the length of a day (i.e. one revolution of the planet) and a year (i.e. one orbit of the Sun) are given in Earth hours, days and years. When talking about the solar system we can refer to our own planet as *Earth* or *the Earth*.

SUGGESTED ANSWERS

2 further/farther   than

3 distant

4 the closest planet to

5 much/far

6 as

7 further/farther/more distant

8 is much further/farther/more distant from the Sun than

9 as   as

10 only

11 twice

12 half

13 about half the length of / half as long as a day on

14 is about two and a half times as long as

15 same

16 longer

17 slightly shorter than a day on

18 shorter

19 22 days longer than [Venus revolves very slowly as it orbits the Sun, unlike Earth which rotates about 365 times during one orbit of the Sun]

20 other   apart from

2 There are, of course, a huge number of possible sentences, so make sure the students have time to compare their sentences in pairs.

If everyone is getting tired of comparing the planets, they could write sentences comparing the countries of Europe or another continent (populations, areas, distance from their own country, etc.) – but this might need further research, which could take more time.

SUGGESTED ANSWERS

1 Mercury is much nearer to the Sun than any other planet.

2 Venus is about the same size as Earth.

3 Earth is about a tenth the size of Saturn and it hasn't got any rings around it.

4 Mars is half the size of Earth.

5 Jupiter is the largest of all the planets.

6 Saturn is very large, but it isn't as big as Jupiter.

7 Uranus is slightly larger than Neptune, but much closer to the Sun.

8 Neptune is further from the Sun than any other planet, apart from Pluto.

9 Pluto is the planet that's the greatest distance from the Sun, and the second smallest after Mercury.

B1 Arrange the class into an even number of pairs. To start things off, in case some students are bemused by this, brainstorm some ideas with the whole class.

2 Combine the pairs into groups of four (or five).

C Back to schools! Please note that the education system in Scotland is different from that in England and Wales.

ANSWERS

1 most/all 2 longer 3 same 4 as 5 almost/nearly 6 many 7 as 8 as 9 as
10 longer 11 than 12 minimum 13 exactly 14 same 15 most

D1 SUGGESTED ANSWERS   (These are debatable.)

Perhaps more informal and more usual in conversation:

is rather like   is similar to   is much the same as   reminds me of   seems like
has a lot in common with

In the same way, . . .

is quite different from   isn't the same as   is nothing like

Perhaps more formal and more usual in writing:

is comparable to   is equivalent to   resembles

Similarly, . . .   Moreover, . . .

is very unlike   differs from   bears no resemblance to   has very little in common with

On the other hand, . . .   In contrast, . . .   Conversely, . . .   However, . . .

2 To start the ball rolling, perhaps discuss the first two topics as a class before arranging everyone into groups of three or four. There's plenty to talk about here and the students may have to force themselves to use the phrases in D1. The topics can be discussed in any order.

(12.6) How does it work?   Reading, Listening and Creative writing

A Dixons (¶10) is a well-known British high street retailer. They sell electric and electronic goods (TVs, computers, cameras, etc.).

The *Radio Times* (¶E) is a magazine that lists the week's TV and radio programmes.

ANSWERS

3 C 5 A 7 E 9 B (D doesn't fit anywhere.)

B If one can't operate a gadget, whose fault is it: the designer's, the manufacturer's – or the consumer's?

C1 Even the non-technically-minded should be able to guess some of the missing information.

 2 Play the recording, perhaps pausing it from time to time.

SUGGESTED ANSWERS

1 25 **2** 90,000 **3** head **4** tilted **5** diagonal/slanting **6** Two **7** 540,000
8 soundtrack **9** quality **10** two **11** reading **12** writing **13** 2,500 **14** 360

Transcript   2 minutes 30 seconds

PRESENTER: How does a video recorder work?

WOMAN: Right, well, to produce a colour TV picture an enormous amount of information is required: on a TV the screen is scanned at 25 frames per second, that means every second 25 separate pictures flash across the screen of your TV. A one-hour recording alone consists of 90,000 separate pictures. Video recorders use magnetically coated tape, it's the same as normal audio tape but wider, inside a cassette. This tape travels fairly slowly and as it travels, the tape first passes an erase head, which erases previous signals and then it travels around a fast-spinning drum. There are two video recording heads on opposite sides of the spinning drum and the video track is recorded in diagonal stripes across the tape.

Well, the system works like this: this drum is tilted slightly at an angle from the tape so that as the tape goes past this rapidly spinning drum the recording heads pass the tape repeatedly many times, and thereby leaving a message in slanting 'stripes'. OK, so two stripes contain the information required for just one picture. A three-hour video cassette for instance would have 540,000 stripes recorded on it. Then after it's left the spinning drum the tape passes two more heads: the audio head and the control head. The soundtrack is recorded along the top edge of the tape and the control track, which synchronises playback speed to recording speed, is recorded along the bottom edge of the tape. Since the tape moves quite slowly the sound quality of a video tape is not as good as on a cassette recorder. Um…and because of this hi-fi stereo videos have two extra tracks which are recorded in the stripes together with the video signals.

So to play back the tape the same process is used but with the recording heads working as playback heads, so…er…sort of reading the information instead of writing it.

A video recorder contains over 2,500 components, a television only has 360, but the greatest wear is on the recording/playback head, which may need replacing after only about three years.

D1 Arrange the class into an even number of pairs, so that they can combine into groups of four or five in D2. Half the pairs look at **Activity 6**, the other half at **Activity 25**.

2 The pairs join together and share the information they've found out about how a movie projector and a movie soundtrack work.

E Begin by working out suitable instructions for someone on how to operate your classroom cassette player, taking suggestions from the class.

In case the students need some guidelines on the language used when giving instructions, here are some useful phrases:

First of all you . . .
After that, you . . .
The next thing to do is . . .
Don't forget to . . .
Make sure you (don't) . . .
I hope that's all clear.
If you have any questions . . .

In writing, instructions are often given in a numbered list (with imperatives):

1 Lift the lid.
2 Inspect the contents.
3 Take out the largest one.
4 . . .

Leo Jones *New Cambridge Advanced English*

12.6 MODEL VERSION

The washing machine
Sort the clothes to be washed and make sure you don't put delicate fabrics in the normal wash. It's better to wash dark and light coloured fabrics in <u>separate</u> washes.

Load the clothes (not more than $3\frac{1}{2}$ kg).

Fill the detergent bulb with automatic powder or liquid and place it inside the machine on top of the clothes.

Shut the door firmly.

Pour a capful of concentrated fabric conditioner into the small left hand compartment in the detergent drawer.

Select the programme you want by turning the dial (front right of the machine) — there is a chart explaining the programmes on the front of the machine.

Pull the dial out to start the machine. The programmes take between 35 minutes and an hour, depending on which one you select.

The dishwasher
To open the door of the dishwasher you pull a grey catch located at the very top of the machine towards the left. You have to use some force as it is not easy to release the catch. The door drops down towards you.

The top basket of the machine is for cups, glasses etc. while the lower one is for all kinds of plates. The cutlery basket is in the bottom section and has slots to fit the various pieces of cutlery in.

Load the dishwasher, making sure that no pieces of crockery can knock against each other. Load larger plates into the back right of the bottom basket and slightly smaller plates back left, leaving the remaining front section of the bottom basket for tea plates, saucers etc. This is to prevent the rotating metal arms hitting the plates.

You put the detergent tablet inside the compartment in the door and close the lid with a click.

Shut the door firmly.

Set the programme by turning the dial at the right of the machine to the desired number; the normal wash and dry programme is 3. This programme takes about an hour.

© Cambridge University Press, 1998

Ⓐ ANSWERS

1 for **2** off **3** out **4** through **5** up **6** up to **7** into **8** out/off

Ⓑ ANSWERS

1 look out for

2 look me up

3 look out for

4 overlooks

5 looks down on

6 gave me a funny look

7 see eye to eye

8 Look here   onlookers

9 have a look at   look alike

10 see her current project through

11 I'll overlook

12 sightseers

13 see to

14 saw through

15 saw red

16 look back on

Ⓒ SUGGESTED ANSWERS

1 He glanced at . . .   . . . the person sitting opposite on the bus.
. . . the small print in the brochure.

2 She stared at . . .   . . . the painting for a long time.
. . . her with admiration.
. . . the person sitting opposite on the bus.
. . . the small print in the brochure.
. . . the view of the mountains.
. . . the people who were making a noise.

3 He gazed at . . .   . . . the painting for a long time.
. . . her with admiration.
. . . the person sitting opposite on the bus.
. . . the small print in the brochure. (?)
. . . the view of the mountains.

4 She peered at . . .   . . . the painting for a long time.
. . . the person sitting opposite on the bus.
. . . the small print in the brochure.
. . . the view of the mountains. (?)

5 He noticed . . .   . . . the person sitting opposite on the bus.
. . . the small print in the brochure.
. . . the view of the mountains. (?)
. . . the people who were making a noise.

6 She watched . . .   . . . television all evening.
. . . her with admiration.
. . . the person sitting opposite on the bus.
. . . the football match until the end.
. . . the people who were making a noise.

7 He glared at . . .   . . . the person sitting opposite on the bus.
. . . the people who were making a noise.

13.1 **The art of conversation** **Listening and Vocabulary**

A **1** Everyone should look at the cartoon to start with.

 2 Play the recording. In some cases Sarah, the expert, gives more than one example, but the students need only note down ONE of each.

SUGGESTED ANSWERS

1 smile / raise an eyebrow encouragingly

2 50–60 cm for North Americans or Northern Europeans / 20–30 cm for Latin Americans

3 sitting next to each other / standing in a relaxed manner / facing each other

4 handshakes

5 'Hello' / 'Nice to see you'

6 'Lovely day' / 'How are things with you?'

7 smile / friendly look

8 looking at your watch

9 'It's been nice talking to you'

10 move backwards / start to go

Transcript   3 minutes 10 seconds

PRESENTER: OK, what is a conversation? Now, a conversation may seem to you and me just to be two people having a chat, exchanging words, exchanging ideas, but it seems that without the right kind of non-verbal behaviour it would probably be impossible to start. Sarah Newby explains why. Sarah.

SARAH: Well, Terry, the stages of a typical conversation can be summarised in a most interesting way. There's nothing new about this analysis, like much of sociology we're just looking at human behaviour in a scientific way and drawing attention to its underlying structure.

PRESENTER: OK.

SARAH: So, let's begin with the so-called 'opening phase'. Now this begins by the two would-be participants making eye contact. In other words, one of them catches the other's eye . . .

PRESENTER: Right.

SARAH: Right? And then both of them have to switch on 'conventional facial expressions'.

PRESENTER: Oh, hang on, hang on.

SARAH: W…no no, all it means really is that th…they smile or one raises an eyebrow encouragingly or something like that . . .

PRESENTER: Oh, I see, yes.

SARAH: Then they reach a…a 'position of comfortable proximity'.

PRESENTER: W…what is…what does that mean?

SARAH: Well, er…basically we're talking about distance. Er…for North Americans or…or…or Northern Europeans 50 to 60 centimetres apart i…is usual. But for Latin Americans: 20 to 30 centimetres.

PRESENTER: Wow! What happens when you get a North American talking to a Latin American?

SARAH: Well, that actually is a very good point . . .

PRESENTER: Yeah?

SARAH: . . . because of course what usually happens is that…that the…the…um… North American will step backwards to try and make some kind of comfortable distance between them.

PRESENTER: Because the Latin American is invading his personal space.

SARAH: Absolutely right!

PRESENTER: I know it.

SARAH: Er…then of course what they do is adopt an 'appropriate posture'.

PRESENTER: Like…?

SARAH: Well, it could be…er…sitting next to each other, or…or standing in a relaxed manner, or…or facing each other.

PRESENTER: OK.

SARAH: Er…at that point they exchange 'ritual gestures and phrases of greeting'.

PRESENTER: W…really? What, even here?

SARAH: Of course, things like: handshakes, 'Hello', er… 'Nice to see you'— all that sort of thing . . .

PRESENTER: I see.

SARAH: Right?

PRESENTER: Yeah.

SARAH: Then they exchange 'stereotyped channel-opening remarks'.

PRESENTER: Now you're going to have to explain that one.

SARAH: Of course, of course: 'Lovely day!'… er…'How are things with you?'

PRESENTER: I see.

SARAH: And then of course the…the main business phase begins, so the actual discussion or conversation takes place.

PRESENTER: The main bulk of the conversation.

SARAH: Absolutely right. Then we come to the 'parting phase', th…the actual ending of the conversation when one or both of them decide it's time to stop. So what they do is they exchange 'appropriate cordial facial expressions'.

PRESENTER: Has to be cordial?

SARAH: Usually. A smile or a friendly look is helpful.

PRESENTER: OK.

SARAH: And then of course we have the exchange of 'ritual gestures and phrases of parting'.

PRESENTER: Wow.

SARAH: This can take the form of…of looking at your watch, er…saying 'It's…er…it's been nice talking to you' . . .

PRESENTER: Oh, right.

SARAH: …and then what usually happens is a…an 'increase of distance between them': y…you start to move, move backwards, starting to go. Er…then both partners break eye contact and the conversation is ended.

PRESENTER: Well! Thank you very much indeed, Sarah. Now, aha, next time I meet someone I think I'll be watching myself to make sure I obey all the rules!

B After the groups have come up with their ideas, reassemble the class to continue the discussion.

CAE exam	In the Speaking paper, some candidates may be paired with a person they haven't met before. It might be helpful to discuss how their behaviour when meeting someone new in real life might differ from how they'd behave in the exam – with a view to minimising the awkwardness of the exam-day situation.

C ANSWERS

1 colloquial   informal   formal   slang   appropriately   swear words   jargon

2 tone of voice   gestures   body language   expression   sarcastic

3 saying/expression   proverbs

Bad language, bilingual, intonation, regional and *stress* don't fit in any gaps.

(13.2) Joining sentences — 2   Effective writing

A1 SUGGESTED ANSWERS

1 A dialect is a variety of a language *which* uses . . .

2 *no changes*

3 *no changes*

4 The office *that* he works *in/where* he works has fluorescent lighting . . .

5 . . . in the new shopping centre, *that* we went to last weekend

2 SUGGESTED ANSWER

Paul has just got engaged to Tracy, who is the daughter of Claire and Frank. They are the owners of Acme Bookshops Ltd, which has just opened a branch in the new shopping centre. We went there last weekend with David, who used to go out with Tracy. Did you know that David's best friend is Paul? It's a small world, isn't it!

B Sentences 4 and 5 are quotes from the extract on 'Symbolic Gestures' on page 115 in the Student's Book.

SUGGESTED ANSWERS

1 Albert Sukoff wrote a long article, doing so without the use of a single full stop.

2 The first island discovered by Columbus was one of the Bahamas.

3 Realising what had happened, she (immediately) called the police.

4 You might rotate your forefinger against your temple, indicating 'a screw loose'.

5 You might rotate your finger close to your temple, signalling that the brain is going round and round.

C **ANSWERS** (Notice the presence or absence of commas.)

1 The person *whose* phone number you gave me was not very helpful.

2 The most important point (*that*) he made was that we should approach each culture with an open mind.

3 The person *I spoke to* / *to whom I spoke* was rather rude, which upset me.

4 Thanks to Pat, without *whose* help the work would have been impossible.

5 *Considering* that you're so clever and you're the one that *knows* the answers (,) I'm surprised you got it wrong.

D **SUGGESTED ANSWERS**

2 After hearing about their plans he was upset and angry.

3 Feeling absolutely furious, he pushed over the table, knocking our best glasses (on)to the floor.

4 While (he was) picking up the broken glass, he cut his finger, which started bleeding.

5 Taking his handkerchief from his pocket, he wrapped it round the cut.

6 After gathering up the broken pieces, which were on the floor, he apologised.

7 Realising how stupid he had been, he offered to replace the broken glasses.

8 He intended to buy us a new set of glasses and, knowing they were good quality ones, he went to a store in town which had/has a good stock of glassware.

9 Looking round the store, he discovered the glasses were very expensive, which gave him quite a shock.

10 Since breaking those glasses he has been careful to keep his temper!

(13.3) Gestures   Reading

A **SUGGESTED ANSWERS**

1 They both communicate information to an onlooker

2 An incidental gesture

3 A primary gesture

4 It's used ironically

5 Six or seven

6 Eleven

7 By approaching each culture with an open mind

If there's time . . .

▼ The extracts on pages 114–5 contain a lot of useful vocabulary – ask everyone to highlight ONE or TWO words in each paragraph that they would like to remember, and use a dictionary to look up the meanings and see further examples.

To start everyone off, look at the first paragraph of the first extract and discuss which TWO 'new' words or phrases seem the most useful. These might include two of these:

signal   deliberately   incidentally   primary   secondary

Here are some of the more useful words and phrases in each paragraph of the two extracts:

GESTURES

¶2 distinction   illuminating   censor

¶3 wink   animatedly

SYMBOLIC GESTURES

¶1 abstract   equivalent

¶2 full-blooded   mime   momentary   stable

¶3 forefinger   forehead

¶4 mistrust   scepticism   alertness   craftiness   chaos   symbolism

¶5 open mind

B These are questions for discussion. Some other examples of incidental gestures: sneeze, cough, sniff, sigh, etc. And examples of primary gestures: thumbs up, wink, point, applause, smacking lips, etc.

Many of the gestures mentioned in the second question can be 'acted' – people sometimes pretend to be puzzled, unhappy, etc.

C Missing from the illustrations are: the rude British two fingers gesture and equivalent American one finger gesture. Also the innocuous British 'Stop', which Greeks may confuse with the obscene *moutza* gesture. Note that some of the British ones shown here may be terribly rude to some nationalities – but this is something everyone should be aware of.

SUGGESTED INTERPRETATIONS

A   Everything's fine

B   I'd like a lift (hitchhiking)

C   Everything's OK

D   Can I pay the bill? (in a restaurant)

E   Two, please

F   He's stupid

G   We understand each other

H   I'm better than you (cocking a snook)

I   Don't tell a soul, keep mum!

J   Come here

K   I'm warning you

L *to O don't really mean anything in Britain.*

13.4 You just don't understand!   Reading

Before **John Gray, Ph.D**, became a relationships guru he had a variety of jobs, including a spell as the press officer for the Maharishi Mahesh Yogi. The extract on page 116 is from his best-known book, *Men Are from Mars Women Are from Venus : a Practical Guide for Improving Communication and Getting What You Want in Your Relationships* (1992). Among his other books are: *What You Feel, You Can Heal : A Guide for Enriching Relationships* and *Men, Women and Relationships: Making Peace with the Opposite Sex.*

Deborah Tannen is Professor of Linguistics at Georgetown University in Washington DC. This extract is from her best-known book, *You Just Don't Understand : Women and Men in Conversation* (1991). Her other popular books include: *That's Not What I Meant: How Conversational Style Makes or Breaks your Relations with Others*, and *Talking from 9 to 5: How Women's and Men's Conversational Styles Affects Who Gets Heard, Who Gets Credit, and What Gets Done at Work*. As an academic she also publishes scholarly books including *Conversational Style: Analyzing Talk Among Friends* and *Talking Voices: Repetition, Dialogue, and Imagery in Conversational Discourse*.

Ⓐ ANSWERS

1 DT   **2** JG   **3** JG   **4** DT   **5** N   **6** DT   **7** DT   **8** JG   **9** JG   **10** JG   **11** N   **12** JG   **13** DT

If there's time . . .

The extracts on pages 116–7 contain a lot of useful vocabulary – ask everyone to highlight one or two words in each paragraph that they would like to remember, and use a dictionary to look up the meanings and see further examples.

To start everyone off, look at the first two paragraphs of the first extract and discuss which TWO 'new' words or phrases seem the most useful. These might include two of these:

glimpsing   awakened   with open arms   intuitively

Here are some of the more useful words and phrases in each paragraph of the two extracts:

John Gray

¶3 reveled (GB revelled)   harmony

¶4 selective   amnesia

¶5 erased

¶6 at odds

¶7 lovingly

¶8 respond   friction

¶9 respecting

Deborah Tannen

¶1 assertiveness training   winding up

¶2 partners

¶3 inclined

¶4 illogical   insecure   put me down   no-fault negotiation   adjustments casting blame

¶5 arising   spiraling (GB spiralling)   stalemate   communication gap

Ⓑ The students may have to read the two extracts again before they can discuss these questions.

Note that this discussion might get too personal for some students' comfort. If any members of your class are recently divorced or in some sort of crisis in their relationship, you may have to skip this section.

(13.5) Advertising   Listening and Creative writing

 Ⓐ Play the recording after everyone has had time to read the questions through.

SUGGESTED ANSWERS

1 the visual aspect   **2** the words   **3** partnership   **4** 30 seconds
5 an individual / lots of individuals at the same time   **6** low   **7** intelligence
8 unknown concept   **9** solicitor   **10** He mentions ALL the qualities except:
adaptability, ambition, listening to others, realism, working in a team

Transcript   7 minutes 15 seconds

BOB: My name's…er…Bob Stanners, and I'm…
er…an advertising copywriter. I write
advertisements, is…is what I do, and…
er…in the advertising business the people
who create advertisements, who write
them and…er…and see them through to
the finished product, they work normally
with an art director, who broadly is
responsible for the visual aspect of…of
advertising…advertisements, and…and a
copywriter, who is responsible for the…
er…basically the words. But in fact jointly
they…really they sit down and they
function like…um…like a…a partnership
and between them they create
advertisements.

INTERVIEWER: Have you had the same partner for
a while, or … ?

BOB: Um…well, one tends to, yes, set up
partnerships and it's all a question
of…of finding someone with whom you
have a good chemistry, er…someone
who you can fight with and…um…
struggle with and have arguments with…
er… and forgive them . . .

INTERVIEWER: Bit like a good marriage!

BOB: It is a bit like a good marriage.

INTERVIEWER: And what do you really enjoy
about the…the job?

BOB: I enjoy I suppose…er…I suppose it's
solving a problem, it's…er…solving a
problem in a way that involves an act of
creativity. And it is working out…it…
it's…it's a very…um…structured thing,
it's a very tight discipline, advertising. It's
much easier, for instance, as you can
imagine to…er…write 15 minutes of
dialogue than 30 seconds of dialogue
where every word has to count. So I…I
enjoy solving a problem and finding
what it is that will *communicate* in a
rewarding, in a winning way…er…to the
consumer. Er…but basically we are
salesmen and if people selling products
could have door-to-door salesmen going
round knocking on the door and putting
an argument person-to-person to people
they would. But that's a very expensive
w…way of doing it, so we are doing it
on a mass basis but it's still one-to-one
s…sell, I mean an advertisement has to
appeal to an individual. But we have to
try and find a way that will appeal to lots
of individuals at the same time.

INTERVIEWER: And what…what do you *not* enjoy?

BOB: Well, what I don't enjoy is … One of the
problems is that you have to please both
your client, the person whose product
you're trying to sell, you have to please

them as well as yourself and the person
that you are selling to. And very often I
think one of the major problems is when
clients basically aim too low. I think most
advertising people, myself included, try
and find the highest common
denominator of communication. I don't
believe you can overestimate the
consumer's intelligence. Provided you
know that you're not going over their
heads, you should give them credit for
intelligence. And I think lots of clients
would rather you didn't give the consumer
any credit for having any intelligence.

INTERVIEWER: What are you proudest of having
done, do you think? Which particular
campaign?

BOB: Creatively…er… one of the things I think
I'm most proud of was, the idea we…that
was used on Perrier, er…which is a
bottled water, which was an unknown
concept to the British, strange as it may
seem now. Twenty years ago if you'd have
suggested that people would happily pay
£1 or £2 for a bottle of water you'd have
been laughed at. We introduced the…er…
the product into this country as 'Perrier
from the people who brought you food',
um…which indicated its French heritage.
And one of the ads which was…um…
well recognised was the one which said
'PICASSEAU', which had a Cubist
bottle…er…with…er…square bubbles
and a square slice of lemon on the glass.
And then another one which…er…
created a lot of stir, which was a young
lad getting his dad to…er…come along to
McDonald's with him, where he knew
that…er…his mother would be – the
parents were estranged – and…er…he
was instrumental in possibly engineering
a reunion, which got us into very hot
water with…er…various people who
suggested we were promising that…
er…a visit to McDonald's would solve
children's problems if they came from a
split home. If you think about it, it was
an understandable worry but then it was
in fact based on a chance remark that my
son, who is a…a solicitor, said which is
that the most frequent meeting place
for…um…divorced couples…er…with
children is McDonald's. So it was…it was
actually taking a truth and writing a little
play about it.

INTERVIEWER: If someone asked you, 'What do I
need to be or to have to make a good
copywriter?'

BOB: Well, I think you have to have an

analytical brain. I think you have to have boundless optimism. You have to have a…an almost childlike faith in what you're doing. Er…you have to be able to get up when you're knocked down and come back with a…with a new solution. You have to like selling, I suppose, you have to like putting over an argument on behalf of something. And you do have to have, I suppose, a common touch.

INTERVIEWER: A good communicator.

BOB: You have to be a good communicator. You have to make sense to people. Er…I think it does help to have a good sense of humour and the ability to put that sense of humour across. You mustn't take yourself too seriously. It's a very difficult balance, advertising is a very very important thing but it's not…er…as important as a lot of people think it is. You have to have a sense of proportion about what you're doing. And I think, possibly, never really been asked this question before, but I suppose from my point of view, I think you have to be honest.

B If you can bring a selection of English-language magazine ads to class they could be shared between the groups, and then compared and discussed. (If you can also get some ads from your students' country to compare, that would be splendid.)

C 1 Reassemble the class after the group discussion – how many different reactions are there to the ad?

2 Make sure everyone plans their report carefully, as suggested in the Student's Book.

If the students need some guidelines on writing a report, remind them how a report is structured:

> <u>Title</u>
>
> Opening paragraph as introduction: purpose of the report, summary of your findings, etc.
>
> 1 points
> 2 you
> 3 want
> 4 to
> 5 make
> 6 in numbered paragraphs
>
> Conclusion (and recommendations)

3 Give everyone time to make any last-minute changes to their report before they hand it in.

> **CAE exam**   Candidates may be asked to write a report in Part 2 of the Writing paper. The report may be related to the candidate's real (or imagined) work experience.

Leo Jones   *New Cambridge Advanced English*

13.5 MODEL VERSION

The magazine I'm reporting on is *Empire*, a movie magazine. The magazine has a wide readership, spanning age and class groups. It's actually difficult to identify a "typical" reader as the magazine cannot be classified as a woman's, man's, young or professional person's magazine. It doesn't address itself to specialist interest groups, like for example a yachting weekly or a DIY monthly.

What we can say is that *Empire* concerns people's leisure activities or more specifically, movie-going or video watching. If people are reading a magazine concerned with leisure then the ads should reflect that area of life and be light-hearted, entertaining and funny. So if we take leisure as our starting point, perhaps the ads ought to be concerned with going out to the cinema, clothes, perfumes, make-up for the occasion, transportation to and from the cinema, etc. They should not be heavy or directed towards one particular segment of the population, such as people in their forties or older, those earning more than £35,000 per annum, teenagers, etc.

Having analysed the content of the ads in one issue, I can report that there were ads for videos, films, alcohol, perfume, newspapers and magazines, cars, sports goods and casual clothes, in descending order of frequency. The ads were not particularly sophisticated and conveyed their message visually in a very clear way: a big photograph with a clear caption; no drawings, cartoons, ambiguous messages or verbal humour and there was little attempt at subtlety or wit. I think the magazine has it about right, appealing to anyone who is attracted by the visual medium. Personally I would appreciate a little more humour and word-play but the range of ads seemed fine. However, one thing I wasn't convinced about was the need for such a high proportion of drink ads.

(13.6) Colours   Idioms and collocations

A ANSWERS

1 with great success
2 slightly unwell
3 realistic details about a place
4 unable to distinguish between certain colours
5 different colours show different applications or categories: green for accounts, blue for imports, etc.
6 way in which different colours are used to decorate the room
7 influence in a negative or biased way
8 understand his character for the first time (usually derogatory)

B ANSWERS

1 blue-collar
2 out of the blue
3 red carpet
4 green
5 green with envy
6 saw red
7 red tape
8 give (me) the green light
9 green
10 once in a blue moon
11 in the red
12 red-handed

C ANSWERS

1 black look
2 in black and white
3 black market
4 black comedy
5 black eye
6 white wedding
7 white lie
8 white-collar
9 blackout
10 white elephant

14.1 English in the world

A1 Looking at the map will help. English is spoken as a major first language in Australia, Belize, Canada (+ French), Guyana, Ireland, Jamaica (and many other Caribbean islands), UK, New Zealand, South Africa (+ Afrikaans, Xhosa, Zulu, etc.), USA, etc.

2 ANSWERS

1 300 million   **2** 400 million (300 + 100)   **3** 130 million (50 + 80) – excluding China
4 250,000   **5** over 60 (official and semi-official)   **6** 120   **7** over 1,000 million
8 two thirds of them

B1 English is used as a second language or *lingua franca* in Bangladesh, Botswana, Ghana, India, Kenya, Lesotho, Liberia, Malaysia, Malawi, Namibia, Nigeria, Pakistan, Papua New Guinea, the Philippines, Sri Lanka, Swaziland, Tanzania, Zambia, Zimbabwe, etc.

2 Hopefully the task is fairly easy, but at the same time interesting. Perhaps point out that some educated people in some parts of England 'lose' their local accent and speak RP (Received Pronunciation: the accent of educated, middle-class people from the South-East of England) – or something approaching it.

C Perhaps also ask:

● How many FOREIGN accents of English can you recognise?

● How many non-British and non-American accents can you recognise?

14.2 Indirect speech

A SUGGESTED ANSWERS

1 *He told us that he had visited Australia in the summer.*
= 'I went there in the summer,' is what he said.
He told us that he visited Australia in the summer.
= 'I (usually) go there in the summer,' is what he said.
He told us that he would be visiting Australia in the summer.
= 'I'm going there / I'll be going there,' is what he said.

2 *She asked me if I had been to New Zealand.*
= 'Have you been there?' is what she said.
She asked me when I had been to New Zealand.
= 'When did you go there?' is what she said.
She asked me whether I had been to New Zealand.
= same meaning as first example

3 *David says he wants to visit his relations in Canada.*
= he wants to go there
David said he wanted to visit his relations in Canada.
= same meaning as first example
  OR this is what he said some time ago so maybe he has gone there by now
David said he wants to visit his relations in Canada.
= same meaning as first example – perhaps emphasising that although he said it in the past he *still* wants to go
David said, 'He wanted to visit his relations in Canada.'
= another person wanted to go there, not David himself

4 *Ruth phoned to say that she would be flying to India the next day.*
   = she travelled the day after the phone call
   Ruth phoned to say that she would be flying to India tomorrow.
   = she is going to travel tomorrow
   Ruth phoned to say that she was flying to India the next day.
   = same meaning as first example

5 *I didn't find out when the show starts.*
   = the show is on soon and I need to know when it starts
   I didn't find out when the show started.
   = same meaning as first example
      OR the show is over or has started already
   I didn't find out when the show will start.
   = same meaning as first example
   I didn't find out when the show would start.
   = the show has started or is over, I didn't know the starting time
      OR same meaning as first example

B The class should be divided into groups of four or five – with a class of 11 students, one group should consist of five and the other of six students. Then, within each group, half the students should look at **Activity 7**, the other half at **Activity 26**.

This is a straightforward transformation exercise, rewriting one short text into reported speech and then another into direct speech. However, Activity 7 contains a 'direct version' of text A and a 'reported version' of text B while Activity 26 contains a 'direct version' of text B and a 'reported version' of text A.

In the end there are several versions of each text to compare: the originals and the versions produced by the two pairs. Step-by-step instructions for this are given within both Activities in the Student's Book.

C1 ANSWERS

1 admit   announce   call out   claim   deny   explain   insist   mention   mumble   repeat   reply   scream   shout   suggest   whisper

2 assure   convince   inform   notify   tell   warn

3 allow   ask   beg   encourage   instruct   invite   order   permit   persuade   tell   urge   warn

D SUGGESTED ANSWERS

2 'No, you'll never guess . . . Give up? All right I'll tell you. I'm from Toronto, so I'm not American, I'm Canadian!' Kate said to me.

3 'What lovely handwriting you have!' Jane said to me.

4 'Why don't you enrol for a course in Japanese?' Jerry suggested.

5 'Look, I'm going to pay for everything. Yes, the drinks too,' Pippa said.

6 'Go on: you really ought to go in for it. You've got a good chance of passing, you know that,' Stephen said to me.

7 'Stephen, don't be too confident. It's a long time since I last took an exam, remember!' I said to him.

8 'Excuse me, I'm sorry to have to say this but would you mind not talking so loudly. It is after midnight, you know,' I said to the people in the corridor.

 E This exercise requires students to report the GIST of what is said in the recordings – just a couple of sentences, summarising the salient points. Pause the tape between each speaker.

Leo Jones *New Cambridge Advanced English*

14.2 MODEL ANSWERS

2 Rupert said that he remembered his childhood with pleasure: he lived in London till he was six and then moved to the country, where he lived on an isolated farm in rather simple conditions.

3 Gay said that she was raised in the South of the United States, where it was warm so much that she spent a lot of time playing tennis and swimming. The good weather gave her a sense of freedom and being spontaneous.

4 Enzo's parents were Italian but he was brought up in the heart of the country in England. This meant that he inhabited two worlds: an Italian world at home and an English one outside the front door of his home.

5 Nick said that he was the son of a doctor in Yorkshire, where he lived in a village. All the villagers knew him as the doctor's son.

6 Ken said that he was brought up in Dover and that he remembered his childhood as always hot and sunny. He felt that the famous castle belonged to him and loved being taken to see the flag flying there.

7 Karen said that she never settled anywhere for very long as a child and had to start school in many different regions. Her difficulty was learning the local accent so that she wasn't treated as an outsider by the other children.

© Cambridge University Press, 1998

Transcript   3 minutes 45 seconds

BLAIN: I was brought up in…er…Northern Canada…um…up in very tiny hamlets, I suppose you might call them, where there might be only two hundred people living. In one of the little towns I lived in – it wasn't a town, it was a camp – there were six families only and the nearest town was 180 miles away. The summers were very hot and the winters were *extremely* cold with masses of snow.

RUPERT: Well, I have very fond memories of my childhood: I was born in Holborn in the centre of London and I went to St George the Martyr Primary School but at the age of six we moved out to the country and we lived on a farm and that has very special memories for me. We were cut off from just about everything, we had a phone v…eventually, an outside lavatory, all those sort of 'romantic' ideas about living in the country, which were reality then and…er…looking back on them, very happy memories.

GAY: I was brought up in Greensboro, North Carolina, which is in the United States but it's down South and…um…it was great being a child there really because it was warm all the time and…er…we had a lot of kind of outdoor stuff that we did: we used to play a lot…um…outside, doing tennis and swimming and stuff like that. Um…I think the weather really affected my childhood a lot because…um…there was a kind of sense of freedom and being spontaneous really.

ENZO: I was brought up in Worcestershire in the Midlands and I'm of Italian parents, therefore I had quite a mixed, or mixed-up, childhood. My parents were from a Southern Italian village, therefore life at home was quite…er…Italian and the minute I walked through the door I suddenly had to become English and…er…and Worcestershire being a very English part of the country, a very typical English part of the country, there…er…this was a…a…a big contrast. And I do have good memories about my childhood, although they're mixed up.

NICK: I was brought up in…er…Huddersfield in Yorkshire, or near Huddersfield. Um…and what I remember most is the fact that I was the doctor's son and so…and we had the surgery in the house, so there were always people coming to…er…to be treated or to see my father and then when I was old enough to be out in the village people would see me as 'Dr Michael's boy' and that was…it was like a little identity without even having to work at it.

KEN: Well, I was brought up in Dover, which is a small town on the south-east coast. Um…I can remember happy sunshiney days…er…paddling in and out of the sea with my bucket and spade and…er…the weather always seemed to be hot and sunny then. Er…there's also a big castle in Dover, which I used to think of as being exclusively mine because it…it's a Norman castle and shaped like a fort, so

a big treat was to be taken up there to see the flag flying on the top of the keep. I have very happy memories of my childhood, yes.

KAREN: I can't actually say where I was brought up because up until the age of fourteen I hadn't lived anywhere for longer than two years. I was brought up throughout Britain: in the areas around London, on the Isle of Man, through the Midlands, in the North of England and in Scotland. And consequently, as I was going to school, I had to learn each accent of the particular area very quickly because children can be very unkind if you don't fit in.

(14.3) Spelling and pronunciation 1 – Consonants
Pronunciation and Word study

 A Play the recording after everyone has done the exercise, either working alone or in pairs. This will give them a chance to make any corrections to the answers they've noted down. (40 seconds)

ANSWERS

/tʃ/	future literature march picture question
/ʃ/	insurance machine moustache opposition partial
/ʒ/	beige decision vision prestige
/dʒ/	average badge cabbage courage damage injury

 B Again, play the recording after everyone has done the exercise. (45 seconds)

ANSWERS

/g/	signature guilty gherkin giggle
/f/	draught laughter
/dʒ/	gesture margarine gypsy gymnasium generation ginger George genuine engineer genius
[silent]	nought sign thorough sigh naughty borough drought

 C Play the recording after everyone has attempted the exercise. (45 seconds)

ANSWERS

/b/	<u>symbol</u> <u>bribed</u>
/g/	<u>hungry</u> <u>ignorance</u>
/h/	<u>rehearsal</u> <u>behalf</u> <u>inherit</u>
/l/	<u>yield</u> <u>failure</u>
/p/	<u>couple</u> <u>hypnotise</u>
/t/	<u>attitude</u> <u>bright</u>
/d/	<u>sadness</u> <u>second-hand</u>

> **CAE exam** Pronunciation is only one of five criteria used to assess candidates in the Speaking paper. Candidates are generally only penalised for non-native sounds where these impede communication by producing ambiguity. Pronunciation also includes stress and intonation for the purposes of assessment, however.

D1 ANSWERS

The only correct ones are:

advertisement   four o'clock   reliable

Correct spellings:

accommodation   argument   committee   developing   embarrassed   independent
medicine   pronunciation   receive   replacing   responsibility   seize   skilful (US
skilful)   therefore   until

▼2 Make sure everyone takes the time to do this.

E1 ANSWERS

draught beer   favour   honour   humour   jewellery   labour   pyjamas   quarrelling
skilful   speciality   theatre   traveller's cheque   travelling   TV programme   woollen

2 Some more examples (British word first):

analyse · analyze   behaviour · behavior   favourite · favorite   neighbour · neighbor
storey · story (building)   plough · plow   axe · ax   tyre · tire (car)

Note that although the nouns *humour* and *glamour* are spelt with a *u* in British English the
adjectives are *humorous* and *glamorous* in both varieties.

CAE exam   Spelling is important in the exam:

In the English in Use paper all words should be spelt correctly to gain
marks. Misspelt words count as wrong answers.

In the Writing paper spelling is only one of a number of criteria used
to assess each task.

In the Listening paper words in note-taking and sentence-completion
tasks should be correctly spelt but the questions don't usually focus
on words that are likely to cause spelling problems for students at this
level.

➡ There's more on British and American English in 14.5 on page 126.

14.4   I ♥ signs   Speaking and Writing

A   The purpose of this activity is to provoke discussion and encourage the students to talk
about the ideas they associate with each slogan. However, to settle any arguments, here are
the origins of some of the slogans:

I ♥ New York	1970s tourist advertisements
Power to the people	socialism
Survival of the fittest	Charles Darwin
Unity is strength	trade union movement
The customer is always right	H. Gordon Selfridge (owner of Selfridge's department store)
Feed the world	Band Aid concert
Make love not war	the 1960s peace movement
All you need is love	Lennon & McCartney
Liberty, fraternity, equality	French Revolution
Workers of the world unite	Karl Marx
Small is beautiful	E.M. Schumacher
Nuclear power – no thanks	1960s anti-nuclear movement
The world's favourite airline	British Airways advertisement
One man, one vote	Basic principle of democracy, better expressed as *One person, one vote*

A few more slogans:

Man was born free but everywhere he is in chains – Jean-Jacques Rousseau
Government for the people and by the people – Abraham Lincoln
The ballot is mightier than the bullet – attributed to Abraham Lincoln
Coca Cola is it   Feel the spirit   Enjoy Coca Cola ice cold

B Again the idea is to provoke discussion, but here are the 'answers':

Mercedes Benz logo   recycling   access for wheelchairs   Woolmark – pure new wool
no smoking   poison   Mickey Mouse   Volkswagen   gents/men's toilet
ladies/women's toilet   telephone   rewind   pause   an environmentally friendly product

C Hopefully the students will encourage each other to explain what each sign tells you to do or not do.

SUGGESTED ANSWERS

Drive slowly: there are children in this area
You're approaching a level crossing without a gate or barrier
You may experience a dangerous sidewind (windsock)
There may be falling or fallen rocks on this stretch of road
The road ahead is uneven
You're approaching a hospital
This way to the car ferry
This way to the beach
No pedestrians are allowed on this road
Wild animals may be crossing the road, drive carefully
You're approaching a speed bump – drive very slowly
The right-hand lane ahead is closed – drive in the left-hand lanes
You're approaching a contraflow: the two lanes on the left change to the opposite carriageway
This path is reserved for cycles and pedestrians only
There's a picnic site ahead
There's a leisure or sports centre ahead
You aren't allowed to park or wait here at any time

D1 First the students speculate on the possible meanings of the signs, all of which are genuine examples of bad English! Do the first one as a whole-class activity to get things going. (This activity gives everyone a chance to feel 'clever' because they wouldn't make the same mistakes themselves!)

2 The rewriting can be done in pairs or alone. Before everyone attempts these brainstorm ideas for the first one, which means:

1 Unsupervised children's play area

SUGGESTED ANSWERS

2 Your luggage will be sent wherever you go.

3 Ladies, leave your washing here and enjoy the afternoon.

4 Our wines are excellent.

5 We are sorry but no ice cream is available today.

6 Heating and air-conditioning: please adjust the controls to the temperature you prefer.

7 Ladies: Children are not permitted in the bar.

8 The chambermaid will be pleased to do any ironing you require.

9 Any complaints can be made at the office between 9 and 11 am daily.

10 Please leave your valuables at the front desk / at reception.

11 Please ask if you require the services of the chambermaid.

12 Visitors are not allowed to feed the animals. Only the keeper is allowed to give food to them.

E Only some of the mistakes are underlined here:

FIRE <u>PROOFER</u> INSTRUCTIONS FOR THE TENANTS

1) <u>Advice</u> the plan which is in front of you <u>in board</u> where <u>are marked</u> the exits, the corridors, the place of the portable fire <u>engines</u>, etc.

2) Ask what the signs mean, <u>where are located at</u> the corridors on each exit, elevators, etc.

3) When the alarm system rings <u>for fire</u> don't be <u>in</u> panic, keep calm and follow the instructions.

4) When you realise that there is <u>fire</u> inform the staff of the hotel <u>with</u> the best possible <u>way</u> and if you are capable act <u>for extinction</u> with fire <u>engine</u>.

5) Follow the instructions which you <u>are listening</u> from <u>microphones</u>.

6) Don't use the elevators in case of fire <u>explotion</u>, but the steps.

7) We inform you that it is not allowed to use spirit lamp stoves in the room, or other heat <u>appartus</u> of open (unprotected) flame.

8) When you leave your room check if there are lighted <u>cigaretts</u> left or any other electric apparatus on.

Leo Jones *New Cambridge Advanced English*

14.4 MODEL VERSION

FIRE PRECAUTIONS FOR RESIDENTS

1) Please look at the plan on the board showing the corridors and fire exits, and the location of the fire extinguishers, etc.

2) If you are in any doubt, please ask a member of staff to explain the signs which are located in the corridors near each exit and elevator.

3) If the fire alarm bell rings, do not panic. Keep calm and follow the instructions you are given.

4) If you believe that there is a fire, inform the staff of the hotel immediately. If possible deal with the fire using a fire extinguisher.

5) Follow any instructions you hear from the loudspeakers.

6) In case of fire use the stairs – do not use the elevators.

7) The use of camping stoves or any open-flame heating appliances in your room is not permitted.

8) Whenever you leave your room, please make sure that all lighted cigarettes have been put out, and that all electrical appliances have been switched off.

F It will probably be necessary to brainstorm ideas for this. If there are already fire instructions on the classroom noticeboard, they may need to be concealed while this is happening!

14.5 British and American English — Word study

As this is a tricky subject, your students may require some extra information: see below. Please refer to *CIDE* or another up-to-date dictionary if you're unsure about the meaning or usage of any of the items in this section.

 A The answers are recorded on the cassette. (1 minute)

Don't play the tape until everyone has finished the exercise. Please note that the words given in the two lists are simply the most common terms used in each variety. The asterisks in the Student's Book show the terms that are also used in the other variety.

ANSWERS

American	British
apartment	flat
attorney	solicitor/barrister
to call someone	to ring someone up
checkmark	tick
closet	cupboard/wardrobe
couch	sofa
downtown	city centre/town centre
drugstore/pharmacy	chemist's
the fall	autumn
faucet	tap
garbage/trash	rubbish
movie theater	cinema
potato chips	potato crisps
schedule	timetable
sidewalk	pavement
zero	nought
zipper	zip

B1 ANSWERS

	British	American
2	ground lift first	first elevator second
3	trousers waistcoat	pants vest
4	underground	subway
5	queue railway	stand on line railroad
6	motorway petrol	freeway/highway (*or* interstate/turnpike/expressway) gas
7	torch	flashlight
8	mobile phone	cellphone/cellular phone
9	CV (= *curriculum vitae*)	resumé (*can also be written as* resume *or* résumé)
10	toilet (*or* loo)	bathroom (*or* restroom *in a public building*)

2 Some more examples:

British	American
pants	shorts
subway	pedestrian underpass
vest	undershirt/T-shirt
dinner jacket	tuxedo
first year student	freshman
handbag	purse
road surface	pavement
prawn	shrimp
sales clerk	shop assistant
second year student	sophomore
sweet or pudding	dessert

sweets	candy
tights	pantihose
to be ill	to be sick
to grill	to broil
bonnet	hood
boot	trunk
car park	parking lot
estate car	station wagon
flyover	overpass
roundabout	traffic circle
saloon	sedan
silencer	muffler
windscreen	windshield
wing	fender
etc.	*etc.*

 There are also a few differences in the GRAMMAR used in British and American English, as shown in these examples of American usage:

Did you go there already?
Did you ever go there?

They had already gotten off the plane.
He's gotten much slimmer since I last saw him.
(but I've got plenty of time.)

If I would have known I could have helped you.   (in some US dialects)
'Do you have a dictionary? / Have you got a dictionary?'
'Yes, I do.'

CAE exam In the Writing paper the use of American English is acceptable as long as it's consistent: students should avoid using a mixture of American and British terms in the same writing task.

In the English in Use and Listening papers American spellings are generally accepted as alternatives.

In the Speaking paper American, or other non-British, pronunciation features are acceptable.

14.6 *Speaking* **and** *thinking*   **Verbs and idioms**

Ⓐ ANSWERS

1 tell

2 tell   say

3 say   told

4 call (me) back   = phone again another time

5 think it over   = consider for a period of time
   talk over   = discuss

6 talk him into   = persuade

7 talk down to   = speak in condescendingly simple language

8 speak up   = speak more loudly

9 call off   = cancel

10 speak out/up   = give one's opinions freely

11 told off   = disciplined

12 tell them apart   = distinguish between

B **ANSWERS**

1 say when
2 talk shop
3 not on speaking terms
4 It goes without saying
5 You can say that again!
6 easier said than done
7 No sooner said than done
8 speaks her mind
9 called his bluff
10 don't think much of
11 thinking aloud
12 thought better of it
13 talking point
14 think again

➡ Some other related idioms:

call someone names	= insult
to say nothing of	= without even mentioning
speak for yourself	= give your personal opinion
so to speak	= as it were, speaking metaphorically
talk of the devil	= you are / here is the person we were just talking about
to say the least	= without exaggerating
to have second thoughts	= change your mind

15.1 Truth or fiction

Speaking and Reading

A 1 Some words that might come up are:

enigma   mystery   weird   odd   déjà vu   uncomfortable   creepy   horror   fallacy
illusion   supernatural   paranormal   occult   uneasy   ambiguous   obscure   scary

> **CAE exam**   Students who are taking the exam could use the pictures to practise talking for one minute, comparing and contrasting the two pictures and saying how they make you feel. Before they attempt this task, encourage them to think of all the things they could say.
>
> There's more practice in comparing and contrasting pictures in the Communication Activity in **15.2 D1**.

2 Play the first part of the story. Ask everyone to suggest what might have happened next.

Transcript   1 minute

WOMAN: OK, well, this happened to one of my best girlfriend's best friends and her father, so I know it's true. They were driving along this country road on their way home from their cabin in the mountains and they saw this young girl standing there by the side of the road hitchhiking. So they stopped and they picked her up because it was really weird that she was out there alone at that time of night, it was really late. And she got in the back seat and then she told the girl and her father that she lived in this house about five miles up the road. And she didn't say anything after that but she just turned around and looked out of the window. OK, so they start driving to her house and she was still really quiet so they sha…thought she was asleep. And then they got to the house, drove up to it, they turned around to tell her that they were there – and there was nobody in the back seat!

3 Play the end of the story.

Transcript   40 seconds

So they were very very confused and they didn't know what to do and they talked about it and they decided they'd knock on the door and they'd tell the people there what happened. OK, so the people in the house answered the door and guess what? They told them that they once had a daughter who looked like the girl that they had picked up, but she had disappeared a long time ago and was last seen hitchhiking on that very road and that that day would have been her birthday.

B   In England the following are thought to be 'lucky': a black cat crossing the road in front of you, keeping your fingers crossed and touching wood. Walking under a ladder is 'unlucky' and if you spill any salt you should throw some of it over your left shoulder! (Also 7 is a lucky number and 13 is unlucky – in many hotels the next room after number 12 is 14!!)

C   ANSWERS

   1 Many of the hopes, fears and anxieties of our time
   2 By the mass media: TV, the press, radio
   3 St George and the Dragon, the Mouse in the Coca Cola bottle

D   ANSWERS

   1 H I   **2** G   **3** F   **4** E   **5** A J   **6** B   **7** D   (C is wrong)

E 1   The cartoon strip in **Activity 8** is 'the Baked Sunbather': a man who used kitchen foil to create reflectors around him while sunbathing, fell asleep and was found later, baked alive.

The strip in **Activity 27** is 'the Poodle in the Restaurant': a couple went into a foreign restaurant with their dog and, unable to speak the language, made signs to the waiter that they wanted him to feed their dog – when their meal at last came the dog had been roasted for them.

2 Here are a couple more:

Some friends of a friend wanted a new carpet, so they went to the shop and chose one and the carpet-fitter came round to fit it while they were out at work. When he had finished he found there was a bump right in the middle. He realised this must be a pack of cigarettes that he'd put down absent-mindedly, so he jumped up and down on the bump until it was completely flat. The family got home and admired the carpet. Then they asked the man if he had seen their pet budgerigar, which was missing. It was then that he noticed his pack of cigarettes on the hall table!

Some friends of a friend went to the woods to gather mushrooms. They were afraid the ones they'd picked might be poisonous, so they fed one to their cat. The cat seemed OK a few hours later, so they cooked the rest of the mushrooms for supper. When they'd finished eating, they looked out of the window and saw their cat lying dead on the pavement outside. In panic they rushed to the hospital to have their stomachs pumped. On their return they found a note from their neighbour explaining that he had accidentally run over the cat in the road.

(15.2) A good introduction and conclusion
Reading and Effective writing

Ⓐ ANSWERS

1 When René Magritte was a *boy* his mother fell into a river and drowned.
2 *Some* of Magritte's paintings are like myths.
3 Magritte's *friends* made up the titles for his paintings.
4 He wanted his viewers ~~not~~ to notice how reality and painting are different.
5 The pictures he painted in the war were *colourful*.
6 Magritte's images have had a *big* influence on advertising.

Ⓑ1 This may take some time to do, but it's worth it! There are obviously no correct answers, but try to get a consensus of views from the class before they look at the concluding paragraphs in B2.

2 The texts in 13.4, 14.1 and 15.1 are the first pages of books – the last paragraph of each isn't a 'concluding paragraph'. But it's still worth considering whether each of their last paragraphs leaves you 'feeling better-informed and satisfied' – or wanting to read on to find out more . . .

Ⓒ All four opening paragraphs have their merits – apart from the fourth, probably! After the students have reached their conclusions, perhaps take a vote on the preferred one.

Ⓓ1 Arrange the class into an even number of pairs (or groups of three), so that pairs of pairs can be formed later. In this Communication Activity each pair has a strange picture to discuss and then write a description of. The one in **Activity 18** is 'The Threatened Assassin', 1926, by René Magritte; the one in **Activity 34** is 'The Street', 1933, by Balthus.

> **CAE exam** | In Part 2 of the Speaking paper candidates have to compare and contrast two pictures, which are more likely to be photos than paintings. Speculating what happened before and what's going to happen next gives candidates more to talk about.

2 The description can be written by the collaborating pairs in class, or done for homework.

3 Each pair comments on the other's work. The model version on the next page (for Activity 18) is rather longer than the students are expected to write in D2.

Leo Jones *New Cambridge Advanced English*

(15.2) MODEL VERSION

A woman has been murdered and her naked corpse is lying on a couch. Her murderer looks calm and shows no signs of remorse. He is listening to a record on an old-fashioned record-player, with his coat, hat and suitcase laid out ready for him to leave.

Two detectives in bowler hats are hiding outside the room. One has a net, the other a club in the form of a human limb, which is strange because detectives would normally use guns.

Three men with their chins resting on the rail of the balcony are observing what is going on. Behind them, in the distance, some hills and a snow-covered mountain peak can be seen.

When the murderer leaves the room, the detective with the net will probably throw it over him and the one with the club will knock him unconscious.

(15.3) A sense of humour   Listening and Reading

Perhaps point out that sarcasm and sincerity can be seen in a speaker's face, as well as heard in the voice. Moreover, what is deemed sarcastic in some situations might be perfectly sincere in others – or even deliberately ambiguous, perhaps.

CAE exam	This activity is useful practice for Part 4 of the Listening paper, where candidates may have to focus on the attitude of the speaker.

SUGGESTED ANSWERS

3 sarcastic **4** sincere **5** sarcastic **6** sarcastic **7** sincere **8** sincere **9** sarcastic
10 sarcastic **11** sincere **12** sarcastic

Transcript   2 minutes

1
MAN: What did you think of my work – was it good?
WOMAN: Yes, it was really good. I liked it a lot.   *sincere*

2
WOMAN: What did you think of my work – was it good?
MAN: Oh yes, it was brilliant. I really enjoyed reading it.   *sarcastic*

3
WOMAN: Need any help?
MAN: Well, I was wondering whether it might be possible for you to help with the
        washing-up.   *sarcastic*

4
MAN: Feeling better?
WOMAN: Better?
MAN: Yes, well, you weren't feeling too good yesterday – I was just wondering if
        you were feeling all right today.   *sincere*

5
MAN: Feeling better?
WOMAN: Better?
MAN: Yes, I was very worried about you because you didn't come to the party
        I invited you to last night.   *sarcastic*

6
WOMAN: Any suggestions?
MAN: Well, I think it might be quite a good idea if you gave up smoking, for example.   *sarcastic*

7

MAN: Any suggestions?

WOMAN: I think it might be quite a good idea if we arranged to play tennis once a week.   *sincere*

8

MAN: How was your skiing holiday?

WOMAN: Oh, it was wonderful – even though there wasn't much snow.   *sincere*

9

MAN: How was your summer holiday?

WOMAN: Oh, we had a really good time – it was sunny *almost* every day.   *sarcastic*

10

WOMAN: Jane . . . I wonder if you'd mind giving us your attention for a moment?   *sarcastic*

11

MAN: Chris?

WOMAN: Yes?

MAN: I was wondering whether it might be possible for you to take notes during the lecture
         tomorrow.   *sincere*

12

WOMAN: Have we finished yet?

MAN: Yes, we have very *nearly* finished, don't worry.   *sarcastic*

B Rita Rudner's humour may be a matter of taste. She is American and these words and phrases are evidence of this:

standing on line   has gotten served   elevator   flat tire   gray hair

C ANSWERS

letting myself down = disappointing myself   victories = examples of success
keep me going = enable me to continue living

1 standing on line = queue up
gloat = be happy at someone else's misfortune

2 peek = have a quick, secret look
rationalize = provide a (reassuring) explanation

4 gives me the giggles = make me laugh uncontrollably
bandage = piece of cloth tied around an injury
blender = kitchen appliance for mixing liquids

7 constant = unchanging

9 glee = happiness and pleasure

D Cartoons are a good 'test' of people's sense of humour. Ask everyone which of the cartoons in this book make them smile. Do they all smile at the same ones?

15.4 Mind control   Listening and Creative writing

The topic of this section and the interview might be upsetting for people who have been involved with a cult – or who have a friend or relative who has. If you suspect this may be the case, perhaps ask any member of the class to send you an anonymous note if they'd rather not discuss this topic in class. However, if anyone has escaped from the clutches of a cult they may welcome the opportunity to warn their fellow students about its dangerous attractiveness.

A The text and the questions will help the students to approach the interview with some previous knowledge. The questions are discussed further by Ian Howarth in the interview.

Depending on the interests and beliefs of your class, perhaps introduce some of this vocabulary. Maybe begin by asking them to note down as many different world religions and sects as they can think of. This is not included in the Student's Book as it may be a sensitive area for some people.

faith   religion   priest   temple   mosque   cathedral   bishop   priest   archbishop   imam altar   parts of a church/temple/mosque   bible   testament   atheist/agnostic   Hindu Buddhist   Muslim   Jewish   Sikh   Christian: Catholic, Protestant, Orthodox, Anglican, etc. born-again

 B1 Play the first part of the interview, which lasts 4 minutes 30 seconds, after everyone has looked through the questions.

SUGGESTED ANSWERS

1 message   **2** attractive   **3** survey   **4** irrelevant   **5** smoke   **6** smoking
7 article   **8** programme   **9** negativity   **10** Devil   **11** eleven

> **CAE exam**   In the Listening paper candidates may have to complete sentences, as here in **15.4 B1** and **2**, or take notes. Generally where sentences have to be completed, a maximum number of words is specified (one or two). Where candidates have to take notes, a single word, a number or a short phrase may be needed, depending on the information that's being summarised.

 2 Play the second part of the interview, which lasts 6 minutes 30 seconds.

SUGGESTED ANSWERS

12 *four of:*   intelligent   educated   good family background   idealistic intellectually curious / enjoy discussions
13 913   **14** money   **15** God   **16** God   **17** sexual   **18** world   **19** power   **20** 500
21 satanism   **22** tarot cards / astrology / palm-reading   **23** methods   **24** beliefs   **25** five

Transcript   11 minutes

PART ONE

IAN: My name is…um…Ian Howarth and… um…I'm a specialist in…in cultism, I represent the Cult Information Centre and I've been working in this field now for 17 years on both sides of the Atlantic, and I'm an ex-cult member.

INTERVIEWER: What is the difference between a cult and a bona fide religion?

IAN: I think it's…it's a matter of the…the methods and we…we question groups for their methods not the message. Er…I think that's an important distinction because in a democratic society we feel people should have a right to believe in whatever they choose as long as they're choosing it. So if the methods used by a group are methods that remove a person's ability to choose through the use of mind control techniques and deceptive practices, then we would…we would have a problem with that.

INTERVIEWER: And you say you used to be a member of a cult?

IAN: Yes, I did.

INTERVIEWER: How were you taken, well, taken in or . . . ?

IAN: Well, um…I used to live in Toronto, Canada. I emigrated to Canada in '72 from…um…where I was brought up in the North of England. And…um…by 1978 all was going well, I was a businessman, I was 31 and…er…life was…was really good to me. And it was August of '78, it was a Saturday, it was a beautiful summer's day, and…er…I was doing some shopping when I was er… suddenly approached by a very attractive woman. She was very attractive, I was very single, so I wasn't at all upset when she approached me. She had a clipboard, a chart and a pen and appeared to be doing a survey and asked me if I could help her with this survey. And I distinctly remember saying 'Yes, please!' and we had a little chat and I answered five questions for her survey and I was just going to walk away when she said, 'You know the way you've answered these questions I think you'd be interested in this community group that I belong to.' Well, I wasn't because I wasn't one that joined groups. Until she said that the group was involved in social work, community work, it was putting back into society. Why not come along and find out more.

And so I went along to this meeting and frankly I was bored to tears. Um… the speaker was a woman in her early thirties, she talked about herself and how she'd become an alcoholic. And I thought, 'Well, how's this relevant to anything?' Anyway she struggled with her alcohol problems, got rid of them but unfortunately became a drug addict in the process and life was going from bad to worse. And then this group came along into her life apparently, and everything was sorted. So I was innocently sort of sitting there but bored, and thought, 'As soon as the break comes along I'll leave'. But when it did I suddenly remembered I'd paid… um…$2 to go in, I thought I'd get my money's worth and have a bite to eat and so on. So I stayed for the food for a little longer and…um…had a plateful of food and wanted to smoke. And I couldn't smoke in the room, you had to go out in the hall to smoke and I did just that. Another lady rushed over, she was very attractive too. (And I mention this because the cults will always use the opposite sex to gain your…er…attention, and they certainly did that with me.) And she said, 'Oh, we didn't know you smoked.' And this is how they got through to me because they said they had a course to show people how to quit smoking. I was interested in doing that.

And…um…so in the end I went on a four-day course to quit smoking, and at the end of it gave the group all the money I had, dedicated my life to it and resigned from my job.

INTERVIEWER: And how long were you a member?

IAN: Well, I…the intent was to recruit me for life, but…um…two and half weeks after the initial involvement, a journalist called Sydney Katz exposed the group in the Toronto Star newspaper, which is a very reputable paper. And I was given this article by someone I'd tried to recruit, and I thought the article would be looking at it favourably, because as far as I was concerned, this was the greatest group on this Earth. So I proudly walked off with this newspaper article that my friend had given me, without reading it I…I went home, opened the thing up in…er…my apartment and nearly fell apart. I was stunned. I hadn't been programmed against the media, the group had slipped up. Most cults will programme members to understand the media is full of negativity or it's run by the Devil.

And having read the article, it reactivated my critical mind. And I actually phoned the journalist and he took things a lot further with me. He sat down with me, er…he gave me his office and all of the literature he'd gathered on the group. He said, 'Look, I'll feed you with food, I'll bring you coffee. Just spend as long as you want. You decide for yourself. There's the information.' I suddenly realised that what he'd written was actually quite mild, because the lawyers had gone through it first. It was far worse than he'd indicated. So I made the break after just two and half weeks, but it took eleven months to fully recover from that. Er…and although it's very unusual for someone to come out of a cult the way I did, it is very normal for people to suffer for a long time. Most people who are fortunate to come out of cults will take a year to…or more to recover.

PART TWO

INTERVIEWER: And what sort of people do get caught up w…in them?

IAN: Well, I think a lot of people want to believe that you have to be weak-willed, easily led, probably a teenager, probably come from a broken home, and you're not very smart. And whilst it is possible that someone like that with one or two of those qualities could be recruited, they're not the majority. It seems the majority…um…of people that are recruited into cults are quite the opposite. They usually come from, shall we say, 'economically advantaged family backgrounds'. Um…they're people who have average to above-average intelligence, they're people who are well-educated, they're people who are idealistic. And…um…they're interested in debating issues with other people and listening to other points of view. Those are the very people that think it would never happen to them, which makes them even more vulnerable.

INTERVIEWER: And so you left the cult after two and a half weeks . . .

IAN: Mm, that's right.

INTERVIEWER: . . . and did you start the Cult Information Centre immediately?

IAN: In November, in other words a month later, on November 18 the murder-suicides occurred in Jonestown, Guyana. And that really hit hard, it rocked me, it… it . . . Those images went right to the core of my being, I felt so sorry for those people and the…the little children lying face down in the mud and I knew it could have been me, I could have been one of those people. And people like me had died. 913 people died. And…um…I just decided there and then that I had to start a charity to get involved in disseminating educational information on this topic and I've been doing it ever since.

INTERVIEWER: So what is the reason behind the group, the cult leader, what is there motivating . . . ?

IAN: Mm, I think it's fair to say that some cult leaders are 'laughing all the way to the bank' and have been all along, so they're there in…for the money. Some cult leaders, however, having programmed people to understand that they're 'God' or special in some other way for ten years, maybe start to believe it themselves. Other cult leaders have believed that they were 'God' right from the word go. I think they're particularly dangerous because they're the less predictable. And some cult leaders are… are clearly quite mad i…in my opinion. Other cult leaders will do it for sexual purposes, they will exploit the men or the women in the group or both. Some will be motivated through maybe some kind of political ambition, they want to take over the world or something like this. And I think some cult leaders just enjoy the power they have over other innocent people. I think the power aspect of it can't be underestimated.

INTERVIEWER: How many different cults are there?

IAN: Well, in Britain alone we're dealing with well over 500 cults. And…and that actually means that on a per capita basis, Britain has the same problem as the United States. It has a fifth of the population and approximately a fifth of the number of cults in operation.

INTERVIEWER: Do you think there's a difference between…um…the occult, those type of groups, and the type of cults we've been discussing? Or do they…do they all come under the same umbrella?

IAN: Well, the occult is referring to beliefs. Um…at one end of the spectrum you've got satanism and witchcraft, and at the other end of the occult spectrum you… you've got things like…um…tarot cards, astrology, palm-reading and so on. Some would say that's 'deep end' to 'shallow end' occult. Um…so the occult revolves around beliefs and…um…practices along the lines that I've just described.

We as an organisation are looking at methods, not beliefs. Most cults do have some kind of involvement with occult beliefs and/or practices. But just because someone's involved in the occult doesn't mean to say that they're necessarily involved in a cult. You can read about the occult. You can however be programmed without your knowledge, without your agreement, to taking on board occult beliefs…er…in a cult organisation. And so it's those groups that we focus on.

Well, the group I was in had an occult basis to it, and…um…was into pyramids…um…that…you know, pyramid power. Um…allegedly one could get some kind of power from pyramid shapes and you could either sit under…under a pyramid or do whatever. But the thing is you go on one of these courses and you finish up under their control and then…um…they will… um…um…get you to do anything they want. The…the group I was in talked about…um…'throwing out white light' to people that was going to 'heal them'. Um…it talked about 'getting closer to ultimate reality', whatever that might have meant. And was very interested in…um…er…astrology and things like this. It's all part of actually the New Age, which we hear a lot about today. Um… actually the New Age is as old as the hills, there's nothing new in it at all, er… it's just a glamorisation of a revival of interest in the occult.

INTERVIEWER: What do you think you're proudest of having done?

IAN: I don't like the word proud, quite frankly. It's very exciting to get a letter from a family. I got one the other day actually, you don't get…um…um…many letters like this. This was from a family I hadn't even spoken to, but they'd lost their daughter to a cult in…in Australia, a British family had lost their daughter while she was travelling in Australia. And…um…friends of the family did contact the Cult Information Centre and…er…we gave them the basics of what the family should do and shouldn't do. And…er…about five years of this had gone by and they were successful in the end, and they were reunited with their daughter. And they wrote to us and said, 'Well, look, we've never actually been in touch with you ourselves, but somebody else was and they gave us this information. And whenever we jumped on the plane to go to Australia, we had to double-check first that we'd packed our "Do's and Don'ts list" from CIC and . . .'. It was very moving, I mean I'm getting goosebumps thinking about it now. And they're back together again!

5 C The students must draw on the information they found out during the interview to do this writing task.

CAE exam

In the exam, of course, candidates don't have to do a writing task in the Listening paper – but the input of information in **15.4 B1** and **B2** is similar to the kind of written information they have to process in Part 1 of the Writing paper.

CAE exam

What are the examiners looking for in the Writing paper?

1 The quality of your composition and how well you have fulfilled the task set: the relevance and organisation of your composition as a whole, as well as the quality of the individual paragraphs.

2 The quality of the language you use: the range and appropriateness of vocabulary and sentence structure; the correctness of grammar, punctuation and spelling.

3 Your ability to display a breadth of experience or background knowledge, and your use of illustration and allusion.

4 A 'balance between accuracy and imagination' in each composition: the examiners try to give equitable treatment to compositions which are 'pedestrian but accurate' and those which are less accurate but 'lively and imaginative'.

5 In Part 1, how well you've accomplished the task, and used the information from the input to do this.

6 The questions in Part 2 provide different tasks, each demanding different responses and techniques: successful accomplishment of the task is important here too.

Leo Jones *New Cambridge Advanced English*

(15.4) MODEL VERSION

Dear Amy,

I'm sorry to hear that you're worried about Tim. It may be that the group he's in is harmless, but it does sound suspicious. I'll write to him and tell him about my experiences and warn him of the dangers. The problem is if he has already been brain-washed, he won't take any notice of anyone. I'll do my best though.

Love,

Phil

Dear Tim,

Amy tells me that you have started going to meetings with the Chimera Group. I was a member of a similar group for a short time and decided to leave after I had found out a few unpleasant facts about them. I know that you're an open-minded sort of person and like discussing issues and listening to other people's views. Perhaps you won't mind if I ask you a few questions about your group and the people who recruited you.

Do you know who the leader of the group is and what his/her beliefs are? Does this person seem like your average person or is s/he special, I mean treated with respect and fear by the other members? Have you been asked to give this person any peculiar or unusual kind of favours or honours? Are there special ceremonies surrounding the presence of the leader? Have you been asked to part with any money?

If you have answered Yes to most of these questions then I think you ought to step back a while and take stock. Perhaps miss a meeting or two and meet me to discuss some of the ideas you've been hearing about. I'd be keen to hear what you have learned and what the meetings are like.

Perhaps I could meet your contact person. Amy tells me that it was a woman you met in a café. Could I meet her too? Perhaps we could all have coffee together sometime.

Please ring me soon. If I don't hear from you by the end of the week I'll give you a buzz.

Look forward to seeing you soon,

All the best,

Phil

  © Cambridge University Press, 1998

Ⓐ ANSWERS

1 every single day
2 stop
3 that's very unlikely
4 special day
5 thinking pleasant thoughts
6 make him happy
7 Eventually
8 a bad day
9 terrified
10 I'm being unlucky
11 That was a wonderful period.

Ⓑ ANSWERS

1 from time immemorial
2 Once upon a time …
3 it's about time/it's high time
4 time limit
5 for the time being
6 time-consuming
7 time and time again   half the time/at times   at times/half the time   wasting my time
8 good timing
9 take your time   in your own time
10 in time
11 the time of your life
12 on time

(16.1) **How are you?**　　　　　　　　　Vocabulary and Listening

A Some common reasons for absence that might be mentioned are:

flu　cough　cold　bad back　bronchitis　hangover　feeling under the weather　bad headache　sore throat　toothache

B To save time in class, ask everyone to prepare this section at home before the lesson.

SUGGESTED ANSWERS

1 Doing exercises　jogging　working out　etc.

2 By dieting　by doing exercises　etc.

3 Flu　mumps　typhoid　malaria　whooping cough　polio　etc.

4 have drunk too much　　　　　*they have a hangover*
have overslept　　　　　　　　*annoyed and perhaps have a headache*
have had a bad night　　　　　*sleepy*
have just run a marathon　　　*worn out*
eat only junk food　　　　　　*guilty?*
have had a bad day　　　　　　*grumpy*
have had a busy day　　　　　*exhausted*

5 have sore feet　　　　　　　　*a chiropodist*
need an injection　　　　　　　*a nurse*
are having a baby　　　　　　　*a gynaecologist*
need an operation　　　　　　　*a consultant / a surgeon*
have a sore throat　　　　　　　*no one or perhaps a chemist/pharmacist*
are having a nervous breakdown　*a psychiatrist*

6 hay fever　　　　　　　　　　*sneezing / a runny nose / sore eyes*
flu　　　　　　　　　　　　　　*headache and nausea*
migraine　　　　　　　　　　　*splitting headache*
food poisoning　　　　　　　　*sickness and diarrhoea*
sprained ankle　　　　　　　　*a painful swollen ankle*
schizophrenia　　　　　　　　*no sense of reality; split personality (?)*
a cut finger　　　　　　　　　*bleeding*
a broken arm　　　　　　　　　*swelling, extreme pain, etc.*

7 hay fever　　　　　　　　　　*tablets perhaps*
a cold　　　　　　　　　　　　*stay at home*
a bruise　　　　　　　　　　　*don't touch it*
scratch　　　　　　　　　　　*clean it, put a plaster on if it's serious*
dog bite　　　　　　　　　　　*go to the doctor if it's serious*
headache　　　　　　　　　　　*take an aspirin or paracetamol*
toothache　　　　　　　　　　*go to the dentist*
graze　　　　　　　　　　　　*clean it, put a plaster on if it's serious*
wasp sting + mosquito bite　　*put up with it or get something from the chemist*
aching back　　　　　　　　　*exercises*
sprained wrist　　　　　　　　*rest it and perhaps put a bandage on it*
a bad cough　　　　　　　　　*take some cough medicine*

8 anaesthetist　consultant　matron　midwife　porter　sister　specialist　surgeon

C Find out from the class what their remedies for hiccups are.

D 1 ANSWERS

1	C
2	D
3	E
4	H
5	G

2 ANSWERS

1	K
2	P
3	J
4	M
5	O

CAE exam **16.1 D** is similar to one of the tasks candidates have to do in the Listening paper. To simulate exam conditions, only play the recording twice.

Transcript 2 minutes

1

NURSE: . . . I'll just have a look inside. If you could just hold her head still while I do this. No, don't worry, dear, it won't hurt at all. Oh, yes, I see, there's just a slight build-up of wax in there – no, there's no inflammation at all. And now let's see the other one . . . mm, that looks fine. Well, it's really nothing to worry about, it should clear itself. But if it doesn't improve in a week, bring her back to see me again.

2

PHARMACIST: Oh yes, I can hear that you're a little hoarse. These are very good – if you suck one every two hours, it should soothe the pain, but try not to do too much talking if you can help it. Now, there are two kinds: these ones contain menthol, or you might prefer these lemon ones . . .

3

PSYCHIATRIST: No, I don't think you should worry about that, it's probably perfectly normal. You may well be suffering from stress at the moment and this is a fairly common reaction. So just lie back, close your eyes and tell me about all about it . . .

4

VET: Could you just hold her quite firmly while I have a closer look … Hmm, yes, it is very dry, isn't it? But her tongue looks fine, her eyes are bright and her coat's nice and smooth, so I really don't think there's anything to worry about. You did say…er…she was eating normally, didn't you?

5

FITNESS INSTRUCTOR: . . . and lift your arms slowly into the air, and try to keep it very straight – straight as you can. Keep your arms above your head for a moment. Now slowly bring your arms down until they point towards your feet, this time curve it very slowly – that's right. Now do the same again . . .

16.2 Prefixes   Word study

A ANSWERS

un-	acceptable bearable conscious desirable foreseen grateful healthy natural sociable willing
dis-	contented obedient respectful
in-	appropriate compatible complete convenient credible discreet experienced flexible frequent hospitable sane sufficient visible
im-	mortal personal polite probable
il-	legible literate logical

B Make sure everyone looks at the examples before they do the exercise.

ANSWERS

mis-	count print read report
out-	last sell

re-	consider count load name open pack play print read record sell sit an exam tell think unite wind
un-	dress load lock pack roll screw wind zip

C Make sure everyone looks at the examples before they do the exercise.

ANSWERS

mid-	air fifties twenties
over	crowded dose enthusiastic estimate loaded polite privileged qualified react simplify valued weight
under	estimate privileged qualified valued weight
self-	catering confident contained defence discipline explanatory respect satisfied
ultra-	cautious fashionable fast polite

➡ Some more prefixes, not included in the Student's Book.

Anglo-	American phone Saxon
anti-	American biotic clockwise nuclear perspirant septic social
co-	educational exist founder leader pilot worker
de-	brief centralise frost value
Euro-	cheque dollar parliament
Franco-	British phone
inter-	departmental personal marry national planetary state
post-	date war
pre-	cooked date recorded school
pro-	American British nuclear
vice-	president captain chairman principal

D SUGGESTED ANSWERS

1 ultra-modern mid-way outlived
2 impatient misunderstand
3 overreacted rewrite unreadable/illegible/inaccurate
4 incompatible self-satisfied/self-confident over-sensitive over-imaginative
5 incredible understaffed reopened
6 self-discipline disorganised
7 unlocked unpacked undressed
8 ultra-modern impersonal unsociable self-catering self-contained

(16.3) Spelling   Word study

This section relates to 14.3 and 18.5 on Spelling and pronunciation.

A 1 The three spelling mistakes are:

laborataries definate classiffied [*laboratories, definite, classified*]

2 ANSWERS

1 substances 2 ✓ 3 therefore 4 appearance 5 roughness 6 launched 7 ✓
8 Regulators 9 ✓ 10 though 11 illness 12 diagnose 13 complaining 14 ✓
15 been 16 According 17 ageing 18 compares 19 older 20 ✓

> **CAE exam**   16.3 **A2** is similar to Part 3 in the English in Use paper, though longer.

B1 Play the recording, pausing it if your students are writing slowly.

Transcript and Answers   2 minutes

NARRATOR: Write down the words you hear. Listen to the example first.

1	handkerchief	I don't carry a handkerchief – I prefer to use tissues.
2	tissues	Have you got any tissues on you?
3	through	We walked through the park feeling excited.
4	excitement	Everyone shows their excitement before a long journey.
5	nuisance	It was a nuisance that we had to queue up.
6	queue	It was a very long queue.
7	gauge	I could see from the fuel gauge that I needed some petrol.
8	awkward	This can is quite awkward to open – can you give me some assistance?
9	assistance	I need your assistance.
10	whether	Can you tell me whether she's an acquaintance of yours?
11	acquaintance	She's not just an acquaintance, she's my fiancée.
12	fiancée	His fiancée's name is Rosemary, she's learning to play the flute.
13	practise	You have to practise a lot if you're learning to play a musical instrument.
14	allowed	Smoking isn't allowed in this building.
15	sighed	Everyone sighed when they realised it was the end of the exercise.

2 CORRECT SPELLINGS

aggressive campaigning diphthong disrupted enthusiastically extinction foreign
inconceivable interrupted sanctuary seize separate underdeveloped weird

3 To make sure everyone takes this seriously it should perhaps be done in class, under your supervision.

CAE exam	Correct spelling is particularly important in the Writing paper as well as in the English in Use paper. Spelling mistakes may cost marks. Candidates should make a habit of checking their work through for spelling mistakes (and other slips of the pen) before handing it in. They should make sure they allow enough time towards the end of the exam to do this.

(16.4) Conditional sentences   Grammar

A SUGGESTED ANSWERS

1 *When it rains our roof leaks.*
   = every time it rains water comes in
   If it rains our roof will leak.
   = it may rain sometime in the future and in that case water will come in
   When it rained our roof would leak.
   = every time it rained (in the past) water used to come in
   If it rains our roof leaks.
   = on the occasions that it rains water comes in (perhaps less likelihood of rain than the first example)
   If it rained our roof would leak.
   = it's unlikely to rain, but if it did water would come in

2 *I'd go first class if I could afford to.*
   = I haven't got enough money
   I go first class when I can afford it.
   = sometimes I have enough money, sometimes I don't
   I'd have gone first class if I could have afforded it.
   = I didn't have enough money, so I didn't travel first class

I'll go first class if I can afford to.
= I may have enough money
I'll go first class when I can afford it.
= as soon as I have enough money I intend to travel first class

3 *He could get a rise if he asked his boss.*
= he's unlikely to ask but if he did it's possible he'd be successful
He might get a rise if he asked his boss.
= he's unlikely to ask but if he did it's possible he'd be successful (perhaps slightly less likelihood of success than in the first example)
He should get a rise if he asks his boss.
= it's possible that he'll ask and if so it's probable he'll be successful
He would get a rise if he asked his boss.
= he's unlikely to ask but if he did I'm sure he'd be successful
He might get a rise if he asks his boss.
= it's possible that he'll ask and if so it's possible he'll be successful
He will get a rise if he asks his boss.
= it's possible that he'll ask and if so it's certain he'll be successful

4 *If you should see him, give him my love.*
= there's a slim chance you'll see him
If you see him, give him my love.
= there's a good chance you'll see him
If you happen to see him, give him my love.
= there's a slim chance you'll see him
When you see him, give him my love.
= you're certainly going to see him

5 *You should save your money in case you want to go on holiday.*
= save up because you might want to go on holiday
You won't be able to go on holiday unless you save your money.
= save up because you want to go – and only by saving up can you afford to go

6 *If only I hadn't spent all my money and had saved some!*
= I wish I had been less profligate
If I hadn't spent all my money and had saved some . . .
= supposing I'd been less profligate

B ANSWERS

1 If I **had been** born rich I **wouldn't need / wouldn't have needed** to work.

2 *no errors*

3 He says that if it weren't for the tax system he**'d** be much better off.

4 There wouldn't be so much poverty **if** less money **were/was** spent on arms.

5   If you **don't** arrive in time they won't let you into the concert.

6 If you **had** bought it last week, the price **wouldn't** have **gone** up.

7 If you **let** me know **when** you arrive **I'll** meet you at the airport.
OR If you'd let me know **when** you arrived / **were arriving I'd have met** you at the airport.

8 I'll be surprised **if** prices **don't** go up next year.

C1 SUGGESTED ANSWERS

1 If it weren't/wasn't for his strict diet . . .
If he weren't/wasn't on such a strict diet . . .

2 If he had realised how long . . .

3 If you see her tonight . . .
If you should see her tonight . . .

2 SUGGESTED ANSWERS

1 Had   been   would/might/could have
2 you not have / there not be
3 there less   would not / might not
4 known   would be / was going to be   would have spent
5 Should you
6 would/might   were it not

D Make sure everyone reads the instructions before they do the exercise. (The words that should not be used are shown crossed out below.)

SUGGESTED ANSWERS

1 completed ~~finished~~ 2 insufficient/inadequate ~~not enough~~ 3 had been
4 would have been 5 restricted ~~limited~~ 6 would be less ~~would have been less~~
7 gained ~~put on~~ 8 unless 9 achievable ~~possible~~
10 had been advised ~~had been told~~ 11 had been recommended ~~been told~~
12 might have been ~~could have been~~ 13 had known 14 have enrolled 15 Should ~~If~~

> **CAE exam** 16.4 **D** is similar to one of the tasks in the English in Use paper, where the same information must be conveyed using different words from the ones in the first text. In the exam there wouldn't be so many conditionals though, and the focus is more on nouns and set phrases.

(16.5) Giving advice   Speaking

A 1 Even people who don't suffer from stress may experience some of the symptoms in the leaflet.

2 If your students are blissfully stress-free they may have to use their imaginations to participate in this activity.

3 Arrange the class into groups of three (or four, with two students sharing one of the roles). Student A looks at **Activity 11**, B at **Activity 15** and C at **Activity 28**. Encourage everyone to use their own words and to experiment with the phrases in A2.

B 1 This is a role-play. It's probably less stressful for everyone to select problems they DON'T have!

✎ 2 This writing task is more necessary for CAE exam candidates than others. Another writing task (for everyone) follows in 16.6.

(16.6) First aid   Creative writing

A 1 This activity encourages the students to assemble their ideas, so that they can compare their own ideas with the recommendations they'll read in A2.

2 Student A looks at **Activity 9** (Snake bite treatment), B at **Activity 16** (Shock) and C at **Activity 31** (Epileptic fit). Make sure they try to explain the treatments in their own words and don't just read the points aloud. The three texts are models for the writing task in B.

B 1 This could be done as a whole-class activity, with notes being made on the board and by the students.

✎ 2 Layout and clarity are important when writing instructions. Remind everyone of the instructions they read in Activities 9, 16 and 31.

Leo Jones *New Cambridge Advanced English*

16.6 MODEL VERSION

Suspected broken/fractured leg

Tell the patient not to move. Stop any severe bleeding and dress any open wound. Splint the injured leg by bandaging it firmly to the other leg (if uninjured). Put soft padding between the two legs. Use any padding you can find – socks or towels will do. You can use belts, ties, towels, stockings, etc. for bandaging if you have nothing else to hand. Wind the bandaging round the areas slowly and carefully and avoid bandaging directly over where you think the fracture lies. Make sure you do not move the injured leg; move the good leg towards the bad one for bandaging. Immobilise not only the area involved but also the joint on either side.

Rescue from drowning

Once out of the water, lie the patient in the recovery position (see illustration). Make sure the head is bent back and the face tilted down so that the airways are open. This position allows any fluid coming from the patient's mouth to escape without choking him/her.

Remove any debris from the mouth and check for breathing visually and by feeling for exhalation on the back of your hand. Feel for a pulse on the carotid artery in the neck. Check the patient's fingers for any blueness. If and only if, there is no sign of life, turn the patient onto his/her back and begin artificial respiration. If, after the first four quick breaths there is no pulse, start external chest compression.

(16.7) *Hearts, hands, legs* and *feet*   Idioms and collocations

ANSWERS

1	heart	lose heart	=	lose courage
2	heart	have someone's interests at heart	=	care deeply
3	hands	in good hands	=	well looked after
4	-handed	short-handed	=	not enough assistance
5	hands	old hands	=	experienced staff
6	heart	by heart	=	memorise
7	hand	hold someone's hand	=	help as if a child
8	feet	find one's feet	=	settle down
9	heart	my heart isn't in it	=	not be enthusiastic
10	hand	give someone a free hand	=	complete unrestricted freedom
11	hands	in your hands	=	your responsibility
12	heart	take it to heart	=	take too seriously
13	heart	a change of heart	=	change decision
14	leg	hasn't got a leg to stand on	=	no justification
15	feet	have cold feet	=	feel afraid to commit yourself
16	hand	keep one's hand in	=	retain a skill
17	hand	give someone a hand	=	help
18	hand	have the matter in hand	=	dealing with
19	leg	pull someone's leg	=	play a joke
20	foot	put one's foot down	=	impose authority
21	foot	put one's foot in it	=	cause embarrassment
22	-hearted	light-hearted	=	not serious
23	feet	put your feet up	=	relax
24	heart	break someone's heart	=	cause someone to suffer despair

➡ A few more idioms (these are connected with BACK and THUMB):

back out of	= withdraw
back up	= support
back down	= yield
back-up	= replacement
behind someone's back	= without their knowledge
rule of thumb	= a rough practical rule
thumb a lift	= hitchhike

(17.1) What do you enjoy reading?   Vocabulary

(A) This discussion deals with one of the two themes of this unit: stories (i.e. books and literature) and love (i.e. relationships).

(B) **SUGGESTED ANSWERS**   (The underlined words should be discussed after doing the exercise.)

1 <u>literary</u> <u>poetic</u> <u>popular</u> <u>predictable</u> thought-provoking ✓ well-written ✓
clear ✓ <u>complex</u> <u>hard to understand</u> lucid ✓ readable ✓ simple ✓

2 <u>appendix</u> <u>bibliography</u> <u>blurb</u> chapter ✓ <u>character</u> <u>dustjacket</u> extract ✓
footnote ✓ <u>foreword</u> <u>index</u> page ✓ paragraph ✓ passage ✓ <u>preface</u>
quotation ✓ section ✓ <u>title</u> unit ✓

3 *The genres are a matter of taste apart from* <u>propaganda</u>.

(17.2) Small World   Reading

> David Lodge, born in 1935, is the author of a number of entertaining novels, mostly dealing with university life, notably:
>
> *Changing Places* – about an American professor and a British lecturer who exchange jobs for a year
>
> *Nice Work* – what happens when a businessman and a feminist university lecturer are thrown together
>
> *Small World* (1984) – an 'Academic romance' satirising the world of academic conferences (this is the opening page)
>
> *Paradise News* – what happens when a reserved Englishman finds himself among the pleasure-seekers of Hawaii

(A)1 If possible, ask the students to read the passage before the lesson as this will save time in class.

2 These are questions for discussion.

In question 8, a *proposal* is a proposal of marriage – *propositions* are suggestions by men that Cheryl might like to spend the night with them.

▼(B) Encourage everyone to try to work the meaning out before they resort to dictionaries.

CAE exam	In the Reading paper candidates will encounter complex texts containing words they haven't come across before. Without dictionaries to hand they may need to work out the meanings from the context, or guess the meanings, or ignore the words they don't understand and concentrate on understanding everything else as best they can.

(C) This can be done in pairs, or by students working alone before comparing ideas with the rest of the class. It may not be easy to find an example to fill every category, by the way.

SUGGESTED EXAMPLES

1 HUMOUR: *Just one of many things that made me smile:*
'Those who were rude or arrogant or otherwise unpleasant she put in uncomfortable or inconvenient seats, next to the toilets, or beside mothers with crying babies.'

2 INFORMATION: *In a novel, information of this kind is usually lacking, though perhaps one might not previously be aware of the routine of the checker's job.*

3 OPINION: *A novel doesn't usually contain many 'opinions', but the passage opens with this one:*
'The job of check-in clerk . . . is not a glamorous or particularly satisfying one. The work is mechanical and repetitive . . . '

4 SOCIAL COMMENT:
'Then the checker bears the full brunt of the customers' fury without being able to do anything to alleviate it.'

5 EMPATHY:
'With half her mind she despised these love stories, but she devoured them with greedy haste, like cheap sweets.'

Preparation

If you'd like to do 17.3 D in the next lesson, ask everyone to look at the Preparation instructions on page 147 now.

(17.3) How romantic are you?   Reading and Listening

Some students might not enjoy 17.3 and 17.4, both of which are intended to be fun. If you feel some of your class might be upset, you may decide to skip some parts. In particular, some students may not be willing to talk about their personal feelings in public.

A **SUGGESTED ANSWERS**   (The words used in the original article are given first.)
1 anybody **2** moment/instant **3** romances/formula/novels **4** book/mainstream/literary
5 titles **6** bookshops/bookstores **7** longer/effort **8** authors/writers **9** life/work
10 strict/detailed/comprehensive/thorough/basic **11** compulsory/obligatory
12 types/kinds/sorts **13** originated/specialised **14** gaze/eyes
15 hero/heroine/protagonist/characters

CAE exam	In the exam candidates should look closely at the context of each missing word and work out first of all what kind of word is missing (noun, adjective, verb, adverb, etc.). Then they should consider various possible words that might fit and choose one which suits the context well. In the exam there's usually only one correct answer for each gap, not several as here in **17.3 A**.

B1 Arrange the class into an even number of pairs. Alternatively, this might be an amusing whole-class discussion.

2 Each pair writes their blurb.

3 The pairs compare their blurbs.

C1 Play the recording only once, without pausing it.

ANSWERS

Yes	6		No	3

2 Perhaps pause the tape after each trio of speakers for the groups to discuss what they said before they hear the next ones.

Transcript   2 minutes

NARRATOR: We asked a number of people this question: 'Do you believe in love?'

KATE: I believe in love. I don't know exactly how to define it but I think it exists and I don't know how long it lasts.

NIGEL: Yes, I believe in love. I don't believe in marriage, but I do believe in love and I think – that…that sounds a bit cynical – but…um…I feel that often marriage can f…can force love when y…you have to keep it going because there's a marriage. So, yes, I believe in love for people and…and specially I do for animals. Yes.

KEN: Yes, I think that love is the finest thing that money can buy.

GAY: Of course I believe in love. If I didn't really believe in love, I wouldn't want to be alive. For me there's everything from personal love to the love that is the healing force, which we need very much right now to help to work with things on the planet, like the rainforest.

KAREN: Well, I have to frankly say that no, I don't, because after four disastrous marriages, it's all just an illusion, you know. It soon wears off.

RUPERT: Yes, I believe in love…er…because there isn't anything else. Um…there's not really a lot more I can say after that, but…er…yes, of course I believe in love.

BLAIN: No, I don't believe in love. Love is a concept created by the marketing men to get men to buy things for women.

KATE: Um…yes, I do. Of course I…I believe in love. Um…I don't believe it lasts for ever and I think it's something that you both have to work on…er…work at if…if you're talking about a relationship between a man and a woman, or a man and a man, or a woman and a woman. Um…but I think…um…having just had a baby recently I'm aware of the love between a mother and a child, which is overwhelming: something I'd never even thought of before.

ENZO: Love's a waste of time. You only get hurt – and you hurt other people.

Preparation

Unless you have already asked everyone to do this, the following activity should be done in the next lesson.

D This activity needs some time to do justice to. It may not appeal to some classes, but others will find it very enjoyable.

(17.4) First meetings   Speaking and Listening

A Depending on the attitudes and age of your class, you might like them also to discuss how gay relationships (and public attitudes to them) have changed in recent years.

B 1 Arrange the class into an even number of pairs.

2 Combine the pairs into groups of four.

3 Play the recording, pausing it after each story for everyone to give their reactions.

Transcript   3 minutes

KATE: I was on my way home from junior high and in order to get to my house you have to walk by this baseball diamond. And there was a game of baseball going on and it looked kind of interesting so I stopped, there weren't very many people watching. And there was this guy and he wasn't really very good-looking but he had frizzly hair and glasses and he was really funny. He did this kind of monologue thing, which was great. And I went home and I told my mother I was going to marry him after talking to him for half an hour. And when I got to high school he was president of the student body and he asked me out and…um… we've got our picture in the yearbook together holding hands, and it's really nice.

KERRY: Well, I'd arranged to have a drink with a…er… friend of mine…a… a…woman friend of mine who's a platonic friend of mine. And she…er…insisted on bringing this friend of hers which…who she said I'd like to meet and…er…I thought she was trying to fix us up and I said, 'Please don't!' Um…but she did bring this friend. Um…and…er… we hit it off. And…er…after the wine bar we went to…er…to have a pizza and we all got…um…had a few more drinks and…er…the other woman who…er…ended up ordering a pizza that had a bunch of stuff on it that I really liked and she…I ordered a pizza that had a bunch of stuff on it that she really liked, so we picked at each other's pizzas all night and we realised that we were sort of… had a…an ideal relationship, so that we could order really any pizza on the menu and…er…we'd both be happy. And anyway we ended up…er…living together and still are.

CORALYN: Um…we met at a party and it was a fancy-dress party. A friend of mine's twenty-first and it was quite big and I went dressed as Alice in Wonderland and…um…this person, this guy that…um…I married was dressed as the Cheshire Cat. And it just seemed so amazing that, you know, we were both from the same thing and we started chatting and ended up being together.

JILL: Well, I'd arranged to go to the cinema with a group of friends and…um…unfortunately I missed the train that would have got me to the cinema on time so all my friends had gone in and I was left standing outside – the film had started, so I wasn't allowed in. And…um…there was a chap outside, he'd also missed the film and we started to talk and…um…we talked for quite a bit and he said, 'Let's go down the road and see that film, because that one hasn't started at the Odeon.' So we went down there and…um…well, we've been going out ever since!

CAROLE: I…I first met my partner…er…when he was on a boat and I was on the river bank, standing and looking generally into the distance and he was coming in to land with his boat and he threw me a rope and said, 'Would you mind catching this?' and I caught it and missed and tripped over it and fell in the river and he had to dive in and rescue me. And that was it!

(17.5) First paragraphs

Reading and Speaking

> **CAE exam**
>
> In the Reading paper of the exam candidates don't normally have to deal with fiction or literature. However, as reading fiction is one of the most painless ways of improving one's vocabulary and reading fluency, I make no apologies for encouraging students to discuss their reading here – and hopefully recommend books to each other.

A As revealed in B, the opening paragraphs are from:
a) *Emma* by Jane Austen (1816)
b) *Three Men in a Boat* by Jerome K. Jerome (1889)
c) *Rebecca* by Daphne du Maurier (1931)
d) *Nineteen Eighty-Four* by George Orwell (1949)
e) *Conundrum* by Jan Morris (1974)

B In this Communication Activity, the students have summaries of the books from which the extracts are taken. Student A looks at **Activity 13** (*Emma, Nineteen Eighty-Four* and *Conundrum*), and B at **Activity 21** (*Three Men in a Boat* and *Rebecca*) – in a group of three, two students should look at Activity 13.

C1 This can be done as homework, or together in pairs in class. The book doesn't have to be an English-language one, but it would be nice if it was.

2 Again this can be done alone or in pairs.

3 As this may take some time, it may have to be postponed till the next lesson.

D1 This may be more relevant for exam candidates than others. There are other writing tasks in 17.6 and 17.7.

2 Encourage everyone to make constructive criticisms.

(17.6) **Expressing feelings**   **Effective writing**

Ⓐ SUGGESTED ANSWERS

delighted	+	overjoyed tickled pink very happy
dismayed	+	disappointed upset sad sorry shocked
amazed	+	surprised astonished astounded taken aback
annoyed	+	irritated angry cross upset
puzzled	+	bewildered confused baffled perplexed flustered

Ⓑ1 Possibly, to add piquancy to this task, everyone could imagine that either Pam or Max is an old flame of theirs, from whom they parted on bad terms!

⤓ 2 The letters could be 'delivered' to another pair who could respond in the roles of 'Pam and Max'.

(There are some useful congratulatory phrases in Activity 33.)

➡ It might also be worthwhile spending time with the class discussing how one might begin and end a **letter of condolence** to someone who is ill, has been bereaved, has failed an exam, etc. Or perhaps a letter to Pam or Max years later when they have split up – or after one of them has failed to turn up at the church?!

Leo Jones *New Cambridge Advanced English*

(17.6) MODEL VERSION

Dear Mr and Mrs Dupont,

Thanks so much for letting me know about Pam and Max's engagement. I am delighted for them and look forward to the wedding. I haven't heard from Pam for ages but shall write to her immediately to get the low-down on her romance! I hope to see you soon.

Best wishes,

Chris

Dear Pam,

Congratulations on your engagement to Max! Your parents have just sent me a card about it. I must confess I was a little mystified to hear the news.

When I last heard from you, you had just turned down an invitation from Max to go out for dinner and didn't sound too keen on him. What has happened?

Please write soon and tell me how things developed between you and Max.

I am sorry I haven't kept in touch with you more over the past couple of years but hopefully we'll see more of each other now. I really am delighted for you both and am looking forward to your wedding.

All my love,

Chris

Dear Max,

How are you? It must be over two years since we were last in touch. That was when you wrote to announce your engagement to Kate. I wrote congratulating you and then never heard any more. I assumed you were having a long engagement.

Now I hear from Pam's parents that the two of you are engaged! Curiouser and curiouser! Please write soon and put me in the picture.

I look forward to hearing from you.

Best wishes,

Chris

(17.7) Four weddings and . . .   Listing and Creative writing

  1 Play the recording – once only should be enough to get the answers, but not to appreciate the stories properly.

ANSWERS

1 Ishia   **2** nobody   **3** Michael   **4** Karen   **5** Michael   **6** Tim   **7** nobody   **8** Tim

2 Arrange the class into an even number of pairs. You may want to play the recording again, pausing it between each speaker for the pairs to compare their own experiences.

3 Combine the pairs into groups.

Transcript   3 minutes 50 seconds

KAREN: I went to a fairly re…typical wedding recently…um…it was one of my cousins, who was marrying the chap she'd been engaged to for four years. They'd actually bought the house, they'd got the house full of all their stuff and they'd been preparing for this white wedding. Er… the whole family was there and…er…it was a competition to see which side of the family could fill their aisles on either side of the church with more people. And then we went on to the reception, where…um…the bride's mother and father who are my cousin and her husband decided that it would be wonderful fun for everybody to put no one next to anybody that they knew, which consequently made for a very boring time with people shouting across the room.

MICHAEL: I guess the biggest wedding I ever went to was my cousin's. She was married in Houston, this is about… er…six or seven years ago. And I'm afraid it was a typical…um…American wedding of total over-the-top excess. Um…the bride and groom arrived in these huge stretch white limos, all the bridesmaids were all dressed in this horrible shade of pink, but it was all very expensive because all the bridesmaids were dressed in silk. And the…the…the groom and his best man were wearing… er…formal dress but one was red and the other was blue. And…er…we all had to wear formal clothes but we…my family…my part of the family turned up in black. Er…and the guy was a dentist, you know, a big Houston dentist: dentists in Houston are *so* rich, you cannot believe how rich they are! The reception was in a big hotel in Houston and they had this really expensive rock band playing, I don't know how much… they said they paid them something like two grand to play for the night, and they were terrible, they were awful. I remember my…the main thing…my main impression after a couple of hours of this…um…reception was of my brother wearing formal dress, because I normally…I had never seen him in anything except jeans and a sweatshirt before, with a full beard and long flowing hair. I think the…the main impression of this wedding was conspicuous consumption. It rained f…drink and snowed food for three hours. It was horrible!

ISHIA: I've just been to an extraordinary wedding reception at the Café Royal… um…which was a Turkish friend of mine and arriving in the middle of London in Piccadilly Circus and walking into the Café Royal was a bit like arriving at Istanbul Airport – full of people, full of children, full of bags and clothes, and I've never seen anything like it in my life, it was absolutely extraordinary. Wonderful food, everybody dancing around like crazy, and then of course the…the wonderful moment where the groom and bride stand there and you have to pin money to them, which can be a bit embarrassing if you haven't brought much with you.

TIM: I don't think it really matters what kind of a ceremony you have to get married. I think the important part about is that it's the day for the bride and groom and the extraordinary feeling is that everybody is there because of you and because they love you and that's the most wonderful feeling and it's a day which is unlike any other day in your life. I got married in a registry office with just my parents there and my wife's parents and nobody else, because we didn't want a ceremony, we just had a *huge* party afterwards, the biggest party that you've…well, the biggest party I've ever thrown. Um…and just the feeling of having all your friends there looking up with this kind of love coming up from them was…was a really, really joyous experience and something that kind of cemented the marriage. I don't think you need a ceremony too much.

B 1 After everyone has noted the improvements in pairs or alone, reassemble the class to compare ideas.

2 Make sure everyone has time to compare their ideas (with a partner, in groups or as a whole-class activity) before they write a concluding paragraph.

C In case everyone wants a change from weddings, alternative events are suggested.

Leo Jones *New Cambridge Advanced English*

(17.7) MODEL VERSION

The last wedding I went to was my friend Petra's. She was marrying a man due to inherit a vast fortune in land and property. His family were quite happy to foot the bill for the festivities as long as they all took place on one of their country estates.

The ceremony was in the chapel (with choir, organ and soloists) and the reception was in the Great Hall. It was quite an event! The room dates back to the 18th century and was amazingly ornate, the ceilings covered in gold painted stucco and the walls lined with mirrors. Vast bouquets and garlands of flowers decorated every available space. There must have been about four hundred guests. Gold, silver and diamonds were dripping from the guests on his side whilst we, the humbler guests, wore our best outfits though we couldn't really compete with the Armani, Gucci and Versace numbers.

The food and drink were phenomenal: caviar, oysters, a hundred kinds of fish, cooked and cold meats. Desserts from paradise. Champagne flowed like water.

The best thing though was Petra's wedding dress. It had been her great-grandmother's and was a plain and simple off-white silk shift. It provided a startling contrast to the extravagant and lavish surroundings and was also a reminder that she too had a family and a history, if from the other side of the tracks.

© Cambridge University Press, 1998

Seventeen Love stories

Ⓐ **SUGGESTED ANSWERS**

1 loves   is devoted to   thinks the world of   can't live without
            is head over heels in love with   is crazy about   is keen on   adores

2 likes   fancies   is fond of   is attracted to   gets on really well with

3 dislikes   is indifferent to   doesn't get on with   has fallen out with   can't bear
            is incompatible with   doesn't think much of   has gone off

4 hates   can't stand the sight of   loathes   detests

Ⓑ **ANSWERS**

1	head	a good head for figures	= aptitude
2	minds	in two minds	= be undecided
3	head	keep your head	= don't panic
4	brain-	a brainwave	= brilliant idea
5	heads	heads	= the side of the coin with the Queen's head on
6	head	over my head	= too difficult
7	head	no head for heights	= suffer from vertigo
8	head	head over heels in love	= madly in love
9	mind	take your mind off	= help to forget
10	mind	keep an open mind	= remain unprejudiced
11	mind	slipped my mind	= forget
12	heads	two heads are better than one	= easier to solve problems with a partner

Ⓒ **ANSWERS**

1	ear	play it by ear	= improvise
2	eye	catch someone's eye	= attract attention
3	eye	keep an eye on	= watch carefully
4	eye	see eye to eye	= agree
5	face	keep a straight face	= not laugh
6	ears	couldn't believe my ears	= be astounded
7	nose	looks down her nose at	= regard with disdain
8	nose	follow my nose	= find way by instinct
9	-faced	two-faced	= not hold consistent/honest opinions
10	face	lose face	= lose dignity or respect
11	eyes	with his eyes open	= fully aware of the risk
12	ear	in one ear and out the other	= heard without making any impression

➡ Some other related idioms:

face up to	= confront problem realistically
save face	= avoid losing respect
with the naked eye	= without binoculars
be nosy	= inquisitive
be down in the mouth	= be miserable
needs his/her head examined	= do something stupid
make up my mind	= decide
off his/her head	= crazy
took the words out of my mouth	= just what I was going to say
with my eyes shut	= without difficulty
splitting hairs	= make insignificant distinctions

Eighteen THE NATURAL WORLD

18.1 FAUNA AND FLORA — Vocabulary and Listening

A 1 Some popular pets in the UK are:

dogs cats budgerigars hamsters gerbils canaries stick insects tropical fish goldfish rabbits snakes racing pigeons guinea pigs

2 Make a list on the board of the issues that the groups come up with. Then ask the students to give their opinions on each one – in groups or as a whole-class activity.

Some environmental issues are:

global warming recycling nuclear waste disposal acid rain protecting fish stocks wearing fur medical experiments on animals

+ topical local issues: new traffic schemes, motorways, power stations, nature reserves, etc.

B Some of the drawings are supposed to be ambiguous, so that students are more likely to disagree about the fauna and flora represented and thereby 'cover' even more vocabulary!

SUGGESTED ANSWERS (+ some extra species added to each group)

1 hare *or* rabbit squirrel bat bear gorilla hedgehog leopard deer goat dolphin
+ wolf chimpanzee baboon

2 owl peacock eagle *or* buzzard penguin parrot *or* macaw pigeon *or* dove stork swan vulture
+ seagull starling budgerigar

3 butterfly *or* moth bee wasp beetle *or* cockroach ant mosquito snail scorpion spider caterpillar
+ hornet bluebottle worm

4 frog dinosaur (diplodocus) lizard snake tortoise newt alligator *or* crocodile
+ iguana turtle toad

5 rose daffodil poppy tulip daisy carnation
+ dahlia buttercup chrysanthemum

6 palm tree cactus fir oak pine mushroom bamboo seaweed
+ apple tree beech maple

7 crab shark octopus squid trout sole lobster oyster mussel eel
+ sole cod scallop salmon

C In this reading activity, student A reads the opening paragraph of *The Transformation* by Franz Kafka in **Activity 5**, while student B reads the blurb of *Woof!* by Allan Ahlberg in **Activity 24**. Then they discuss the questions.

After they've discussed what they've read, you might like to ask your students to write a couple of paragraphs on this topic:

'What would it be like if YOU woke up one morning to find yourself transformed into a cockroach, a dog – or another creature?'

D These clips give students practice in using the 'clues' they hear to work out more information when they are listening to a conversation or a broadcast. Perhaps pause the tape after each clip.

ANSWERS

1	giraffes	6	unleaded petrol/fuel
2	harmless	7	acid rain
3	environment	8	recycled
4	greenhouse effect	9	nuclear energy/hydro-electric power/solar power
5	extinct	10	spiders

Transcript   3 minutes

NARRATOR: You'll hear ten extracts from conversations. In each case the last word or phrase is not audible. Decide what the missing word or phrase might be. Listen to the example first.

1

MAN: . . . no, they live in Africa and they feed on leaves. I don't think they roar or make any noise. Oh, they've got these wonderful, long necks. You've been to the zoo, haven't you? Now, when you were there, did you see the . . .

2

WOMAN: . . . but actually they're not slimy at all, their skin is dry. And they aren't all dangerous because some types don't have a poisonous bite, in fact…well…to humans they're perfectly . . .

3

MAN: . . . well, it's pollution, the overuse of chemical fertilisers and insecticides in agriculture all cause damage to the . . .

4

MAN: . . . carbon dioxide and other gases has led to an irreversible situation where the ozone layer is being damaged and the earth is likely to become warmer – this is known as the . . .

5

WOMAN: . . . felled and burned, all sorts of rare plants and animals are killed and we'll never see them again – these species'll all become . . .

6

MAN: . . . all new cars take it, but if you're not sure about your car ask your garage if your car can be adjusted by them to run on . . .

7

MAN: . . . the reason why the trees are dying is basically because the smoke and exhaust gases from industry, power stations and vehicles is full of sulphur dioxide and this poisonous substance falls to earth again as . . .

8

WOMAN: . . . yes, you see, paper, glass bottles and metal can all be used again more cheaply and without causing pollution or needing to cut down more trees. All these products can easily be . . .

9

MAN: . . . may be true but the article I read said that we should cut down on the amount of energy we use if we want to conserve fossil fuels and reduce the pollution they cause. Apparently, the only way of producing electricity without pollution is by using . . .

10

MAN: Hit it or something, go on, kill it! I can't stand them!

WOMAN: Calm down, and don't be so silly. It won't hurt you – you're not a fly, are you? – and I'm certainly not going to kill it because I like . . .

(18.2) Compound words   Word study

Ⓐ1 Compound nouns   Deal with any questions arising from the examples before the students begin A2.

You may like to point out to your students that in most compound nouns the main stress is on the first element but with a strong secondary stress on the second element:

blackbird	/'blæk,bɜːd/	classroom	/'klɑːs,ruːm/
toy shop	/'tɔɪʃɒp/	lighthouse	/'laɪt,haʊs/
greenhouse	/'griːn,haʊs/	coursebook	/'kɔːs,bʊk/
rainforest	/'reɪn,fɒrɪst/		

But in these NOUN PHRASES (i.e. adjective + noun) the main stress is often on the noun with a secondary stress on the adjective:

black bird	A crow is a large black bird /ˌblækˈbɜːd/ with a yellow beak – it's much bigger than a blackbird /ˈblækˌbɜːd/.
green house	They have a green house with a red roof.
toy shop	Little Timmy was playing with his toy shop – we can also imagine him playing with toy soldiers. (He probably bought his toy shop from a toy shop!!)

➡ However, in context, this pattern is often NOT followed, especially when we are making a special emphasis.

2 ANSWERS These are recorded on the cassette (1 minute 45 seconds).

charter flight   committee meeting   computer screen   drinking water
flight attendant   food chain   holiday brochure   language teacher   meeting point
ozone layer   palm tree   pet food   post office   pressure group   progress test
safety precautions   steering wheel   telephone call   traffic lights   typing paper
video recorder   waiting room   washing machine   wastepaper basket   water pressure
window cleaner   zoo keeper

ⓑ1 Compound adjectives
Again you might like to point out to your students that most compound adjectives have the main stress on the second element but with a secondary stress on the first element:

self-employed	/ˌselfɪmˈplɔɪd/	duty-free	/ˌdjuːtiˈfriː/
ozone-friendly	/ˌəʊzəʊnˈfrendli/	two-day	/ˌtuːˈdeɪ/
fourth-floor	/ˌfɔːθˈflɔː/		

2 ANSWERS These are recorded on the cassette (1 minute 40 seconds).

good-looking   green-fingered   hard-hearted   hard-working   heart-broken
home-made   ill-informed   loose-fitting   narrow-minded   quick-witted
record-breaking   self-employed   short-staffed   time-consuming   under-paid
user-friendly   well-behaved   well-meaning

⓲⁸·³ Protecting the environment   Reading and Listening

Ⓐ1 ANSWERS
1 C   2 D   3 I   4 E   5 K   6 B   7 G   8 L   9 F   10 J
(A and H don't fit anywhere)

> **CAE exam**   18.3 A1 is similar to one of the tasks in the English in Use paper. Candidates may need further practice using *Practice Tests* if they found it difficult.

2 The discussion could be in groups rather than pairs, if you prefer.

Ⓑ Play the recording after everyone has looked through the multiple-choice questions.

ANSWERS
1 C   2 B   3 D   4 C   5 C   6 274   7 395,000   8 255,000   9 39   10 71   11 29
12 20   13 hopeful/optimistic

> **CAE exam**   In the Listening paper there may be a text with multiple-choice questions, as here in questions 1 to 5 in **18.3 B**.

Transcript 8 minutes 15 seconds

CYRIL: My name is Cyril Littlewood and my job is that of founder and director of the Young People's Trust for the Environment and Nature Conservation.

INTERVIEWER: How did you start becoming interested in the environment?

CYRIL: When I was evacuated from London at the start of World War Two – er…children were evacuated away from London in case of bombing raids – er…I was sent about 40 miles…er…into Sussex in the South of England to a small town called Three Bridges. At that time it was still quite a rural area, there was lots of forest land nearby.

And one day my friends and I were out in the forest playing and we came across some poachers setting snares. We watched them for quite some time before they realised we were there and…er…they said, 'Oh, please don't tell on us because if you do we shall get into terrible trouble, and we're only trying to catch a few rabbits because we're hungry. If you don't tell we'll show you where you can come back and watch foxes and badgers.' Now this seemed a pretty good deal to us and so we said, 'Yes, OK.'

Um…and they actually did show us badger setts and fox's earths and they told us to come back and what time to come back. And in fact we went back, and we did see badgers and we did see foxes and that really got me hooked, there in those woods in Sussex.

INTERVIEWER: Why do you do it?

CYRIL: It's because it's something so important to me. I would hate to think of all the fantastic wildlife and plant life and wild places disappearing from our world.

INTERVIEWER: What sort of things then do you do on a typical day?

CYRIL: Luckily I don't have such a thing as a typical day. Er…this is one of the beauties of my job, i…it varies so much. I might be involved in design work for leaflets, um…or I might be required to go out and give school lectures, which I do fairly often. On other occasions I might be taking a group of children out…er…into the countryside, the local countryside. I should stress that the area around Guildford, where our offices are, is very beautiful. It's…er…well, I think some of the nicest countryside in Britain, except that I'm from Yorkshire and therefore I think Yorkshire's even better. But, um . . .

INTERVIEWER: Second nicest!

CYRIL: Yes, second nicest! Although then there's Dorset too, you see, where we spend so much of our time…er…running environmental discovery courses for children, that's a lovely place too.

INTERVIEWER: What form would they take?

CYRIL: The courses?

INTERVIEWER: Yes.

CYRIL: We spend eight or ten yea…weeks of the year down on the Dorset coast in a very small town called Swanage. It's surrounded by some of the most beautiful countryside, it's wild coastal scenery. And…er…we welcome parties of children to spend a week with us. During the course of each day we take the children out to different places. We look at habitats, we look at geology, we look at the history too. And all around us there we've got reminders of animal life, we've got three species of deer, we've got badgers, foxes, we've got seals, and…er…whales and dolphins that come round the coast, the occasional basking shark. In fact, couple those things with the scenery and Dorset is a fantastic place for children to visit to learn a bit more about nature.

INTERVIEWER: And do you think children take it…take it all for granted?

CYRIL: They don't take it for granted once they've spent the week with us. They begin to understand that there are wonders they'd never noticed before. We like to think that by the time those children go home, after six days, we've opened their eyes to some of the secrets of the countryside. And it's rather nice that so many school teachers have said, 'They've learned more with you in six days than they've learned in a whole term back at school.'

INTERVIEWER: And is there any particular animal that you…is your favourite?

CYRIL: The giraffe is one of my favourite animals, I always think the giraffe is such a lovely creature. I've followed them in East Africa with cameras and sort of got quite close to them. And I've found that as long as they can see you, they don't seem to worry too much about you, as long as you stay in sight. If you try creeping up on them, then they get nervous.

And as I tell children when we're out in the local woodlands, 'Talk at a normal level. Don't shout because that frightens animals away. Don't whisper because a whisper can sound threatening to an animal.' So if we're trying to approach some deer we do it with the children chatting in… talking away in sort of low tones and…er…it gives us a chance to get quite close to the animals.

INTERVIEWER: What can the average person do to help the environment, do you think?

CYRIL: The sad thing really is you say initially, 'There's so little you can do'. In an industrialised country such as Britain or most of the countries of Europe we'd say, 'Please don't waste energy, turn off all unnecessary lights, don't throw rubbish, don't throw litter. Perhaps use your car less if it's going to help reduce the amount of pollution in the air.' I…I'm saying this and yet I have to use my car to get around and do my job as so many other people do, so that becomes very difficult.

INTERVIEWER: But things have improved in the last five years or ten years, haven't they?

CYRIL: Attitudes have improved and some things have improved. Er…sadly animals like the tiger, for instance, are going down quite rapidly. And despite the fact that…er…charities raised £27 million to help the tiger, hardly any of that money has actually been used to do anything.

We don't have enough respect for animal life in the world. But then you see, every minute or so another 274 human babies are born into the world. We get people pouring into the world at a rate of 395,000 babies every day, and if you allow for the death rate and…er… subtract the death rate from the birth rate you'll find that at the end of each day we've gained approximately 255,000 more people on Earth. That's about 39 million people a year.

So, as 71% of the Earth's surface is covered by the oceans, we only have 29% left. Of that 29%, 20% is too hot and dry for agriculture, 20% is too cold for agriculture, 20% is too wet or too wooded for agriculture, and 20% is too mountainous or hilly for agriculture on a big scale. And that leaves us just 20% of the land surface on which to grow the majority of our food.

And these are all problems that we try to get across to children. You know, if you get a child to – as I did yesterday in a…a school – I say, 'Now put your hands on your heart.' I said, 'Can you feel it beating?' And some looked rather worried. 'Every time your heart beats "boo-boom" like that three more babies have been born into the world.' And things like that make the children think and remember. I've got great hopes for the future because children really are more genuinely concerned than ever I've ever known them to be.

INTERVIEWER: And much more aware as well.

CYRIL: And much, much more aware. They're more aware than most adults. A child can tell you a great deal more about acid rain and global warming. This is a hope for the future that these children of today are growing up to be more responsible…er…members of the public in the future. It doesn't matter where they are in the world, it…er . . . The African children are showing the same interest, children in parts of Asia are showing the same interest. In Japan there is a…a gradually growing movement against whaling, er…stimulated by young people once again. So young people throughout the world are beginning to realise that our world is a very beautiful and wonderful place and we've got to keep it that way.

INTERVIEWER: And quite fragile as well.

CYRIL: Very fragile.

C This is a follow-up discussion – and also preparation for the writing task in D.

D This is more vital for CAE exam candidates than others. (If necessary, remind everyone how to approach report-writing – see 13.5 in the Teacher's Book.)

18.4 The future and degrees of certainty   Grammar

A SUGGESTED ANSWERS

1 *I'll write to her tomorrow.*
   = offering or promising to do so
   I'm going to write to her tomorrow.
   = straightforward statement of intention
   I was going to write to her tomorrow.
   = I originally intended to do so, but now I won't OR I may not do so

I'll be writing to her tomorrow.
= sometime tomorrow this is what I'm going to do
I will write to her tomorrow.
= an emphatic offer or promise OR expressing determination to do so
I'm writing to her tomorrow.
= this is already planned (I've set aside time to do it tomorrow)
I'll have written to her tomorrow.
= I'm going to write today, so tomorrow the letter will have been written
I'll have to write to her tomorrow.
= it's necessary for me to do so tomorrow.

2 *Are we going to make the first move?*
= do we intend to do this?
Shall we make the first move?
= is it a good idea: do you agree with this suggestion?
Do we make the first move?
= are we expected to do this (is this the accepted procedure)?
Will we make the first move?
= is this what will happen in the future?

3 *I'm just going to phone them now.*
= I'm going to make the call straight away
I'm about to phone them now.
= I'm going to make the call straight away (as first example)
I was just about to phone them now.
= my intention was to make the call but now I'm not going OR I'm going to make the call straight away (as first example)
I'm phoning them now.
= I'm on the phone now OR I'm going to make the call straight away (as first example)
I've phoned them now.
= I have made the call and so you don't need to remind me again
I'll phone them now.
= I'm offering to make the call straight away OR I'm going to make the call straight away (as first example)

4 *Will you help us later?*
= I'm asking you to help us (a request)
Are you going to help us later?
= is it your intention to help us?
Will you be helping us later?
= is this what will be happening later?
Won't you be helping us later?
= I thought this is what would be happening later, but perhaps I was misled
Are you helping us later?
= is it your plan to help us?
Were you going to help us later?
= do you intend to help us? OR did you intend to help us (and now you've changed your mind)?
Won't you help us later?
= please, I'm asking you to help us (a more persuasive, cajoling request than the first example) OR I thought this is what you promised, but perhaps I was misled.
Aren't you going to help us later?
= I thought this is what you intended, but perhaps I was misled

B ANSWERS

1 *Shall* I help you to carry the shopping?

2 *no errors*

3 I'll have a drink while I'm *waiting* for his plane to land.

4 The meeting *won't/can't* begin until everyone *has* arrived.

5 *no errors*

6 I'm sure it *won't* rain tomorrow.

7 I'll be glad when it *is* time to go home.

8 *no errors*

C ANSWERS

1 will be cut down / will have been cut down

2 will be devastated

3 will have been destroyed

4 will accumulate

5 will (have to) be imposed

6 will have become / will become

7 will lead

8 will   be causing

9 will (have to) take

10 will have to come / will come

D SUGGESTED ANSWERS   (with second column rearranged)

1 I don't think he'll be here on time.

2 He's very unlikely to be on time.

3 I'm sure he'll be late.

4 He'll probably get here on time.

5 He may get here on time.

6 I know he'll get here on time.

7 I expect he'll be here on time.

8 I'm almost certain he'll be on time.

e I think he'll be late.

g I'm pretty sure he'll be late.

a He can't possibly arrive on time.

h He's unlikely to be late.

d I don't know if he's going to be late.

c He's not going to be late.

b I doubt if he'll be late.

f There's a slim chance he'll be late.

E

Notice that we tend to be suspicious of someone who says they are absolutely sure about something – just because they say they're sure it doesn't mean they're right!

SUGGESTED ANSWERS

100%	It's going to get warmer.	= I'm certain it will
↑	I'm absolutely sure it will get warmer.	
	It's sure to get warmer.	
	It's bound to get warmer.	= probable
	In all probability it's going to get a great deal warmer.	
	There's a very good chance that it will get warmer.	
	In all probability it will get warmer.	
	I wouldn't be surprised if it got warmer.	
	It's likely to get warmer.	
↑	I bet it will get warmer.	
50%	It looks as if it will get warmer.	= I'm uncertain
↓	I guess it might get warmer.	
	I suppose it might get warmer.	
	I'm fairly sure it won't get warmer.	
	I doubt if it will get warmer.	= improbable
	I don't think it will get warmer.	
	I'd be surprised if it got warmer.	
	There's not much chance that it will get warmer.	
↓	There's no likelihood that it will get warmer.	
0%	Of course it won't get warmer.	= I'm certain it will not

F

Allow enough time for this freer discussion, which gives everyone a chance to use the expressions from E.

(18.5) Spelling and pronunciation 2 – Vowels

Pronunciation and Word study

A **SUGGESTED RHYMES** (Some of these only work in R.P. and not other accents.)

calm · farm   caught · bought   bird · third   sleep · creep   slip · pip   pot · got
look · cook   lunch · crunch   cool · fool   bite · fright   now · cow   toy · boy
there · hair   here · fear   make · fake   note · goat   fuel · dual   tired · hired
tower · power   royal · spoil   player · greyer   lower · grower

B1 The two examples are recorded on the cassette as well as the three sentences that have to be highlighted in B2. (15 seconds)

2 Play the recording after the students have done this exercise. (30 seconds)

SUGGESTED ANSWERS

1 We all enjoyed your talk very much – the subject was very interesting.

2 The damage caused to the environment by industry *is* often overlooked.

3 Against all odds, Greenpeace has brought the plight of the natural world to the attention of caring people.

C This is a time-consuming, but important exercise.

No correct answers are given for all these homophones – consult a dictionary, if necessary, to settle any arguments.

D **ANSWERS** These are recorded on the cassette. (4 minutes)

i   (mile · title   film · kitchen   fright · island   firm · sir)

a   watch · yacht   father · castle   bald · yawn   share · scarce
    ache · vague   hand · factory   says · any

ea bear · pear   team · weak   break · steak   threat · jealous   hearty · sweetheart
    fear · dreary   search · earnest

au sausage · cauliflower   naughty · daughter   laugh · draught

ei receive · perceive   weight · neighbour   leisure · Leicester   their · heir
    height · either

ie chief · believe   fierce · pier   friendship · unfriendly   die · pliers

u   bury · guess   bullet · butcher   butter · mustard   business · busy   refuse · flute
    murder · burst

o   monkey · frontier   lose · movement   folk · ghost   crowd · shower
    orange · soften   boy · joyful   ordinary · glorious

ou enough · rough   found · plough   bought · court   cough · trough
    dough · although   through · throughout   should · could   thorough · borough

oo food · loose   flood · blood   floor · door   foot · book

(18.6) *Keep, hold, stand* and *turn*   **Verbs and idioms**

ANSWERS

1	turned	turned a blind eye	= deliberately not notice
2	turn	turn back	= return
3	held	held over	= postpone
4	stand	stand on ceremony	= be very formal
5	keep	keep in with someone	= stay on friendly terms with them
6	stand	stand up for	= support
7	keeps/kept	keep a record	= documents
8	holds	hold a record	= the fastest/biggest/etc.
9	keep	keep a diary	= write regularly in a diary
10	keep	keep someone company	= stay with them
11	turning	turning point	= point where significant change takes place
12	turned	turn down	= reject
13	hold	get hold of	= reach
14	Hold	hold it	= wait
15	kept	keep something back	= withhold
16	stands	stand in for someone	= deputise
	hold	hold the fort	= take charge temporarily
17	keep	keep your head	= not panic
18	stand	stand on her head	= do a headstand
19	stand	stand in your way	= prevent someone from doing something
20	stand	stand up to	= withstand

➡ Some other related idioms:

keep up with the Joneses	= maintain same material standards as one's neighbours
keep up appearances	= continue to do what's expected in public, to hide something
keep from	= prevent oneself from doing
hold off	= not begin
hold out	= last
stand out	= be conspicuous
stand up to	= resist and confront
standpoint	= point of view
stand-by	= backup
turn in	= go to bed
turn against	= become hostile to
take (it in) turns	= do one after the other

19.1 In the headlines

Vocabulary and Speaking

A Perhaps write up the names of some British newspapers and news magazines and explain what they are like. Bring some samples to class if you can.

In the UK the actual size of a daily newspaper is an indication of its readership and content:

- A tabloid is a small-format popular newspaper, with many human interest stories, scandal, gossip and sport. There are also Sunday tabloids.
- A quality daily 'broadsheet' is a more serious newspaper, with more extensive coverage of home and foreign news, the arts, business news and sport. There are also Sunday broadsheets.
- Every city or region also has a local evening newspaper (tabloid format) which covers local news and events.

B **SUGGESTED ANSWERS**

Tu   The manager of the bus company said that some bus services will/may have to be withdrawn in order to save money.

W   A number of bus passengers are critical of the bus company manager's intention to withdraw some services.

Th   The Minister (of Transport, presumably) said that he or she supports the bus company manager's proposal.

F   The bus company manager has resigned because of all the controversy over the proposal to withdraw some services.

S   Members of the Cabinet disagreed about the proposal to withdraw bus services and the Minister of Transport has resigned as a result.

C1 **ANSWERS**

axe/scrap = reduce/dismiss   **back** = support   **call** = request   **clash** = disagree
curb = restrict   **grab** = confiscate   **loom** = be imminent   **oust** = replace   **quit** = resign
slam = criticise   **soar** = rise   **swoop** = raid   **vow/pledge** = promise

2 ANSWERS

battle/clash etc. = disagreement   **bid** = attempt   **blaze** = fire
chief = person in charge/leader   **drama** = happening   **fury/outrage** = anger
link = connection   **riddle** = mystery   **split** = division   **threat** = possibility
war = rivalry

D1 Arrange the class into groups of three. All the original stories are in the Activities in D2, but make sure everyone tries to guess them before they start D2.

2 Student A looks at **Activity 17**, B at **Activity 30** and C at **Activity 36**. The stories are all genuine newspaper reports.

✂ **Preparation**   Make sure everyone does this before the next lesson. If English-language newspapers aren't available at local kiosks, you may have to supply some or they could photocopy articles in the library.

19.2 Don't believe everything you read . . .   Reading

A 1 They assumed the TV celebrity Dr Wolff had died, and didn't check their facts before publishing the article.

2 ANSWERS

1 Prof   **2** Prof   **3** Prof   **4** Dr (Hampstead Garden Suburb is not part of Hampstead, though it is near)   **5** Prof   **6** Dr   **7** Dr + Prof   **8** Prof   **9** Dr   **10** Dr   **11** Dr + Prof
12 Dr   **13** Prof

> **CAE exam**   19.2 A is similar to a task in the Reading paper where candidates have to find where particular information is given in one or more texts.

B These questions for discussion depend on the students having prepared a newspaper article. If they haven't done so, this should be postponed to the next lesson.

19.3 Danger – Hippies!   Reading and Listening

➡ IMPORTANT:

Allow plenty of time for these integrated activities. The whole sequence is likely to require at least 90 minutes, together with time for preparation and follow-up at home.

Follow the procedure suggested in the Student's Book for each stage of the sequence.

All the activities should be done by students in pairs, though some of the reading can be prepared at home before the lesson. No 'correct answers' are given here, as most of the questions are a basis for discussion.

30 MAY

 1 to 3 This is a listening activity. Follow the procedure suggested in the Student's Book.

Transcript   1 minute 15 seconds

Thursday 30 May

MALE NEWSREADER: Here is the news. The group of 300 hippies who set up camp on a farm in Somerset earlier this week have promised to leave quietly. The convoy of 100 vehicles had been on the move for several days, after being prevented from setting up camp at Stonehenge, where they wanted to hold a free pop festival to celebrate the summer solstice. Wiltshire police banned this festival and escorted the slow-moving convoy out of the county into Somerset.

The hippies, who call themselves 'peace people', live off social security handouts and collect weekly unemployment benefit. There are also many school-age children amongst them. Their homes are primitive home-made tents, called 'benders', and ancient converted buses or vans. According to the police many of these vehicles are unroadworthy and their drivers are breaking the law and causing a hazard to traffic. A number of hippies have been charged with drug offences since they first set up camp at the farm.

The owner of the farm at Lytes Cary near Somerton, Mr Les Attwood, who suffers from heart disease, claims that the uninvited campers have caused serious damage to his crops.

A High Court injunction ordering the hippies . . .

31 MAY

1 to 4 This is a reading activity. Follow the procedure suggested in the Student's Book.

 31 MAY TO 9 JUNE

1 & 2 As they listen to the broadcasts, students have to mark the route on the map in the Student's Book AND note down the single most important event of each day. Perhaps pause between each news bulletin for everyone to complete their notes.

Halfway through (at the point marked with ★★★ in the Transcript) stop the tape for everyone to discuss what they have heard so far.

The news broadcasts, although they do report the events that actually did happen, are slanted against the travellers in a decidedly non-BBC manner.

3 Working in groups, the students discuss their reactions to the story so far.

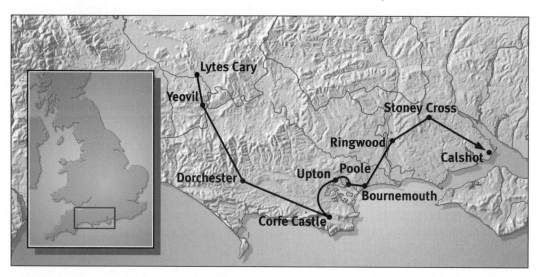

Transcript   5 minutes 20 seconds

Saturday 31 May

FEMALE NEWSREADER: Here is the news. The so-called peace convoy finally left Somerset today but were met by 300 police in riot gear who blocked the main road into Dorset. As Somerset police would not allow them to turn back into Somerset, for most of the day they were parked along the main Yeovil to Dorchester road. Finally, after the intervention of local MP, Mr Paddy Ashdown, the police agreed that the convoy could move on but only in five separate groups at half-hourly intervals. Local farmers, fearing that their own land might be invaded like Mr Attwood's, blocked all gates and access along the route. At the moment the five groups are reported to be heading in the direction of . . .

Sunday 1 June

MALE NEWSREADER: Here is the news. The so-called peace convoy reassembled last night near the village of Corfe Castle. This morning the convoy was forced to move on.

A police road block was set up at Upton and, after angry scenes, a police vehicle rammed the leading vehicle and forced it off the road. Following this incident, the twelve occupants of the vehicle were arrested. So far today there have been twenty arrests.

The convoy has just started moving again, but police are blocking all roads into the holiday resorts of Poole and Bournemouth. After leaving . . .

Monday 2 June

MALE NEWSREADER: Here is the news. Last night the 115 vehicles of the so-called peace convoy began a slow-moving journey through the outskirts of Poole and Bournemouth. At about midnight they crossed the Dorset border at Ringwood and drove into Hampshire finally stopping in the early hours at Stoney Cross, a picturesque beauty spot in the New Forest.

This morning, Hampshire police officers toured the area in loudspeaker vans informing them that they must leave by 3 pm, but many vehicles are now out of fuel and the 300 hippies have apparently decided to defy the police by refusing to move on again.

Chief Constable of Hampshire John Duke described them as 'anarchists who were spoiling a beauty spot and harassing residents and holiday-makers alike'. He said that they were . . .

Tuesday 3 June

FEMALE NEWSREADER: Here is the news. In the House of Commons today the Home Secretary described the peace convoy as 'a band of medieval brigands, who have no respect for the law or for the rights of others.' In a statement to the House . . .

Wednesday 4 June

MALE NEWSREADER: Here is the news. In a court hearing today one member of the so-called peace convoy who was arrested at the weekend has been sent to prison after his hearse ran into a police vehicle and damaged it. Local residents near their camp in the New Forest have complained that . . .

★★★

Thursday 5 June

MALE NEWSREADER: Here is the news. This morning the Cabinet discussed the matter of the so-called peace convoy and some ministers are understood to have urged changes in the law to prevent a reoccurrence of the events of the past two weeks. According to the Home Office, the present situation remains a matter for the police to deal with and there is no likelihood of the army being called in . . .

Friday 6 June

FEMALE NEWSREADER: Here is the news. As expected this morning the high court issued an order for the so-called peace convoy to disperse and leave the area of Stoney Cross in Hampshire. They have been given one week to organise their departure so that they can leave in an orderly way.

During the night a flock of sheep was attacked by stray dogs from the convoy and the owner of the flock, Mrs . . .

Saturday 7 June

MALE NEWSREADER: Here is the news. According to our reporter the so-called peace convoy at Stoney Cross shows no sign of moving on, despite warnings from police. A large tent has been erected where . . .

Sunday 8 June

MALE NEWSREADER: Here is the news. The 300 hippies in the New Forest today appealed for extra time to organise their departure. They say that their vehicles need repairs and they will be unable to drive away for several days. The site at Stoney Cross has been described by local residents as 'noisy, unhealthy, dangerous and filthy'.

Meanwhile in London . . .

Monday 9 June

FEMALE NEWSREADER: Here is the news. The so-called peace convoy is no more. At 4.30 this morning, in a carefully planned operation, 440 police officers from four counties under the command of John Duke, Chief Constable of Hampshire, entered the camp, woke up the hippies and forced them to leave the site. 124 out of 129 vehicles were impounded because they were unroadworthy or unlicensed. 38 people were arrested for possession of drugs. The hippies, now on foot, started to walk through the rain in the direction of Ringwood but as the rain became heavier most of them accepted the offer of free buses to Calshot, where they were given food and free rail tickets to their homes. The police operation which took . . .

10 JUNE AND 12 JUNE

1 Reading the two texts on page 164 could be set as homework, but they should be discussed in class.

⚆ 2 & 3 SUGGESTED ANSWERS

1 Sympathetic

2 No need to go in at 4 am
No need for so many police officers
No consideration given to the consequences of 'neutralising' the Convoy

3 They seem more concerned with criticising the police and the Government. Perhaps the main point is that 'someone' is going to have to come up with a permanent solution, rather than a series of temporary ones.

4 To avoid further violence

5 He doesn't seem to like them very much

6 To point out that the police behaved kindly – 'the firm, caring operation by the police'

FINALLY . . .

Ask everyone to what extent reading the editorial and the letter has changed their view on the events of May to June.

19.4 Connecting words   Effective writing

Parts of this section depend on the students having done 19.3.

A1 Highlight the relevant words in your own copy of the Student's Book.

2 And also highlight the five rhetorical questions in your copy of the Student's Book:

Fine – but then what?

Does that mean that hundreds of police are to spend the next fortnight marching around the lanes of southern England in case someone makes a fraudulent social security claim or someone else steals some firewood?

. . . is it really as great an eyesore or disruption as all the Ministry of Defence's convoys, ranges and no-go areas?

Has the Peace Convoy destroyed rural England on a scale to match the grain baron farmers?

Are all the road traffic, drugs and criminal damage offences that have piled up around the Convoy really so overwhelmingly serious that everyday crime prevention across large tracts of the south-west needs to be suspended to deal with it?

B1 Studying the expressions needs time – including more time as homework.

2 SUGGESTED ANSWERS   (Many variations are possible.)

Sure, . . . Sure, . . . Sure, . . .   *While it is true that . . .*
But . . .   *In spite of this . . .*
It doesn't . . .   And it doesn't . . .   *Furthermore . . .*
First, . . .   Second, . . .   Third . . .   *First of all . . ., Secondly . . ., Finally . . .*
Sooner or later . . .   *Eventually . . .*

C Continuing the article can be done for homework.

SUGGESTED ANSWERS

Although (*it must be admitted that*) hard drugs can never be totally eradicated, there are a number of steps that should be taken to reduce their use. *Furthermore* / *What is more* these steps must be taken at once – before it is too late.

Firstly / *In the first place* / *First of all*, national governments throughout the world must control the use and supply of drugs within their borders. *This means that* / *It follows that* international organisations must coordinate individual states' policies. States which 'supply' drugs may be pursuing contradictory policies to states that 'consume' them and *as a result of this* / *consequently* / *this means that* time and effort is frequently wasted.

Secondly, . . .

19.5 Crime and punishment   Vocabulary and Speaking

A1 ANSWERS

1 B **2** C **3** B **4** A **5** C **6** D **7** D **8** B **9** B **10** D **11** A **12** B **13** B **14** A
15 A **16** B **17** A **18** B **19** B **20** D

> **CAE exam**   **19.5 A1** is similar in format to Part 1 in the English in Use paper. In the exam there are only 15 gaps to fill – and the text is not about such a specialised topic as here. (The alternatives are words with similar meanings, not different spellings, as in the example.)

2 The text in A1 will help everyone to structure their description.

> **CAE exam** 19.5 **B**, **C** and **D** are similar to Parts 2, 3 and 4 of the Speaking paper.
>
> Part 1, which your students should have no problems with by now, requires the candidates to talk about each other for about 3 minutes (= $1\frac{1}{2}$ minutes each).
>
> In Part 2 each candidate has one minute to speak, plus 20 seconds to comment on the other candidate's task.
>
> Part 3 takes 3–4 minutes with both candidates participating as equally as possible. It's the candidates' joint responsibility to manage the interaction and marks are awarded for global achievement and interactive communication accordingly. In the exam the stimulus for this conversation is visual (illustrations, diagrams or photos), not a list of ideas as here in **19.5 C**.
>
> Part 4 takes 3–4 minutes. The examiner/interlocutor will encourage a more reticent candidate to speak more and discourage a more talkative one from dominating the conversation.

B 1 to 3 Arrange the class into pairs and keep the same pairs in C and D. Follow the procedure suggested in the Student's Book.

C 1 & 2 This is a collaborative task to be done together.

Some other more serious offences that might be mentioned are:

hijacking an airliner   blowing up an office block   killing a child   rape

Some other less serious offences that might be mentioned are:

parking in a disabled driver's space   taking stationery home from the office
letting down the tyres of someone's car   letting off a firework in a public place

D Finally, the students continue their discussion of crime and punishment/treatment.

19.6 Reports and opinions

Creative writing

A 1 to 3 Follow the procedure suggested in the Student's Book. Your students might prefer to use their own news photos instead of or as well as the ones in the Student's Book.

B 1 & 2 Exam candidates should do this 'against the clock' in one hour.

Leo Jones *New Cambridge Advanced English*

19.6 MODEL VERSION

It had been raining heavily all week. There was a rumour that the river might burst its banks, as it had done before, but none of us believed it.

When I woke on the Friday morning and looked out of my bedroom window I could hardly believe my eyes: the whole village had become a lake and it looked quite beautiful. There was nobody about – everyone was upstairs indoors, like us. The cars parked in the square were half-submerged and as the water was far too deep to wade through and we didn't have a boat, we were stranded. Downstairs everything was waist-deep in water, which went on rising all day and by late afternoon was nearly all the way up the stairs – but then it began to go down.

Everything on the ground floor in our house was ruined and had to be thrown away. It took us months to clear up the mess. Surprisingly, once the car had dried out it started first time – but the upholstery still smells of river water.

Dear Sir,

It was a miracle that nobody was drowned in the floods recently, but millions of pounds of damage was caused. How much longer do we have to put up with this?

There are three things which should be done right away:

1 The river banks need to be strengthened and raised by at least two metres.

2 A dam should be built in the mountains above the town, so that the flood water can be controlled. This could also generate electricity and the reservoir would be a fine tourist attraction and leisure facility.

3 If there is likely to be a flood, an official flood warning should be given by the authorities. If we had received adequate warning this year, we could have moved our furniture upstairs, driven our cars to higher ground and stayed out of danger.

It is high time something was done about this – what are we paying our taxes for?

Yours faithfully,

(19.7) Presenting a radio show

Listening

A Play the recording after everyone has read through the questions.

ANSWERS

1 O **2** A **3** E **4** G **5** P **6** K **7** H **8** M **9** B **10** L **11** N **12** D

The ones that don't match at all are: C F I J Q

Transcript 9 minutes

JoAnne: I'm JoAnne Good and I'm a radio presenter for a BBC station, a local BBC station although it covers three counties, it covers Sussex, Surrey and north Hampshire and also some of South London and it's the only BBC all-talk radio station. It did use to play discs, then they were removed and so it's specifically speech-based, which is supposed to deal with news, it's basically a news station but obviously there's a lot of entertainment involved as well and I deal with the arts programme and I present a four-hour arts programme… er…called the Late Show. We have a quarter of a million listeners.

INTERVIEWER: And how did you start?

JoAnne: I started by going into the radio station and doing their travel bulletins. If you're a travel presenter you have to find the travel information yourself and then present it, but you have to do this at 30-minute intervals throughout the day and you're not allowed to repeat yourself. So

if there's a traffic jam…um…that's recurring throughout the morning you can only mention it like once every two hours. And then you get into the whole thing where you have to mention the three counties as well, so if you mention a traffic jam in Sussex you have to make sure you also mention a traffic jam in Surrey and north-east Hampshire, otherwise you get the listeners phoning up from all these counties saying, 'We don't care what's happening in Sussex.' So all the time you're being a diplomat.

And so I was doing these early morning travel bulletins and…um…they became a bit of a cult actually, because I used to say, 'If you are in a traf…in a traffic jam do ring this number and let me know.' And I got a lot of people who would ring me on their mobile phones and say… um…'I don't think you mentioned the A27, JoAnne. And I found it particularly foggy this morning.' So…I would then say, 'Michael on the A27's just phoned through and he says it's foggy, look out!' And so people would just tune in in the end for these traffic bulletins and…um… I suppose I became a bit of a celebrity so they thought this would transfer well into my own show. Well, doing three-minute bulletins and then being given a four-hour nightly show was quite a big leap.

INTERVIEWER: And what do you most enjoy about what you do?

JOANNE: It's a four-hour show, two hours of which is…um…dealing with interviews with celebrities, but the first hour and the last hour are phone-ins. And the first hour is a phone-in advice hour, when we have a doctor…um…or an agony aunt or a gardener, or a cook. And those are great because you can actually learn, so I enjoy those because you put the questions forward that you really want to know, so you are the 'voice of the listener'. And then hopefully you get people on air phoning up to correspond with the specialist.

INTERVIEWER: Any funny experiences of people ringing in?

JOANNE: My managing editor never wanted anybody on air who was older than 50, um…they…they were called 'down-market listeners', and he wanted them off immediately. Well, one night . . . you…you…you pray you're going to get phone calls and you can judge the success of your broadcast by the amount of red lights which are flashing up throughout. These are the people that want to come on air, 'the caller'.

And I'd got Dr Colin Lewis in the studio with me and…um…we had Dorothy from Eastbourne phoned up, and she was 85 if she was a day. And she said, 'Doctor, I just can't sleep, I'm suffering from insomnia.' And Dr Colin Lewis went…launched into his …um… solution towards this, but Dorothy wouldn't get off. And often they will do this, um…a listener will 'milk' the…the expert for as long as they can. But if you're not getting many calls you're thankful for that. And we weren't getting many calls, Dorothy from Eastbourne on this particular evening was the only call! So I was helping the doctor along by saying, 'Dorothy, have you tried a lavender pillow?' and things like this.

Suddenly Line 5 started to flash. Now, Line 5 is an internal line which only the Managing Editor rings through on. If Line 5 goes it has to be answered. So my producer answered and…and flashed up on my screen: 'Kill Dorothy from Eastbourne,' which means: 'Get rid of Dorothy because she's too old.' So Dorothy was mid-conversation and I just had to wind up and said, 'Dorothy, have you ever tried taking a con…a good holiday and relaxing?' and then cut her off totally, which is very bad but that's…those are the odds you're up against, you see.

So the phone-in at the beginning is one of the best things but the phone-in at the end of the evening now that's when all the listening figures . . . That's what people tune in for and that's what is the best part of the whole job because you never know what is going to happen. That's why I do it for that hour because you never know who's going to come on air, you never know what they're going to say. And you have no 'delay button' – er…commercial radios have a 30-second delay but the BBC have no delay – so *you* have to judge if that caller is going to be dangerous or not. And you're in charge of the station: the BBC head office can close it. If you have somebody who comes on air who's libellous, if somebody swears, you can lose the station.

It was my fault, some kids went a step too far, they were on mobiles and I should have realised. If people phone through on mobiles…um…usually you have to be wary of them because they can turn the mobile off and you'll never get back to them, but on a mobile people take risks. And these children were all ringing from a rave in London, South London. They were all at this thing, ringing me through. They'd driven there listening to my show and they were ringing through. Now, you could tell that they were under the influence of alcohol and goodness knows whatever. But they were also being very very witty, and they were punctuating my show. So I was having normal calls from people in Eastbourne or whatever, but these kids would come in at other times. And it was like a running theme throughout. But one of them at the very end just came out with a – well, I won't repeat it on this – but a stream of abuse, which I was too slow at cutting him off. And it killed…it actually killed the whole hour. Because it wasn't witty, it wasn't clever, it just killed it. Even though there's no live audience you can sense the shock it was just…it ruined a very good hour.

What you do…what you have to do is you create 'waves'. You…you…you come out with…with very obvious statements to get a reaction really. And there was a wonderful … When I arrive just before the show I go through every newspaper and try and find news stories that will 'take'. Some news stories … You can guarantee if it's…i…in England the stories that will get people ringing in are language, anything to do with language, um…and the Royal Family, they will all . . . But that's the easy way out. A good radio show . . . the best thing to do is to stick with *one* topic, to be…to be brave enough to just deal with one topic, to go through every aspect of it so that you're, you know, the people listening, the people driving will think, 'No, I don't agree with her. She's saying . . . That's not right. I don't think . . . ' So if you cover every aspect of one topic there'll be something there for everyone. And that's what makes it an interesting discussion then…um…by the end of the hour. But if you're throwing in all different topics it's usually because the presenter's panicking.

INTERVIEWER: What have you done when there haven't been enough people ringing in?

JoAnne: It is…it is literally like running naked through the streets. It is…it…never are you more vulnerable, never are you more vulnerable. And what I have done, and… and I have…I've heard other presenters do this, and it is such a mistake, is to ring your friends to get them to ring in. Um…and if you listen you can always tell when it's not a genuine caller: genuine callers, there's…there's something about their apprehension about coming on air, or their passion about a subject or something. Um…or you have…there is a…a 'hit list' in the studio of people who call in regularly and we keep their numbers back and will ring them. So they might be watching a television programme and they'll get a call from the station saying, 'Can you come and help her out, we're talking about . . . cyclists, have you any opinion on this?' And you get them on air and you just milk them for as long as you can until other lights, the red lights, start lighting up, and you get other callers. But it can be a very very lonely hour. And because you can't break for music there is no…there's no one to help you. No one to help you, you just have to sit there and pray that the calls are going to come through.

(19.8) *Back*, *front* and *side*　　　Idioms and collocations

ANSWERS

1	back	behind my back	= without my knowledge
2	back	background	= family, interests, etc.
3	side	on the side	= unofficially
4	side　side	side by side	= next to each other
5	front-	front-page news	= important news
6	front-	front-runner	= favourite
7	back	back you up	= support
8	backed	back out of	= withdraw
9	back-	back-up copy	= reserve
10	back	backwards	= in reverse
11	back	backbencher	= non-office-holding MP
12	side	side effect	= secondary result
13	back　front	back to front	= the wrong way round
14	front	a front	= a way of hiding
15	front　back	front and back	= first pages and last pages of a book
16	side　side	from side to side	= swaying
17	backed	back down	= accept defeat
18	side	sidetrack	= distract

20.1 Earning a living   Vocabulary and Speaking

A Some words that might come up:

routine customers clients passengers counter desk computer responsibility
promotion prospects wages salary lunch hour shift work office hours white
collar blue collar paperwork memo fax e-mail correspondence

B1 This is intended to be provocative and controversial!

2 Some more jobs that might be added:

forestry worker fashion model clerk film director assembly line worker travel
guide street cleaner surgeon undertaker nursery school teacher coal miner

C1 Encourage the students to use their imagination in this discussion.

2 Each partner from C1 could do a different task because they might find it interesting to
compare their work later. This can be done in class or set for homework.

20.2 A satisfying job   Reading

A ANSWERS

0	the		5	conductor		11	✓		17	alone
00	✓		6	in		12	how		18	an
1	✓		7	✓		13	✓		19	away
2	the		8	on		14	past		20	✓
3	will		9	was		15	out		21	for
4	✓		10	✓		16	being			

> **CAE exam** **20.2 A** is similar to Part 3 in the English in Use paper, except that in
> the exam the text is less idiomatic, shorter and has fewer lines to
> proofread.

B She enjoys: driving passengers thanking her being in control

She doesn't enjoy: breaking down telling passengers to get off working at night
abuse (people swearing at her)

20.3 Satisfaction and success   Speaking

A Arrange the class into two groups: A and B. Explain the procedure to them (see the
Student's Book). If you have a large class it might be a good idea to issue the two groups
with different coloured badges or stickers so that they can see who's in which group.

In a large class there could be two Group As and two Group Bs.

1 To do this it's probably best if everyone mills around finding members of the other group
to interview. It doesn't really matter if people are interviewed twice, even if this may seem
rather unscientific.

If you prefer everyone to remain seated, re-form the class into pairs consisting of members
of different groups, so they can carry out the interviews.

2 The groups reconvene and process their findings.

3 Each group presents its findings to the other – try to make sure that most of the group have a chance to speak.

B Everyone writes a report summarising their findings.

20.4 Word order   Effective writing

A SUGGESTED ANSWERS

2 We should get in touch with them as soon as possible.

3 We should send them a fax immediately.

4 We also ought to send them a letter.

5 We shouldn't send them an e-mail every day.

6 We should never phone them in the morning.

7 We really shouldn't have taken so long to reply to their letter.

8 When will you have completely finished?

B SUGGESTED ANSWERS

1 They have a brand new office block in the heart of busy downtown Manhattan.

2 She has got a splendid well-paid job in an up-and-coming new computer software company.

3 The most reliable permanent member of our staff is taking early retirement.

4 I always stay in a lovely little traditional family hotel beside a beautiful mountain lake.

5 First I attended a long-winded monthly staff committee meeting and then I made an important business phone call.

C SUGGESTED ANSWERS

1 The River Thames in London is spanned by over twenty bridges, of which Tower Bridge, built in 1894, is the most famous.

2 The first stone bridge was London Bridge, which was built in 1209, lasted six hundred years and was the only bridge across the river until 1750.

3 In 1968, Robert McCulloch, an American millionaire, found out that London Bridge was about to be demolished because a new one was to be built.

4 He decided to buy it and have it shipped to America and rebuilt in the desert at Lake Havasu in Arizona as a tourist attraction.

5 His offer of $2.4 million, plus an extra $1,000 for every one of his sixty years of age, was accepted.

6 It was only later that he realised he had made a slight mistake.

7 He had assumed that it was Tower Bridge that he was buying and he hadn't realised that London Bridge was just an ordinary stone bridge dating back to 1908, so he was very disappointed.

8 If you visit Lake Havasu now you can see London Bridge rebuilt there, which is an impressive sight!

> **CAE exam**   **20.4 C** is like Question 6 in the English in Use paper. Candidates should make sure that they spend enough time on it and check their sentences very carefully afterwards, making sure they've included the relevant information, not distorted any of it, and not imported any extra information. They should also make sure their spelling, punctuation and grammar are correct! Further practice using *Practice Tests* is recommended. This task type will be replaced in the exam with a 15-item word formation task after June 1999.

20.5 Great business deals? Reading and Listening

A 1 The original titles were:

1 The best real estate deal in history
2 Not again, Josephine!
3 Nice ice at a reasonable price

2 SUGGESTED ANSWERS

1 $24 worth of kettles, axes and cloth*
2 $80,000,000
3 $27,000,000
4 (about) 12 cents
5 (about) 800,000 square miles
6 (about) 1,600,000 square miles
7 $7,200,000
8 (about) 5 cents
9 $750,000,000 worth
10 100,000,000,000 tons (estimated)

* On a serious note: Perhaps you should remind everyone that the European colonists and settlers in North (as well as Central and South) America not only ruthlessly deprived the Native Americans of their land and hunting grounds by theft, trickery and force of arms, but actually killed most of them – millions of Native Americans died in bloody massacres, in concentration camps and on death marches, from alcoholism, from starvation, and from imported diseases like smallpox, measles and cholera. Before 1492 over 10 million Native Americans lived north of the Rio Grande; by 1890 only half a million survived.

 B SUGGESTED ANSWERS

1 STEAMSHIP 2 20,000 3 Aristotle Onassis 4 depression 5 millionaire

6 £6,000 7 Big Ben 8 2,000 9 100,000 10 The Statue of Liberty 11 Australian
12 5 13 California

14 scrap metal 15 bank notes 16 50,000 17 Al Capone 18 1945 19 134,000,000
20 1947

Transcript   6 minutes 30 seconds

In the…er…late 1920s, early 1930s, there was a…a young Greek businessman who…er…made quite a lot of money…er…by importing tobacco into Argentina. Um…he then moved up to North America…er…this was in about…er…1933, when of course the world was in the middle of a…a trade slump. Er…he…er…decided he wanted to get into shipping, and to get into shipping he needed ships so he…he started looking around for some ships to buy with his tobacco fortune and he found ten vessels…er…which belonged to the Canadian National Steamship Company…er…the problem being that they were frozen into the ice in the St Lawrence River in Canada. They'd been rusting away there for two years and were now completely filled up with snow and ice. Er…in fact the story goes that when he went aboard to…er…inspect one of the ships, he fell into a snowdrift and…er…ended up on the deck below. Well, the ships had cost $2 million to build…er…about ten years before, and the owners were prepared to let them go just for a…a scrap price of…er…$30,000 each. He offered $20,000 and the owners accepted.

He left them there, stuck in the ice, there was nothing more he could do. Er…but a few years later, the…the world depression…er…came to an end and…er…world war seemed to be looming in Europe and of course that led in its turn to a…a bit of a shipping boom. So the young man, there he was with his ships and…er… he became one of the richest men in the world. His name was . . . Aristotle Onassis.

Once upon a time there was an enterprising Scottish actor, called Arthur Furguson, who discovered that he could make a very good living selling things that didn't actually belong to him, in other words he was a con man.

He first got the idea when he was sitting in the middle of Trafalgar Square (in London that is). Um… this was in 1923, and he saw an American tourist admiring the stone lions and the fountains and Nelson's Column. He introduced himself as the 'official guide' to the Square and started to explain the history of the place. And while he was doing this he also slipped in a little mention that as Britain was heavily in debt, the British government was looking for the right kind of person to buy the Square. He said that he was the official government salesman and that the asking price was around £6,000. The American said that this was a good price and offered to pay by cheque right away, so Mr Furguson went off to okay this with his superiors – in other words he went off for an hour and a half and kept the American waiting. Well, he then came back and said: yes, they were willing to sell to the American at that price. The American wrote a cheque and Furguson gave him a receipt and the address of a company who would dismantle the Square and get it ready for shipping it to the States. Then he went off to cash the cheque.

Soon after that he sold Big Ben for £1,000 and took a down-payment on Buckingham Palace of £2,000. Two years later he went to the United States and leased the White House to a Texas cattleman for 99 years for $100,000 per annum. Later he arranged to sell the Statue of Liberty to an Australian for $100,000, but unfortunately Furguson allowed the buyer to take a photograph of him, and the Australian, feeling slightly suspicious, showed the photograph to the police. Furguson was identified and sent to prison for fraud for five years. When he came out he retired to California, where he lived in luxury until he died in 1938.

In 1925, in Paris, there was a man called Victor Lustig, he was actually a…a Czechoslovakian but he was living in Paris. And one day, he noticed a news item in the paper that said that the Eiffel Tower was badly in need of repair. He used his connections and got hold of some official notepaper from the Ministry of Posts and wrote letters to five businessmen inviting them to a meeting with, as he signed it, 'Count Lustig', at a famous hotel.

All of them attended this meeting and they were told in so-called complete confidence that the Eiffel Tower was in a terrible condition and would have to be demolished and rebuilt, and they were invited to submit tenders for 7,000 tons of scrap metal.

Well, after the meeting, Lustig got in touch with one of them, Monsieur André Poisson, and told him that the deal would go through more smoothly if he could manage to pay a little extra money, in other words a bribe. Well, Poisson being greedy, er…agreed to this and paid the full price for the scrap metal and the bribe. Now, he paid it in a banker's draft, er…so Lustig took the banker's draft and left the country. Now, Poisson was so ashamed of what he'd done that he didn't dare tell the police so Lustig came back again – and repeated the trick on another businessman. However, this time after this he left the country and emigrated to America, where he continued his trade on that side of the Atlantic.

Now, one of his deals here was to sell a machine to a millionaire that would duplicate bank notes and for this he got $50,000. In the 1920s he persuaded Al Capone, the famous gangster, that he had a system by which he, Capone, could double his money on Wall Street and Capone gave him $5000 for this. However, Lustig, probably for obvious reasons, thought better of this deal and paid Capone back his money. He became an associate of Capone's and started a new line of business: printing bank notes. But in 1934 he was caught and imprisoned. However, he escaped. Eventually, after eleven years, in 1945 he was rearrested and found guilty of printing $134 million!! He died in prison in 1947.

(20.6) Abbreviations and acronyms   Word study

Ⓐ ANSWERS

i.e. = that is   **e.g.** = for example   **fig** = figure   **pp** = pages   **qv** = see another entry
cf = compare   **ch** = chapter   **ed** = edited by   **para** = paragraph   **NB** = important note
intro = introduction   **cont'd** = continued

Ⓑ ANSWERS

2 personal assistant

3 15 thousand pounds per annum

4 not applicable

5 enclosed curriculum vitae and (photograph)

6 as soon as possible

7 reference number

8 at £19.99 (including Value Added Tax) per dozen   15 per cent

9 Limited   public limited company

10 telephone number   extension

11 on behalf of   Department

C   ANSWERS

1 Dr Brown doesn't live at 13 St Albans Ave any more – she's moved to no. 30, hasn't she?

2 This VHS VCR can record NICAM stereo broadcasts in hi-fi sound, and it can also play either NTSC or PAL system videos.

3 The USA is over 9 million sq km / km^2 in area: it's 38 times larger than the UK.

4 This CD-ROM player operates at 220 v AC, not DC.

5 At the end of the talk there wasn't time for a Q & A session.

D 1 If you can bring copies of some English-language newspapers to class this can be done right away without preparation.

2 In France, for example, where the TV system is SECAM (séquentiel électronique couleur à mémoire) this might be explained like this:

'SECAM is the system we use for TV in France – it's not compatible with PAL, which is used in the rest of Europe, or NTSC, which is used mainly in the USA and Japan.'

3 The abbreviations used should be English ones!

➡ Some more common abbreviations:

EU (European Union)   NB (*nota bene* – note well)   UN (United Nations)   BBC (British Broadcasting Corporation)   P.S. (post script)   PC (personal computer *or* politically correct)   ASAP (as soon as possible)   Rd (road)   Sq. (Square)   PTO (please turn over) RSVP (*répondez s'il vous plaît* – please reply)

AIDS (Acquired Immune Deficiency Syndrome) and HIV (human immunodeficiency virus) BSE (bovine spongiform encephalitis – mad cow disease) and its human equivalent CJD (Creutzfeld-Jakob disease)

and acronyms:

UNESCO = United Nations Educational, Scientific and Cultural Organization
UNICEF = United Nations International Children's Fund
OPEC = Organization of Petroleum Exporting Countries
NATO = North Atlantic Treaty Organization
SABENA = *Société anonyme belge d'exploitation de la navigation aérienne* (the Belgian airline)
QANTAS = Queensland and Northern Territories Air Services (the Australian airline)

20.7   *-ing* and *to* . . .   Grammar

A   SUGGESTED ANSWERS AND CONTINUATIONS

1 **We stopped to eat our sandwiches when . . .**   *. . . we saw a suitable place to sit down.*
= we were walking along and then stopped in order to have a picnic
We stopped eating our sandwiches when . . .   *. . . it started to rain and we ran for cover.*
= we were eating our sandwiches but stopped doing so, perhaps suddenly

2 **I won't forget to meet her because . . .**   *. . . I've made a note in my diary about it.*
= this is something I'll remember to do (*in the future*)
I won't forget meeting her because . . .   *. . . it was a memorable occasion.*
= this is something I remember vividly (*in the past*)

3 *He'd like to study alone because . . .*   *. . . he has an important exam next week.*
    = this is what he wants to do now or soon.
    He likes studying alone because . . .   *. . . he finds it easier to concentrate.*
    = this is what he always/generally prefers
    Studying alone is what he likes because . . .   *. . . he can spend all night at it if he wants to.*
    = this is what he enjoys

4 *I used to write a lot of 250-word*
    essays but . . .   *. . . not any more: now I write much longer ones.*
    = this was what I customarily did in the past
    I usually write a lot of 250-word
    essays but . . .   *. . . recently I haven't written any.*
    = this is what I normally do
    I'm used to writing a lot of 250-word
    essays but . . .   *. . . this subject is really causing me difficulties.*
    = this is what I am accustomed to doing (now)

5 *Sometimes she didn't remember to hand*
    in her work because . . .   *. . . she used to be so absent-minded.*
    = this is what she forgot (*in the past*)
    Sometimes she doesn't remember to hand in
    her work because . . .   *. . . she is so absent-minded.*
    = this is what she forgets to do (*in the present*)
    Sometimes she doesn't remember handing
    in her work because . . .   *. . . she has such a short memory.*
    = she does hand in the work but she forgets whether she has done so or not

6 *The lecturer went on to tell the audience*
    about . . .   *. . . his eventful voyage home.*
    = this is what he did next
    The lecturer went on telling the audience
    about . . .   *. . . the theory of relativity.*
    = after an interruption he continued the same story

7 *We tried to get through to her on the*
    phone but . . .   *. . . there was no answer.*
    = this is what we attempted to do
    We tried getting through to her on the
    phone but . . .   *. . . without success, so one of us went round to her flat.*
    = this is the method we tried and perhaps another method succeeded
      OR this is what we attempted to do (as first example)

8 *I regret to tell you that your application*
    was unsuccessful because . . .   *. . . your qualifications are not suitable.*
    = I'm telling you this bad news now (*rather formal style*)
    I regret telling you that your application
    was unsuccessful because . . .   *. . . I didn't think you'd burst into tears about it.*
    = I'm sorry that I told you this, perhaps because you reacted so badly

B1 This is a time-consuming exercise, but important. It could be prepared at home.

SUGGESTED ANSWERS

allowed – B   appreciated – E   arranged – A   asked – B   assumed – E   attempted – A
avoided – C   **began** – A + C   chose – A   consented – A   considered – C
continued – A + C   **decided** – A + E   **denied** – C + E   **discovered** – D + E
disliked – C + D   encouraged – B   enjoyed – C   expected – B   failed – A   felt like – C
found – D + E   found out – E   finished – C   forbade – B   forced – B   **forgot** – A + E
got – B   gave up – C   guessed – E   happened – A   **heard** – D + E   **helped** – A + B
hesitated – A   **imagined** – C + E   **intended** – A + B   invited – B   knew – E
managed – A   **meant** – A + B   **noticed** – D + E   ordered – B   persuaded – B
postponed – C   **pretended** – A + E   promised – A   proposed – A   realised – E
recommended – B + C   refused – A   saw – E   spent some time – C   **suggested** – C + E
told – B   thought – E   **tried** – A + C   understood – E   **wanted** – A + B   watched – D
wished – A + B + E

▼ **2** Some students may want to highlight more than ten verbs.

3 This can be begun in class and continued as homework.

Ⓒ ANSWERS

1 Although I was looking forward to *meeting* her, I was afraid *of making* a bad impression.

2 *Smoking* is not allowed in the office but employees are permitted *to smoke* in the canteen.

3 Everyone was beginning *to get* nervous before the exam, but once we began *to realise* that we were all in the same boat we began to feel better.

4 The man denied *having* committed the crime but he failed *to convince* the magistrate.

5 They made me *sit* down and wouldn't let me *leave* without *apologising* for being rude to them.

6 To get a good job you have to *have* the right qualifications.

7 Don't forget *to make* notes before you start to write the essay, and remember *to check* your work through afterwards.

8 You can't expect *to achieve* success without *working* hard.

20.8 Applying for a job   Creative writing

Ⓐ This could be done as a whole-class discussion, rather than in pairs.

Ⓑ1 In real life there's no word limit to job applications, but such a letter should probably be one side of paper if it's word-processed or typed.

2 The students read each other's work.

CAE exam	A job application letter might well be a task in Question 1 (Part 1) of the Writing paper – and there may be more information to process than in **20.8 A**. In this case, the application must include all the required relevant information.

Leo Jones   *New Cambridge Advanced English*

20.8 MODEL VERSION

Dear Mr Western,

I am writing in response to your advertisement for part-time hosts and guides for your clients.

I am a 51-year-old retired teacher of English as a Foreign Language and have worked and lived in Greenwood for 15 years. As well as being used to dealing with groups of people, I am a seasoned traveller, having spent my twenties working in Europe and the Far East. I think I can appreciate the position of people away from home, in a country whose language they may not know well.

In my last job I was the Social Organiser for the language school. This involved coordinating a social programme for over 400 students per month with an age range from 16 to 70+. I have good contacts with most of the local cultural, sporting and tourism fraternity and certainly have a knowledge of what's on where.

As a student I acted as a guide in art galleries and museums, so I do have some direct (if rather distant) experience of guiding.

I am available for this work from Monday to Thursday, including evenings and would be prepared to work on Sundays if necessary.

I enclose my resumé.

Yours sincerely,

Pat Matthews

P.J. Matthews

(20.9) *First, second, third . . . and last* Idioms and collocations

Ⓐ SUGGESTED ANSWERS

1	*Max arrived late.*	= he didn't arrive on time
	Max arrived last.	= everyone else arrived before him
2	*I decided to catch a late train.*	= not an early one
	I decided to catch the first train.	= the first of the day
	I decided to catch the early train.	= the only early one
	I decided to catch the last train.	= the last of the day
	I decided the train was late.	= I worked out that it wasn't on time
	I decided to catch an early train.	= one of the early ones
3	*A second-hand watch*	= not a new one
	The second hand on a watch	= the hand that shows the seconds, not the minute hand
4	*Her first husband*	= the first of her husbands
	Her last husband	= her most recent husband OR the final husband of several
	Her latest husband	= her current husband (of many)
	Her ex-husband	= her previous husband
	Her second husband	= the husband after the first
	Her late husband	= she is a widow
	Her former husband	= her previous husband
	Her husband is late.	= he hasn't arrived yet

Ⓑ ANSWERS

1 *lasts*   the *last* straw

2 *first* things *first*   *first* thing
on *second* thoughts   at the *latest*

3 *first* come, *first* served

4 at *first*   *lasted*

5 *second* nature   on *first* name terms

6 *last*-minute   *later* on

7 at *first* hand   *first*-rate

8 *second*-rate   as a *last* resort

9 the *last* word

10 a *second* chance / a *last* chance

11 a *second* opinion

12 *first* cousins   *second* cousins

13 *latest* news   at long *last*

14 *first* aid   the week before *last*

15 in the *third* person   in the *first* person

16 *Last* but not *least*

READING

1.1	Landings
1.4	The Castaways
2.5	Japanese beach lovers & Push-button lover
3.3	The rage of Rambo
4.2	Cat canteloupe
5.2	Trouble in paradise
5.5	Travel writers
6.2	Politically correct?
6.5	Horoscopes
7.3	Different styles
7.4	The unstoppable Albert Sukoff
7.5	Spammed and Writing unlimited
7.6	The secrets of writing business letters
8.1	The good old days?
9.1	Life begins at 50
9.2	The Greys
9.4	Family life
10.2	Island
10.3	The best of all possible worlds
10.5	Brasilia
11.3	Remarkable Charlie
11.5	Record-breaking lottery winner
12.3	The Cat Sat on the test
12.4	That sixth sense
12.6	Clock of ages
13.3	Gestures
13.4	You just don't understand!
14.1	English in the world
15.1	New legends for old
15.2	Odd, odder, oddest
15.3	Inhuman nature
16.3	Mirror, mirror
17.2	Small World
17.3	In her arms, he melted
17.5	First paragraphs
18.3	Protecting the environment
19.2	Don't believe everything . . .
19.3	Travelling tribe . . .
20.2	Rosalyn Clark, bus driver
20.5	Great business deals?

LISTENING

1.1	A year on a desert island
2.2	World Music
2.5	See the world?
3.2	One of my favourite films . . .
6.1	Seven descriptions
7.1	Handwriting
7.7	The differences between spoken and written English
8.3	Fourteen ninety-nine
8.5	In other words . . .
9.3	Granny power
10.1	An ideal home?
10.2	The perfect society

11.1	Role models
12.1	Ten clips
12.2	First day at school
12.6	How does it work?
13.1	The art of conversation
14.2	Indirect speech
15.3	A sense of humour
16.1	Five clips
17.4	First meetings
17.7	Four weddings and . . .
18.1	Ten clips
19.3	Danger – Hippies!
20.5	Great business deals?

INTERVIEWS

1.5A	Pen Hadow – an Arctic explorer
3.1B	Maev Alexander – an actress
5.1C	Susan Davies – a traveller
7.2	Isabelle Amyes – a television scriptwriter
9.1D	Geoffrey Smerden – founder of a University of the Third Age
11.6A	Anita Roddick – founder of The Body Shop
12.1A	Wendy Fielder – a research scientist
13.5A	Bob Stanners – an advertising copywriter
15.4	Ian Howarth – founder of the Cult Information Centre
18.3B	Cyril Littlewood – a conservationist
19.7	JoAnne Good – a radio presenter

WORD STUDY

2.6	Synonyms and opposites – 1
3.4	Making an emphasis
4.5	Words easily confused
6.4	Synonyms and opposites – 2
8.4	Forming adjectives
10.6	Synonyms and opposites – 3
14.5	British and American English
16.2	Prefixes
16.3	Spelling
18.2	Compound words (nouns and adjectives)
20.6	Abbreviations and acronyms

GRAMMAR

2.3	The past – 1
4.4	Simple + progressive aspect
6.3	Modal verbs
8.2	The past – 2
10.4	Articles
12.5	Comparing and contrasting
14.2	Indirect speech
16.4	Conditional sentences
18.4	The future and degrees of certainty
20.7	*-ing* and *to* . . .

SPEAKING AND PRONUNCIATION

2.4 Really? That's amazing! (expressing reactions)
4.3 Appropriate language (formal and informal styles)
6.1 What do they look like? (describing people)
11.2 Emphasising the right syllable
11.5 Sharing opinions
14.3 Spelling and pronunciation 1 – Consonants
16.5 Giving advice
17.4 First meetings
18.5 Spelling and pronunciation 2 – Vowels
19.5 Crime and punishment (discussion in the style of the CAE Speaking paper)
20.3 Satisfaction and success (conducting a survey)

EFFECTIVE WRITING

1.2 Joining sentences – 1
3.5 Punctuation
4.2A Spelling and punctuation
5.3 Making notes
7.4 Long and short sentences
7.6 Formal letters and personal letters
8.5C–D Formal and informal style
9.2 Paragraphs
11.4 Style, tone and content
13.2 Joining sentences – 2
15.2 A good introduction and conclusion
17.6 Expressing feelings
19.4 Connecting words (conjunctions)
20.4 Word order

CREATIVE WRITING – the main Creative writing sections are in bold type

1.3 **Writing a narrative**
2.5D A letter to a friend
3.8 Planning ahead and writing a review
4.2C Instructions (a recipe) and a note
5.4 **A complaint letter and a note**
6.4E A letter of reference
7.8 **A tactful (informal) letter**
8.3C Descriptions of the lives and achievements of two historical figures
9.5 **A letter to the editor (of a magazine)**
10.3C A description of your own Utopia
10.5D A letter describing the attractions of a city

11.5E A letter to a friend who has won the lottery
11.6C **Descriptions of three household names for a guidebook**
12.2B A letter about your first day at a new school or in a new class
12.4B A letter to the writer of the article OR an account in the same style as the article
12.6E Instructions on how to operate household equipment
13.5C **A report on advertisements in a magazine**
14.4F Instructions on what to do in case of fire
15.4C **A letter giving advice and a note** (based on information in the Interview)
16.5B Another letter giving advice
16.6B **Instructions for a first-aid manual**
17.5D An article describing a favourite book
17.7C **An account of a wedding or a family event**
18.3D A report on measures to protect the environment
19.6 **Reports and opinions (a report and an opinion column)**
20.1C An account of someone's day at work
20.8 **A letter applying for a job**

IDIOMS AND PHRASAL VERBS

1.6 All's well that ends well! — idioms and collocations with *all*
2.7 You can't lose! — verbs and idioms with *lose*
3.7 At . . . and by . . .
4.6 *Bring, carry* and *take*
5.6 *High, middle and low*
7.9 *In . . . and out of . . .*
8.6 *Get*
9.6 *Ages* — idioms and collocations with *age, fresh, new, old* and *young*
10.7 *Hard, soft, difficult and easy*
11.7 *For and on*
12.7 *Look* and *see*
13.6 Colours — *red, blue, green, black* and *white*
14.6 Speaking and thinking — *say, tell, call, speak, talk* and *think*
15.5 *Day* and *time*
16.7 *Hearts, hands, legs* and *feet*
17.8 Head over heels . . . — *head, brain, mind, face, eye, nose* and *ear*
18.6 *Keep, hold, stand* and *turn*
19.8 *Back, front* and *side*
20.9 *First, second, third . . .* and *last*

READING

1.1	Landings
1.4	The Castaways
2.5	Japanese beach lovers & Push-button lover
3.3	The rage of Rambo
4.2	Cat canteloupe
5.2	Trouble in paradise
5.5	Travel writers
6.2	Politically correct?
6.5	Horoscopes
7.3	Different styles
7.4	The unstoppable Albert Sukoff
7.5	Spammed and Writing unlimited
7.6	The secrets of writing business letters
8.1	The good old days?
9.1	Life begins at 50
9.2	The Greys
9.4	Family life
10.2	Island
10.3	The best of all possible worlds
10.5	Brasilia
11.3	Remarkable Charlie
11.5	Record-breaking lottery winner
12.3	The Cat Sat on the test
12.4	That sixth sense
12.6	Clock of ages
13.3	Gestures
13.4	You just don't understand!
14.1	English in the world
15.1	New legends for old
15.2	Odd, odder, oddest
15.3	Inhuman nature
16.3	Mirror, mirror
17.2	Small World
17.3	In her arms, he melted
17.5	First paragraphs
18.3	Protecting the environment
19.2	Don't believe everything . . .
19.3	Travelling tribe . . .
20.2	Rosalyn Clark, bus driver
20.5	Great business deals?

LISTENING

1.1	A year on a desert island
2.2	World Music
2.5	See the world?
3.2	One of my favourite films . . .
6.1	Seven descriptions
7.1	Handwriting
7.7	The differences between spoken and written English
8.3	Fourteen ninety-nine
8.5	In other words . . .
9.3	Granny power
10.1	An ideal home?
10.2	The perfect society
11.1	Role models
12.1	Ten clips
12.2	First day at school
12.6	How does it work?
13.1	The art of conversation
14.2	Indirect speech
15.3	A sense of humour
16.1	Five clips
17.4	First meetings
17.7	Four weddings and . . .
18.1	Ten clips
19.3	Danger – Hippies!
20.5	Great business deals?

INTERVIEWS

1.5A	Pen Hadow – an Arctic explorer
3.1B	Maev Alexander – an actress
5.1C	Susan Davies – a traveller
7.2	Isabelle Amyes – a television scriptwriter
9.1D	Geoffrey Smerden – founder of a University of the Third Age
11.6A	Anita Roddick – founder of The Body Shop
12.1A	Wendy Fielder – a research scientist
13.5A	Bob Stanners – an advertising copywriter
15.4	Ian Howarth – founder of the Cult Information Centre
18.3B	Cyril Littlewood – a conservationist
19.7	JoAnne Good – a radio presenter

WORD STUDY

2.6	Synonyms and opposites – 1
3.4	Making an emphasis
4.5	Words easily confused
6.4	Synonyms and opposites – 2
8.4	Forming adjectives
10.6	Synonyms and opposites – 3
14.5	British and American English
16.2	Prefixes
16.3	Spelling
18.2	Compound words (nouns and adjectives)
20.6	Abbreviations and acronyms

GRAMMAR

2.3	The past – 1
4.4	Simple + progressive aspect
6.3	Modal verbs
8.2	The past – 2
10.4	Articles
12.5	Comparing and contrasting
14.2	Indirect speech
16.4	Conditional sentences
18.4	The future and degrees of certainty
20.7	*-ing* and *to* . . .

SPEAKING AND PRONUNCIATION

2.4   Really? That's amazing! (expressing reactions)
4.3   Appropriate language (formal and informal styles)
6.1   What do they look like? (describing people)
11.2 Emphasising the right syllable
11.5 Sharing opinions
14.3 Spelling and pronunciation 1 – Consonants
16.5 Giving advice
17.4 First meetings
18.5 Spelling and pronunciation 2 – Vowels
19.5 Crime and punishment (discussion in the style of the CAE Speaking paper)
20.3 Satisfaction and success (conducting a survey)

EFFECTIVE WRITING

1.2   Joining sentences – 1
3.5   Punctuation
4.2A Spelling and punctuation
5.3   Making notes
7.4   Long and short sentences
7.6   Formal letters and personal letters
8.5C–D Formal and informal style
9.2   Paragraphs
11.4 Style, tone and content
13.2 Joining sentences – 2
15.2 A good introduction and conclusion
17.6 Expressing feelings
19.4 Connecting words (conjunctions)
20.4 Word order

CREATIVE WRITING – the main Creative writing sections are in **bold type**:

1.3   **Writing a narrative**
2.5D A letter to a friend
3.6   **Planning ahead . . .** and **Writing a review**
4.2C Instructions (a recipe) and a note
5.4   **A complaint letter and a note**
6.4E A letter of reference
7.8   **A tactful (informal) letter**
8.3C Descriptions of the lives and achievements of two historical figures
9.5   **A letter to the editor (of a magazine)**
10.3C A description of your own Utopia
10.5D A letter describing the attractions of a city
11.5E A letter to a friend who has won the lottery
11.6C **Descriptions of three household names for a guidebook**
12.2B A letter about your first day at a new school or in a new class
12.4B A letter to the writer of the article OR an account in the same style as the article
12.6E Instructions on how to operate household equipment
13.5C **A report on advertisements in a magazine**
14.4F Instructions on what to do in case of fire
15.4C **A letter giving advice and a note** (based on information in the Interview)
16.5B Another letter giving advice
16.6B **Instructions for a first-aid manual**
17.5D An article describing a favourite book
17.7C **An account of a wedding or a family event**
18.3D A report on measures to protect the environment
19.6 **Reports and opinions (a report and an opinion column)**
20.1C An account of someone's day at work
20.8 **A letter applying for a job**

IDIOMS AND PHRASAL VERBS

1.6   All's well that ends well! — idioms and collocations with *all*
2.7   You can't lose! — verbs and idioms with *lose*
3.7   *At . . .* and *by . . .*
4.6   *Bring, carry* and *take*
5.6   *High, middle* and *low*
7.9   *In . . .* and *out of . . .*
8.6   *Get*
9.6   Ages — idioms and collocations with *age, fresh, new, old* and *young*
10.7 *Hard, soft, difficult* and *easy*
11.7 *For* and *on*
12.7 *Look* and *see*
13.6 Colours — *red, blue, green, black* and *white*
14.6 Speaking and thinking — *say, tell, call, speak, talk* and *think*
15.5 *Day* and *time*
16.7 *Hearts, hands, legs* and *feet*
17.8 Head over heels . . . — *head, brain, mind, face, eye, nose* and *ear*
18.6 *Keep, hold, stand* and *turn*
19.8 *Back, front* and *side*
20.9 *First, second, third . . .* and *last*